FAITH & DUTY

FAITH & DUTY

NICKY CURTIS MM

André Deutsch

First published in Great Britain in 1998
by André Deutsch Ltd,
76 Dean Street,
London W1V 5HA
www.vci.co.uk

André Deutsch Ltd is a VCI plc company

Some names in this work
have been changed for security reasons.

A catalogue record for this title is available
from the British Library

ISBN 0 233 99415 7

Typeset by Derek Doyle & Associates
Mold, Flintshire.
Printed by MPG Books Ltd,
Bodmin, Cornwall.

Contents

For the lads that didn't come back,
and in recognition of Chris Mather's outstanding
courage and leadership

PROLOGUE

A BLAST FROM THE
PAST: BELFAST 1995

Funny, the little jokes life plays on you. There I was, in the unstable confines of McKenna's Bar, deep in the Republican heartlands of Armagh city, being betrayed by my own bladder. That last half-pint of Guinness, along with the other three I'd had, was now screaming for release with about the same insistence as the Guildford Four. I wanted to piss so badly my teeth were floating.

I pushed my way through the crush around the bar, hoping that the concrete stares, hard mouths and half-turned faces didn't mean what I already knew to be true; during my last conversation at the bar-end phone I'd let my Irish accent slip. I'd hung up slowly, closed my eyes, and opened them again to see the black bone of the receiver hanging there. Shit.

I was deep in the war zone here, and no matter what they tell you, there's no such thing as a safe house for an ex-soldier on foreign soil. The most you can hope to do is to continue to 'get away with it'. I remembered what it had been like in the early days.

As a new recruit in those old pictures of me with the cocked beret and cocky grin, I'd been armoured by adolescent innocence. All young men are sure that they'll never die. And graveyards are full of the innocent and the sure.

Christ, I thought, what am I doing here?

I'd come back to Ireland to close a business deal with Seamus, an old mate of mine. He ran a string of market stalls in border towns and was interested in the used Levi's that I was now importing from America, many of them pre-worn by US prisoners.

Jail seemed a pretty safe place to be right now.

Surprisingly, I'd felt quite good about being back in the city. There's that hearty Irishness to it all that no amount of Troubles can ever completely destroy. Walking the streets I'd noticed builders reordering the rubble back into walls. But entering the bar I also saw that damaged lives aren't so easily rebuilt. They're there to see: the lines; some visible, most not. The laughter lines still there in spite of it all, the worry lines there *because* of it all, the scar-tissue lines, and the invisible battle lines. McKenna's Bar, like all the others, was a dark, windowless hole full of good-time drinkers and bad-time bullies. The kind of place to make you long for home. The bad lads were always the ones slapping backs and lapping up the attention from their loud stories and hard laughs.

It had always been a high-wire act for me, but with no net if you got it wrong, and no applause if you got it right.

But that was then, in the days when I'd come in search of information that often led to deaths or internment and when I was armed and backed up with Intelligence guys sat at other tables ready to call in the uniforms if needed. And this was *now*, 1995, and I'm unarmed and I couldn't feel more exposed if I was stood here in my Y-fronts.

Bloody Seamus. Why hadn't he turned up? Why hadn't he been home? I'd called his wife three times. And why had I drunk so much? Because I was as nervous as a big-balled Alsatian waiting for the chuffing vet to chop 'em off, that's why!

If the bar that you're in is dangerous then the toilets will be its killing fields. In McKenna's Bar you wouldn't even guarantee the Pope wouldn't get the living shite kicked out of him.

The toilet door slammed shut behind me, immediately muffling the bar music to a dull thump. I sighed with relief as I pissed into the steel trough, hearing the warm stream drum, and watching the steam rise. The dirty details of the place jumped out at me – the spiralling fag-ends heading for the drain, my own warped reflection in the steel, and the scrawled graffiti greetings – *Fuck Off Brit Bastards!* and *See You In Hell*.

BANG! The door swung open and a wave of music crashed back in and was then sucked back out again when the door slammed shut, BANG! I turned around and saw the two of them stood there. One tall, one stocky. In black leather jackets, arms swaying, cocky. And dangerous with it. Bad lads. Both with long, greased-back hair and trouble faces. Provisional IRA these guys may have been but hardened professionals they weren't. If they had been, I'd have died with my dick in my hand. Still my heart revved and the old familiar adrenalin rush hit me hard. I zipped myself up and faced them. I saw the pendulum swing of their arms and recognized the glint of metal swaying in and out of the dark. I found myself thinking, where's my mother right now? What is she doing? Fussing over dinner? Slumped in her chair.

So after all those years of dodging down back alleys, bullets skipping off cobbles or zipping past my face (only missing because I happened to be running *this* way and not *that* way), after all that, it's come to this; two automatics emptied into my face, leaving me starfished on the floor of an Armagh bog. Well, I thought, at least I'm in the right place to shit myself.

I looked into their faces, trying not to make it look like a challenge but as if I was just being open. I didn't like what I saw. Despite being young enough to be my sons, they looked as hard as the nails in Christ's cross. I thought, I'm in big, big trouble here.

'All right there, lads?' I said, trying to control the fear in my voice and failing. Try to keep the fear back, Nicky, I thought, just try to sound puzzled. After all, if I had nothing to hide then I'd have nothing to fear. I fought to convince myself so that I could convince them.

'You English bastard!' the tall one barked, 'What the *fuck* are you doing here!'

'Look, lads. I'm a businessman,' I said, and was immediately struck by how weak it sounded. I chastised myself, come on now, stay calm, you can do it. It can't end here. Not now, not like this. God, what I would have given for the holy weight of a 9mm in my hand right now.

'Here's my business card,' I said, and handed it to him. 'I don't want any trouble. I'm here on business. I'm a Catholic. Have I done something wrong?'

Sweet Jesus, talk about famous last words. I imagined that on my gravestone, 'Have I Done Something Wrong?'

'You're still English,' the taller one said, not even showing the card to the other one, who wasn't interested anyway. 'You're still one of *them*!'

The card hit the floor. I saw the gun fully for the first time when he brought it up to my eye. Beautiful things, some guns. God, how my ma's gonna cry when they tell her. I saw her crying on the doorstep. I heard the click of the slide hammer as he snapped a bullet in line with the barrel.

My own life didn't flash before me, like they say it does, but someone else's. Robert Nairac's. He was an old colleague of mine who had found himself in this same position twenty years ago, confronted in the toilets and then followed out into the car park. They reportedly kicked him about like a football, threw him in a car, took him to the outskirts of town, beat him some more with bricks and planks and then shot his body in every limb. Until there was nothing left to shoot.

'English bastard!' spat out again brought me back to the present. Looking down the business end of a Browning makes you remember the damage you've seen it do in the past, the black dot it puts on the forehead and the great sucking wet hole it leaves at the back.

'Get ter fuck out of here and don't fucking come back! If you do you're a fucking *dead* man!'

It took a few seconds to sink in and then I nodded and glanced at the tall one as I squeezed past, arms still raised. Yeah, I thought, you and me out in the alley, one-to-one, and it'd be a different story, son. But as much as it turned my stomach, I had to give them their moment of glory, just to get out alive. Live to fight another day and all that crap.

I reeled out into the car park. With short, quick steps and shorter, quicker breaths, I lurched towards the car. The back of my neck tingled with the fear of a bullet suddenly booming out of the dark and throwing my brains on to the windscreen. I noticed for the first time now how my hands were trembling. After-shock. I fumbled the key around the lock (get in you bastard!) and dropped down into the driver's seat. I wished that I felt safe enough just to sit there, but I didn't. I gunned the engine and threw the car down Portadown Road towards the safety of Prodland. The car weaved slightly as I turned and let fly a rope of vomit on to the passenger seat.

The panic was gradually replaced by anger: at myself for landing in that position; and an older, deeper anger I'd built up in streets of blood and lies.

I slowed down as soon as I felt that I was in a safe enough area of Prodland to relax a little. I swung the car in behind the Templeman Bar, entered, and downed a double whiskey in a single swig. Something as simple as the clink of the ice-cubes against my teeth made me feel glad to be alive. I immediately ordered another.

I was still breathing heavily at the thought of what might have happened. If they'd searched me they would have found my credit card with MM after my name, the abbreviation for Military Medal.

Then the blood would have really hit the fan. That would have condemned me to death, of that I'm sure.

I considered calling my brother-in-law, Jimmy, who was part of the RUC Special Branch in Belfast, but decided against it. I didn't think he'd be interested in pursuing it. For one, the two gunmen would be long gone by now and protected by the standard wall of silence from everyone else in the bar. And second, Jimmy would be reluctant to get involved in anything that might cause unnecessary ripples in light of the recent truce that had been called.

And I could imagine his response after finding that I was in a bar in the Catholic heartland – 'What the hell were you doing there anyway, you daft bastard!'

I had to admit, he would have had a point. What *was* I doing there? I could have met Seamus anywhere. Somewhere safe. Looking back, I think, deep down, that I still missed the excitement of the old days and wanted to recapture it. I know now that this is quite common among war veterans. It happened to men who came back from Vietnam: the inability to readjust to ordinary, everyday civilian life. You get addicted to the adrenalin, the fear-driven, heightened awareness of yourself and your surroundings. And there's also something that only ex-soldiers have felt but rarely feel free to acknowledge: the sheer thrill of it.

I know how that sounds, like a schoolboy excitement over being in battle which, you'd think, the sight and smell of real blood would destroy. But it isn't always true, it doesn't always do that. Sometimes, nothing can make you feel more alive than having death at your elbow.

Yeah, sod it, I decided that it was a bad idea to call Jimmy. I just wanted to get my head down for the night and catch the bloody ferry back to England tomorrow morning and see Sarah, my wife.

As I drove down the Larne Road towards the M2 motorway, I started to relax. The panic had faded. By now I felt distant enough from it even to smile. Jesus, if those two lads had known who they'd had at gunpoint. In my time I'd probably done more damage to their 'cause' than they could imagine. They didn't realize how narrowly they'd missed their chance to be hailed as local heroes.

As in the past, I went from being shit-scared to feeling elated that I'd been able to bluff them. I'd had to do it years ago when a small group of us had found ourselves hopelessly outnumbered by an angry mob in one of the back alleys of Belfast. I'd call out orders to non-existent squadrons in order to convince the mob that we weren't alone.

I also knew I was only trying to make myself feel better. The fear fades but never completely disappears. I still have the nightmares to prove it. In fact it's always the same nightmare: I'm facing an angry mob ready to tear me limb from limb and I reach for the only thing that will save me, the pistol I always kept tucked in my waistband. But it's not there. I search for it frantically, backing off from the advancing crowd, praying that the weapon is there. But it isn't. Then I awake, shaking and covered in sweat.

The sliproad to Cookstown suddenly flew towards me and I snapped out of my daydream to fling the car across the road towards it. The back end weaved out and severely injured a few contra-flow traffic cones in the process. I felt the car judder and saw the cones bounce behind me in the rearview mirror. What I didn't see was the RUC Land-Rover until it overtook me with its blue light flashing. Great, I thought, this really puts the tin lid on it.

I slowed down and pulled over. They did the same, got out and walked towards me. I thought how strange it was that the RUC now felt safe enough to drive around in marked cars with flashing top-lights. In my day their usual form of transport had been unmarked Cortinas with steel plating and thickened glass. And the fact that it was always Cortinas made the Ford motor company furious because it effectively killed stone-dead their hopes of ever selling one to any civilian. No one wanted to be mistaken for the RUC and shot: 'Oh, sorry for shooting yer, mate. Thought you were Special Branch. Cortina, yer know . . .'

I suddenly realized that, after the Guinness and whiskey, I was probably well over the limit. In the past, a flash of the ID would result in being waved on by the RUC as if you were an old mate. They always had more important things to worry about than a few over-the-limit squaddies; some of their own officers in the same state, for instance.

The RUC constable approached me. I spoke slowly and carefully to try to convince him I wasn't as far gone as my last manoeuvre suggested. 'Yes, Officer, how can I help?'

'Stand still, sir,' he ordered and let his hand hovver over the standard-issue 38 Reuger Special in the opened holster on his waist. He was young, but I still felt confident about my ability to talk my way out of it. After all, we were once on the same side, part of the same forces, and if the worst happened, and I was charged, I could always ask Jimmy to pull the file.

'My name's Nicky Curtis,' I said. 'I have a lot of friends in the RUC.' I knew straight away that it hadn't come out right and had gone down even worse. 'Some of them pretty senior,' I added for effect. I could tell that he wasn't impressed, his impassive face showing nothing. I was becoming frustrated now at my own inability to gain control of this situation.

'Been drinking, sir?' he asked firmly.

'I have, yes,' I admitted, 'but I've just had a very bad experience in Armagh. You know how it is . . .'

He obviously didn't, interrupting me to say, 'Blow into this, please.' It was no surprise when the digital readout said I was twice over the limit. He showed no emotion as he looked at the result. I exercised my right to wait twenty minutes to retake the test and used the time to attempt to get on friendlier terms, drop a few more names. No joy. I felt my anger returning. The second test confirmed the first and I was arrested. I decided to make the journey to Antrim police station in their vehicle so his partner could follow in my car. If I'd left it there overnight it would certainly have been stolen by the next morning.

I didn't waste any more time arguing or trying to persuade them. The lad was too young to realize, I reasoned. I'll sort it all out with his superiors back at the station. But the adrenalin of the evening's earlier event was now back on the boil. This is all I need, I thought. I should be halfway home by now. We passed through the gates and up to the fortified station. I've been inside a few of these places in the past, but this was the first time I had been under arrest.

The duty sergeant behind the desk had a shock of white hair and been-there, done-it-all eyes. We had something in common: he looked as tired as I felt. He looked up, took me in with a glance and then read me my rights and asked if I understood.

'I don't bloody believe this! I spent my entire fucking youth in your shithole of a country, protecting the likes of young Danny Boy here.' I jabbed my finger at the young patrolman. 'Who was probably still on his mother's tit when the Provos were scaring the shit out of you lot. I've saved more lives than the whole fucking lot of you put together. If it wasn't for the likes of men like me you'd have Gerry-fucking-Adams for President. And as it happens you still might, if you don't get off your arses and get some real work done instead of wasting your time on me.' I was laying it on a bit thick by now, but I was too far gone to care. I let my hands slip off the desk where I'd been gripping it and waited for the anger to subside. Or for them to say something that would refuel it. They waited too, hoping I'd burned myself out.

The sergeant spoke first. 'If you would just calm down, sir, before you make matters any worse than they already are.'

I pushed my face up to his. 'If you charge me with this poxy offence you can be sure that as well as pleading guilty to this, I will also plead guilty, in open court, to all the other offences that I committed on your behalf. You know what I'm talking about, like planting ammunition in the houses of known Provos before you searched them. I'll also admit to helping SAS squads come into the Republic to kill IRA members and staff captains. You and me both know about the shoot-to-kill policy. Seven shades of shit will really hit the fucking fan then.'

I met his stare, and in it I saw that I'd suddenly introduced a little unexpected unease in the middle of the usual Friday-night boredom. He leaned back, holding my gaze, only breaking it to turn and exchange a few whispers with another senior officer. Out of the corner of my eye I could also see the young officer shift against the wall, but I resisted the urge to turn to him.

The older one eventually leaned forward, on to the desk. 'Perhaps, sir, you would like to follow me.'

He led me to a small office next to the processing area and closed the door quietly behind us. He gave a slight sigh. For the first time, I really looked at him. He was nearing the end of his career, probably a good man who'd just seen too much and was sick of it all. We did have a lot in common.

'Look, Mr Curtis, I know who you are and what you've done here in the past *but,*' and here he paused expecting another outburst, but I just raised my eyebrows expectantly, 'you have to understand that the Province is in a time of change. The fact that you were arrested by young Danny should tell you that much.' I looked to the ceiling. I knew all this meant that he couldn't do anything.

He also knew that I knew he was just trying to soften the blow. He moved closer, looking genuinely apologetic, and there was a this-is-off-the-record tone to his voice. 'Look, if you still have friends here you should contact them because once the process at this station has started . . .' He spread his hands. 'Your friends may be able to do something when the paperwork leaves here.'

I nodded silently. As I sat down by the telephone I heard the door click behind me as he left. I knew the phone would be bugged but I was beyond caring. I made a few calls but it was after midnight now and I didn't get any answers. I hung up and for the second time in the last few hours found myself staring dejectedly at the deaf skull of a telephone. Sod it. I'd sort it all out tomorrow.

There was no cell for me at the station so they took me to a nearby hotel. I called Sarah again in England and managed to get through and tell her the whole tale. She said she'd ring her father to ask him to get in touch with Jimmy. He must have done, because Jimmy rang me back. 'Don't worry,' he said. 'I'll tell them you were working for us as a source.'

It didn't make me sleep any easier. In fact I hardly slept at all, just tossed and turned in the single bed, twisting the sheets into a straitjacket around me.

I couldn't calm down, and running things over in my mind just made me angrier. As I stared at the ceiling, I almost laughed at the irony of being treated like this. After all those years risking my life on the streets as a soldier and as an undercover agent in bars and clubs. The undercover work was always the most stressful: 'sleeping with the enemy' some call it. The 'sleep' was always fitful, and the 'enemy' prone to murdering you in your bed.

I knew of men working undercover who had been sussed out and were later found crucified in their own dirt on a disused factory floor. Actually *nailed* there.

I remembered how my name had become known in the ranks after I was the last guy to fire a shot during an infamous gunbattle in Belfast. Amazingly, from over 300 yards away, we hit one of them slap-bang in the 'T-zone' (or the 'T', as we called it, the intersection of the eyes and nose). It turned out he was one the IRA's highest-ranking officers. Next day the picture of his body was splashed over the front pages of the national papers. The awful destruction to the back of his head was carefully hidden, of course.

Watching headlight beams slide silently across the ceiling, I eventually fell asleep.

Next day I left, not knowing that I would later be fined £200 and banned from driving in Northern Ireland. Cheers, you bastards, I thought. The feeling's mutual.

I was far more upset than I would let them know. On the way back to the ferry I felt incredibly saddened. I felt let down; betrayed, in fact. There was no other word for it.

I turned on Classic FM and by some strange coincidence they were playing Elgar's *Nimrod*, just as the Guard's Band had been at Buckingham Palace the day I'd arrived for the medal ceremony.

I decided it was time to tell my story and the truth about what happened all those years ago on the streets of Belfast. It really was a war, and one that the university-educated officers were unable to fight. To me and my men it was our war. And sometimes, at the lowest points, when I felt all alone, it was just mine. A corporal's war.

PART ONE

IN UNIFORM

*'You shall hear of war and
rumours of war.'*

1

FROM YORKSHIRE TO BORNEO

As a child I'd always looked forward to Saturday nights. That's when Dad would come back from the pub, well oiled after a night down the road with his pals. What he smelled of was still a mystery to me but they were things I hoped to discover one day soon, like beer and cigarettes.

I'd sit cross-legged at his feet, which seemed huge to me. Right then he was the biggest man in the world. You never look up to anyone else again in the way you once did to your dad.

So I'd sit there on the floor as he spun tales of his time in North Africa, his capture by an SS panzer division and his escape from the POW camp in Italy. It had happened during one of the camp's organized football games, this one English versus Scottish prisoners, which were held outside the perimeter fence with all the other prisoners cheering through the wire. Dad got the players to start a fight and during the chaos he rolled over a wall, picked up the clothes he'd previously left there, and legged it into the woods. The second part of his plan didn't run so smoothly. He criss-crossed Italy for ten weeks before he managed to cross the enemy lines and find the Allies. He always had a dodgy sense of direction, the daft old bugger. He was later featured in the *Daily Express* as the first POW to escape and return to England.

You can imagine the effect on a young lad: war heroics and football – what a combination! Little wonder that I headed for the Army Careers Office as soon as I was old enough to apply, at seventeen.

Besides, I'd seen enough of life underground, down the pit, to know that I didn't want to blacken my arse down there for the rest of my life. I remember Dad coming home covered in soot, looking like one of those cartoon characters after a bomb's exploded in its face. The only other alternative for me then in a northern pit-town was either the unemployment office or some mundane job.

It was 1964, and while most lads of my age were growing their hair and then shaking it to the Beatles I had a regulation Army crop and began travelling the world. As part of the Strategic Reserve Brigade stationed in Colchester we could be deployed within seventy-two hours to anywhere in the world where Britain held a colonial interest. From the heat and noise of Hong Kong to the still deserts of Aden; from scouting through the dense jungles of Malaya to help training Yanks in Panama before they went out to Vietnam, I loved it all.

On returning to Britain in 1969 with my passport stamped black with destinations, I found that we were being posted to Minden in Germany as part of a Battle Group and as infantry support to the tank regiment, the 7th Army Brigade. Unfortunately I was to spend three years there as part of the British Army of the Rhine. I say 'unfortunately' because it was so bloody boring that even a trip to the dole office back home would have seemed like a big adventure. This was one part of my Army life that I wouldn't be thrilling *my* kids with.

I never realized there were so many words for 'boredom' until I started writing my letters home. As squaddies, we had nothing to do but drink (which was always easy for us), lay on our bunks flicking through porn mags and, after we got randy, try to get acquainted with the local Fräuleins (which was very difficult for British soldiers: a classic case of 'don't mention the war' if ever there was one).

Just before we left Colchester for Germany I had moved up the ranks to gain a lance-corporal's stripe. This little bit of authority meant I could exercise my gift for delegation; in other words I was a naturally bossy little sod, given half the chance. That was one of the joys of promotion – you could get the lower ranks to do all the crappy jobs you'd always hated doing yourself. It also gave me the chance to skive, big time, which is an art in itself when you're a member of the forces during peacetime. It's a shame they never gave out stripes for it: my uniform would have been stiff with them.

Carrying my clipboard as if it was something that gave me the power of invisibility, I'd wander around the camp and blend into all the useless activity that was invented to keep us all busy. I'm sure this is where I learned valuable camouflaging techniques that would later save my life.

I'd move purposefully around the camp until I found an opening that I could exploit to slip off and play cards and snooker with the other non-commissioned officers. Or sometimes we'd just sit out the afternoon, gossiping like old spinsters until our day ended at around four. Then it was off with the uniform and into our civvies so we could head for the bright lights of town. No bar or disco was safe as we attempted to leave no local girl unturned. That was our contribution to Anglo-German relations, you might say.

Despite the shirking on camp and the distractions of town, I was still getting good reports for my soldiering. I was a good shot and orienteer, and I ran for the battalion which made me very fit. I also got a little leeway because of my success at cricket and footie. That would have pleased Dad.

Then, one freezing day in December, I thought I'd been rumbled. A platoon of soldiers was being put through its paces in a drill session on the huge tarmac square at the centre of the barracks. They marched to and fro, stomping and arm-swinging as a senior NCO screamed blue-murder at them. I thanked God that I had something much more important to do, like inspecting the fire hydrant in front of me. I'd already seen a second-lieutenant approaching and had knelt by the hydrant, my forehead knitted in concentration as I made notes on the clipboard.

As he passed, I stood and saluted in the appropriate manner and he returned the salute and walked on by. I congratulated myself on my cunning. Many of the young officers were trained at Sandhurst, which may have taught them the correct way to twirl a lady at a tea-dance but, as far as we were concerned, they knew bugger-all about soldiering.

Nice one, Curtis, I thought.

'Corporal Curtis! To me!'

It was Sergeant-Major Allen roaring at me from an open HQ Block window. The fact that the HQ was over thirty metres away showed that whatever else he may be, softly spoken he wasn't. It's the job of men like Sergeant-Major Allen to bore their way into your brain until they make it theirs. They don't call it drill training for nothing.

I marched to the open window with dread, banged my feet to attention and shouted, 'Sir!'

'Corporal Curtis, what are you doing?'

'I'm standing in for Corporal Williams, sir,' I stuttered, squinting up at the window. The winter sun hung behind the HQ, blinding me and turning the sergeant-major into an ominous, black silhouette. 'Corporal Williams, as you know, is Battalion Orderly today but has had to visit the doctor with a severe dose of the shits. Sir.' The shape didn't move or reply, which I took to mean that I was managing to get away with it again. I carried on with growing confidence. 'It was probably the curry we had last night, sir. Come to think of it, I'm feeling a bit on the loose side myself. I think I should see the doc as well,' I added as a final flourish, and made a move to leave.

The shape in the window spoke, 'Corporal Curtis, you are a skiving git! *You* know that, and *I* know that.'

'Oh no, sir, essential info, sir.' I held up the clipboard as if it was proof.

'For your information, Curtis,' he barked, 'I have just talked to Corporal Williams' – he paused for effect – 'and he looks as fit as a butcher's dog. As fit as you look to me, in fact. So get your lazy arse up here, now!'

Shit. I'm in for it now. As well as a major bollocking, lying to the company sergeant-major could get me extra duties. That would mean that I'd miss my date with the local lovely that I'd hoped to spend my Christmas break with. I made my way up to his office with my heart in my boots.

I stamped to attention, stared at the wall behind him and steeled myself for a ferocious bawling-out. 'Curtis,' he said in a softer tone than I expected. I looked down from the wall and directly at him. 'You have been selected as the Green Howards' nomination to attend the Parachute Regiment's battle school.'

I stood there stunned. I wondered if it was some kind of cruel joke he was playing before he got down to the real business of screaming in my face until it was flecked with spit.

'The course starts in three weeks at Brecon in South Wales,' he finished, and then stared at me.

I knew that only the best of the battalion and normally only sergeants were chosen for this, and I felt elated. As if to bring me back to earth he explained, 'The sergeant who was nominated can't make the course. His wife has just given birth to twins and there are complications.' He stepped up to me, nose to nose. 'You're next in line, so get your arse in gear, get your act together, and don't disappoint me.'

I recovered from the shock to protest at the short notice. Usually you'd get six months in order to prepare.

'Tough. If you wanted an easy life, laddie, you should have gone down the pits not joined the bloody army!'

For the rest of the day I lay on my bunk. With my boots kicked off and my hands behind my head, I stared at the ceiling and tried to take it all in. We'd all heard talk about Brecon, of course. It was standard training for the elite parachute regiments and the speciality of the Special Air Service, the SAS.

Being chosen to be trained in this company filled me with a mixture of pride, excitement and horror. Christ, I thought, I've only got three weeks to get ready for this one. And I'd also have to face the prospect of returning here to the fury of Sergeant-Major Allen, who, if I failed, would take great pleasure in tearing off my head and shitting down my neck.

One thing that kept my spirits up was the prospect of running into Johnny Jones again. Johnny was one of the trainers at Brecon and a former comrade-in-arms. We'd served in Malaya together: I was his lead scout, hacking away at the head of our squad as we trekked through the jungle. The trees were as wide as houses. Manoeuvring around them, we had to climb over roots as thick as fallen chimneys. The trees rose to form a great canopy of leaves far above us and even though the sun was blocked out, the heat was unbelievable.

Johnny had been kept on as an instructor at Brecon because he'd done so well on the course a few years earlier. Well, at least Johnny will look after me, I thought.

With any chance of a Christmas break with young Helga suddenly disappearing down the Swannee, I set out a training regime for myself. So while everyone else was getting legless and singing their heads off in the warmth of town, I was pounding over the frozen ground of the camp's playing fields in full combat kit with a ninety-pound pack and an automatic rifle. Merry bloody Christmas, I thought. As I staggered under the weight of the backpack, I swore to God that if I bumped into Santa Claus I'd shoot the fat, cheery bastard myself, point blank.

Despite my frostbitten fingers and blistered feet, my determination to succeed kept me going. I knew that success on the course might bring me a promotion. But time was against me, and when I arrived at Merthyr Tydfil one bleak January morning, I knew I wasn't ready.

Along with about three hundred other soldiers, I boarded one of the three-ton trucks. We were all drawn from every part of the British army: infantry, marines, guardsmen and paras. But whoever we were, we all shivered the same from the cold and the apprehension. As the truck bounced along with the wind whistling through the canvas, I thought of what lay ahead – the cold nights in the field, the days of exhaustion, the nights of no sleep – and I shivered some more.

Originally, the course was devised so that every British soldier would attend at some point in his career, resulting in the world's most highly trained fighting force, ready to deal with anything, anywhere. But the idea was too impractical and so the course became a much more selective one for senior NCOs only. They could then pass on everything they'd learned down through the ranks to their men.

The first three days lived up to expectations. We were initially split into eight-man sections as we attacked known positions, eventually moving to larger, organized platoon and company attacks. Each task was separately commanded by different course members. As well as the physical hardship of being out in the field (trying and failing to get some kip in freezing, waterlogged trenches during 'dug in training', for example), there was also the mental stress of having to assume leadership. This isn't something that had worried me in the past as it had always come naturally. I remember the very first time it was acknowledged by someone, a nun as it happens, although it wasn't entirely meant as a compliment. I was only twelve, and a typical, troublesome, dirty-kneed little twelve-year-old I was. Even as the school bell was still clanging, I was out through the door tugging my tie off and my shirt out, belting down the street with my mates to make the most of those long summer evenings. We'd run from the cobbled streets full of grown-ups and make for the nearest scrap of waste ground. Suddenly, we were in the jungle! Jimmy and Gaz were Germans and John and I were British commandos winning the war with twig rifles and stone hand-grenades, or duelling with reeds over who would be Errol Flynn in *The Crimson Buccaneer*.

One day we stole some reeds from old Mrs Sutcliffe's garden. Unfortunately, she spotted us and called the police. Dad's slipper, the headmaster's office and the local court were followed by a twelve-shilling fine. I'm sure that I wasn't supposed to, but I couldn't help feeling quite proud of Sister Mary's pronouncement – 'Nicholas is a born leader but seems to have a natural talent for leading others astray!' That clinched it for me in the gang: *I* was Errol Flynn!

Brecon wasn't exactly the waste ground behind Mrs Sutcliffe's garden, however, and I was painfully aware of my lack of command experience. Also, my position as a temporary acting sergeant made me very uneasy. Mess etiquette was a minefield that couldn't have unnerved me more than the real thing.

I was equally worried by Johnny Jones. My cheerfulness at seeing him again was short-lived. He didn't speak to me for three days. I was stunned. This was a man I'd considered a close comrade during our combat missions in the past.

The fourth day brought another surprise. I thought that all my fellow course members had performed brilliantly but the senior instructors thought differently. They methodically ripped apart the performance of each soldier, one by one, until I was the only one left. Jesus wept, they'd bollocked guys that I thought had done well so what the fuck did they make of me? I steeled myself for the prospect of being fired out of the nearest cannon.

Johnny turned to me and said, 'Lance-Corporal Curtis!', accentuating my rank for all present. I cringed. 'I would like you to let us all in on the secret, Curtis, of how you became bullet-proof during your brief and so far unspectacular career in the British army?' His demand echoed around the barracks and hung in the air. I stared straight ahead, trying not to flush red. 'I have to ask,' he continued, 'because you stood on the skyline of those hills shouting orders. And you stood in open ground doing the same bloody thing. You're either bullet-proof or the invisible fucking man! But I could see you, and if I could see you then so could the enemy. What's your secret?' Humiliation was pushing tears up behind my eyes and I blinked quickly to keep them back, determined not to show my hurt. This would be seen as weakness and in the army weakness is something to be derided, stamped and spat on. I could also feel the relief of all the men around me at not being on the receiving end of the biggest bollocking of the day. They were safe now and enjoying it. I'd have felt exactly the same in their position, no doubt about it. Well, so much for being Errol bloody Flynn, I thought.

'This tosser,' he carried on, 'was my scout once, and he displayed exactly the same disregard for his life then. Why he didn't get his bloody head shot off is still a constant mystery to me. I've had sleepless nights about it,' he shouted, really playing to the gallery now, 'thinking what a lucky fucker that Curtis is! Bloody bullet-proof.' He scanned the faces that were all now riveted to him and then spun back on me, 'While you are on this course, under my command, Lance-Corporal, you will do things my way!' I suddenly had a vision of him bursting into a Frank Sinatra impression and, despite the hurt, I fought against even the faintest smile. If I hadn't overcome it, death would at least have been instant. I could sense the storm abating slightly. 'So, there's no fucking comic-book hero-ics! No fucking gung-ho John Wayne wank! And *definitely* no fucking backsliding! Just pure, professional soldiering. Then maybe, just maybe, I can keep you, and the unfortunate bastards under you, out of an early hole in the ground.'

I continued to stare straight ahead, not wanting to offer him the slightest hint of a challenge. Besides, I wouldn't have offered any, he was right, and that realization made me as angry at myself as he was. Later, after the shock and shame had eventually subsided, I realized that as with Sister Mary, there had been a coded message in there that I could take some succour from. I was still on the course, I hadn't been thrown off, and what Johnny Jones was saying was that he thought I had leadership qualities and would one day lead men of my own platoon, so I had to learn how to do it right. I took comfort from the fact that he must have thought that there was something in me worth pursuing. And he really was just trying to save my life. That's something that I was to appreciate later on the streets of Belfast.

Over the next few months I learned how to hone the qualities that enable you to lead soldiers confidently in a time of war. Some of the conditions were horrendous but I learned how to cope. We had to live, night and day, in wet clothing weighed with rain; sleep in ice-hardened holes for only a couple of hours at most; reassem-ble and clean a gun with our frozen fingers, and do it correctly. One of the toughest tests was 'Escape and Evasion', which is exactly what it says: you're thrown out into the field with a head start, no food, and plenty of fear, and you are expected to survive.

In preparation for this, one of the SAS officers showed us the army's version of a fast-food takeaway. With one of the local sheep bucking and baaing between his knees, he slit its throat with a quick, easy motion. As its blood spurted on to his boots, he produced a container and caught the rest until the can was full, all the time calmly giving instructions: 'Use anything you can find, an old can or tin, and save it for when you might need it later. It makes excellent black pudding.' Some of us looked at each other and then back at the tin. The blood was black. He then demonstrated the skinning technique by ripping off the poor creature's hide like a wet blanket. At that point several of us nearly turned to vegetarianism.

Looking back, it was funny watching this big, burly soldier stood out in a field giving cooking instructions like a butch Delia Smith.

The next stage, 'Capture and Interrogation', was the most feared. From what we'd heard there were no laughs at all to be had here. In battle, even if you're outnumbered or cornered you still, literally, have a fighting chance. On training manoeuvres the heaviness of your rifle feels like a burden, but under real enemy fire it's the most comforting weight you've ever had to bear.

Capture by the enemy robs you of this protection and even before they strip you to inflict a beating, you already feel naked without that familiar dull weight in your hands. We had to be prepared for this ugliness by having it thrown right in our faces by men who had already experienced it. No laughing matter.

The day of our 'capture' came. A dozen of us climbed tensely into the open back of a truck that was knitted with barbed wire. We knelt down while black sacks were placed on our heads. I saw the grey sky and green hills black out as the hood was snapped down over me. The idea was to replicate capture and interrogation as real-istically as possible. This included our hands being rope-tied behind our backs. Or it should have done. Recently, this practice had been abandoned because one of the locals, who also happened to be an MP, had run to London and objected in the Commons to 'the utterly appalling sight of bedraggled men being led through the district to an apparent mass execution'.

I have to admit it must have looked pretty hideous. And it could have easily led to some poor old, half-senile granny thinking that the Germans had finally invaded before keeling over clutching her chest. So we just knelt there with our untied hands behind our backs.

I felt the truck jump away and as we bounced along with other trucks before and behind us, I began to think. I knew this wasn't one of those situations where you could make yourself feel better by thinking, Nah, it can't be *that* bad. Probably just barrack-room exaggeration. From my cold toes to my colder nose, I *knew* that this was going to be every bit as bad as they said. I don't need this, I thought, I'll take my chances in the field when it happens, if it ever does. One thing that played on my mind most was a story I'd heard about one of the humiliation techniques. This involved the trainees all being tied stark-bollock naked to their beds, whereupon the foulest-looking prostitutes from the local town would be brought up to walk at the foot of the bunks, pointing and laughing at the trainees and their fear-shrivelled dicks.

I actually thought, Sod this for a game of soldiers! The hoods were thin enough to leave you a little vision. I looked around at where the three guards were positioned on the truck bed beside us. Then I whispered to the guys nearest to me, 'Fuck this. I'm going over the side. Follow me.' I heard a few muttered exclamations of, 'You nutter! You serious?' Over the engine noise, I hissed back through the cloth, 'It's supposed to be like the real thing, isn't it? So let's fucking make a break for it!'

I felt the gears drop, heard them deepen in sound, and knew that we were slowing for a hill. It was now or never. Before I had more time to doubt the wisdom of this brilliant idea, I jumped up and flung myself at the nearest guard. He immediately keeled back over the side without a sound, a look of such utter disbelief on his face that it still makes me smile. I ripped off the hood and jumped. As I hit the ground I heard the brakes slam and quickly turned to see three others following me and the guards leaping after them. I threw myself over the nearest wall and dived into the stream that I found there. I was used to being completely piss-wet by now so I didn't mind. I thought that I'd just jump back up and leg it like crazy, but I hadn't counted on one thing – the steep, fast-flowing streams of the Welsh hills. I hit the water and flew off downstream like shit off a shiny shovel. I was so shocked that I didn't even cry out.

Along with three others, I scrambled out of the water and ran for cover. I dived into some undergrowth and lay there panting, my heart thudding. I could hear the guards' shouts becoming louder and clearer as they got nearer. I kept my head down and my eyes shut, thinking that if I couldn't see them then they wouldn't see me. One of them walked up to me and stopped. I was almost on the verge of standing up to avoid the embarrassment of crouching there as he watched me, when an unexpected thing happened. He hesitated, turned and walked back to the group shouting, 'No. Nothing.' He hadn't seen me.

After what seemed like an eternity, I eventually popped my head up and peeped out. If this is how a fox feels when it's being hunted by a dozen pillocks in red coats, I thought, then I'm on the little fella's side right down the line. I also had that awful, sick feeling you get inside when you think you just might have done something drastically wrong. Too late now. I stood up and nearly had a coronary when I saw what I thought was a guard standing over me.

Except it turned out to be one of my fellow escapees, a geordie called Terry.

I recovered enough to say, 'You stupid bastard! What are you doing sneaking up on me. Jesus H Christ!'

'Sorry, man. I thought you were one a them as well! Where's the other fellas, then?'

'I don't fucking know! Do I look like a fucking shepherd?'

'Hey, it were you're bloody idea, Nicky! What do we do now then?'

'Fuck me, I'm on the run with Little Bo Peep.'

Our slanging match brought the other two out of cover. One of them, a big lad called Mikey who had an annoying habit of always cracking his knuckles, moved over to us. 'Now, now, girls. Don't bicker.'

I saw one of his hands move to the other and decided to nip this in the bud right away. 'Crack one fucking knuckle, Mikey' – I pointed at his hovering hand – 'and I'll crack your fat head.'

'Bloody hell! Who died and put you in charge?'

'*I* put me in charge when I was the first to have the balls to deck that guard!' The fourth member of our little gang, John, started laughing. 'Yeah, did you see his face? Fuck me, I've never seen a face like it. Did ya see the face on 'im?'

Eventually we set off in the direction of the base, but before we got too close we veered off towards a nearby farm. I found the farmer's wife (and a big, ruddy ox of a woman she was, too), told her that we were on an exercise and asked if we could sleep in their barn. ' 'Course you can, my love,' she said, and off we trotted into the hay.

Sitting up in the dark musty loft, we found a new satisfaction at what we'd done, mostly through laughing at what we knew the others must be going through. 'Those poor bastards,' and 'Bet they wished they'd joined us,' were typical comments that night.

'I could eat a scabby horse's head,' said Mikey.

And I'd have fought him for it. I was bloody starving. So there then followed another bickering session over who should go to the farmhouse. As usual, I got pissed off before anyone else.

'I'll do it. Christ, you lot are a right bunch of schoolgirls. And make the most of cracking your knuckles while you've got the chance,' I said to Mikey.

Outside it was as black as a miner's arse but I used the glow from between the farmhouse's curtains to guide me there. The wife looked even bigger and ruddier than before as she filled the small open doorway. No wonder her poor bugger of a husband's never home, I thought. Yet, when I asked if she could spare us some food, she was so friendly that I felt guilty for thinking bad of her. That was until she returned with four measly pieces of stale bread. 'Thanks,' I muttered and turned back to the barn. Tight bastard Welsh!

'Are you fucking joking?' they all said in a chorus. 'What did you do, Nicky, grab this out of the dog's dish?'

'Look, I'll have it all if it doesn't come up to your high standards!' They all made a grab for their share. I have to say, that bread tasted like the finest food on God's green earth.

That night was a strange mixture of unease and bliss. There was the simple pleasure of doing something as basic as sleeping rough with nothing around me but silence and dark country. In unguarded moments, laying there in the shadows as the others deep-breathed in sleep, I felt really free. Like I was my own man. I savoured it because I knew that tomorrow I would be theirs.

Based on what I already knew, I tried to imagine what the ones we'd left behind were going through. I was to learn later that I wasn't too far wrong. After we'd jumped ship the guards had returned in a fury. The other squaddies had all remained knelt there, just lifting their hoods to catch sight of us four mad bastards making the Great Escape. The constant stream of effing and blinding by the guards as they made their way back made the others glad that they'd stayed; it sounded like we were going to get an even bigger kicking than the one they were in for. And there we were in the barn like the Famous bloody Four, thinking that *they* must be jealous of *us*.

Back at the camp, the rest of them had been pulled off the truck and pushed into a room for hour upon hour of mental and physical torture. When they weren't being kicked to crap or beaten with bricks and bars, they were made to stand on tip-toe whilst leaning against a wall using only their fingertips for balance. A slight slip would result in another fresh thump. Time disorientation was achieved by gradually lightening the room, then darkening it again. With only limited vision from under the hoods, they quickly lost track of minutes and hours and wondered if they had been in there for days.

When the hoods were finally pulled off there was still no respite as each man was thrown into a chair and screamed at. They had each been given pieces of 'secret' information which should never be revealed. But the trainers were as cunning as any enemy would be. After the beatings, the kindness and coaxing would start. 'Look,' they'd say, 'your mate's already told us,' and the guy in the chair would turn to see one of his fellow prisoners through an open door, laughing with a coffee in his hand. The guy would turn back completely demoralized. What he didn't realize was that the prisoner was flanked by two other trainers either side of the door, out of sight, hissing, 'Laugh you little bastard. Look like you're enjoying yourself or I'll fucking hammer you!' Which they did anyway as soon as the door was closed.

Some real hard-as-nails blokes went in there, and even they came out shaken.

We got back to base and immediately walked into the sharp end of a world-class dressing down. I was held responsible. I suddenly had the shocking realization that I was in line for the worse thing that could possibly happen to any soldier here – to be R.T.U.'d, or Returned To Unit. It was worse than not coming up to scratch – that was just undertraining and you could always reapply; this was being ignominiously kicked out for not fitting in: something much more difficult to rectify in the army's eyes.

It was too near the end of the course now to put me through what the others had endured, which elevated the seriousness of my offence.

With my career on the line – no, more than my career, my life – because by this time the army was my life, I tried everything: I pleaded ignorance of rules, misunderstanding of orders, before eventually settling for 'using my initiative during engagement with the enemy'.

The fact that I wasn't R.T.U.'d was mostly down to the guard commander's own embarrassment at not posting enough men to guard us and I was released with a commendation for initiative!

Even by my standards, it was a close call. To this day, I still can't quite believe that I got away with it.

I returned to Minden walking on air; flying in fact, because I felt like Superman. Or at least superfit and supertrained. Despite my first doubts about what the trainers were putting us through, I came to understand their wisdom and experience in doing what they did. I left feeling ten times better for the confidence and self-belief that they had helped to instil in me. I felt I could achieve anything that I put my mind to.

Back on base I strode into the HQ office, ready for anything they cared to throw at me. I felt more than a little deflated when I was told that most of the regiment was out on exercise. If I'd thought I was now indispensable, then this was quickly dashed by my subdued homecoming. But that's the army for you. At almost every level you have to subjugate yourself to the greater good, to the most effective overall plan. It just cannot function without that understanding and the discipline that it requires. Yes, there are moments for personal decision-making and individualism, but by and large you are a part of a much greater machine.

I leaned down on the desk and chatted to what was, apparently, the only man left on base from the First Battalion Green Howards. Corporal 'Happy' Applegate was a deeply mournful individual with a face like a warped fiddle.

'What's new then, Happy?' He gave me the news that I had been promoted to full corporal, as of two weeks ago. I figured out that it was just about the same time that I'd been wheeling around a Welsh hill after a sheep that seemed reluctant to be my dinner.

Happy didn't look up from his paperwork. 'And you've got a new platoon commander for your lot, Six Platoon. He's arriving soon.'

Now that was interesting. Happy told me the new commander was called Chris Mather. 'Sounds like a bit of a plonker to me, Hap. No doubt he'll be another bloody "Rupert".'

'Rupert' was the disparaging name we gave to a certain type in the infantry; as in, 'He's just a bloody Rupert, what does he know?' They were always public school twits, over-privileged gits who scraped through Sandhurst with barely enough experience to clean a rifle, let alone fire one. The kind of men that sent thousands over the top to certain death in the First World War. They came flying in at a high level and demanded a respect that they could rarely earn.

'Pull his file for us, Happy,' I said, 'let's see what's in store.'

Against regulations, Happy showed me the file before it had even been inside the adjutant's office. It didn't make for a good read; in fact I felt about as happy as Happy looked after I'd finished reading it. Mather's military service was about as short as my patience. After initially good reports, he had been recommended for a parachute regiment course. There he got further good reports until, amazingly, he backed out from his first of three mandatory jumps over Salisbury Plain. Bolstered by my recent success and my confidence in myself as a 'real' soldier rather than a tin one, I felt justified in dismissing him as a wanker. Little did I know then that this was the man who would soon change my life.

A few days later I caught sight of Lieutenant Mather for the first time and felt satisfied in my earlier opinion. He was in the process of being put through a joke sword drill by a fat bastard of a jumped-up captain playing at being a sergeant-major. The captain's fellow officers stood on the edge of the parade ground laughing at the performance. I felt for Mather. A prat he may well have been, but in his present company that was a compliment.

The next day, as we had no platoon sergeant, I found myself in charge of Six Platoon. I stood out in front and surveyed the three ranks of three sections; all present, correct, and awaiting inspection by the company commander. This was first muster parade at eight-thirty in the morning. The company was brought to attention and the company commander began his march from the HQ to inspect his troops. Behind him marched the other platoon commanders, including our new one, Lieutenant Mather. I could hardly believe what I saw and closed my eyes in a silent prayer. When I opened them he was still there, and getting closer.

Seeing him walk, I realized he was what we'd call in Yorkshire, a 'gawk'. He lumbered forward towards us with such gormless neglect that I half expected to hear muffled titters from the men behind me. He got closer and closer, as large as life and twice as clueless. How come his combat suit doesn't fit, I thought, doesn't the army make them in his size? Even his beret was the wrong size; sitting on his head like an afterthought. Now, I was a big fan of the *Carry On* films, but I didn't want to be in one.

Shortly afterwards we were told that we would be moving out to be stationed in Northern Ireland for three months on an emergency tour. It didn't come as a surprise. Trouble had been cooking on a slow heat on the streets of Belfast and Derry for almost a year and we wondered if it was now coming to the boil. Advance warning signs had already been posted: several Irishmen in the regiment had gone back home on leave and never returned. We knew that they had given themselves over to the 'cause', and with all their military training they were welcomed with open arms by the para-military organizations. We even received postcards from some of them with scribbled greetings on the back which were as ominous as they were ambiguous: 'WISH YOU WERE HERE!', 'LOOKING FORWARD TO SEEING YOU'.

But I didn't spend any time worrying about it. I was just glad to leave the endless boredom of Minden behind and get a chance to see some action. I was hoping to put some of my new-found, hard-won soldiering skills into practice.

We started to prepare a training routine for what was to come. But before it could begin I was called into Colonel Ronnie Eccles's office. My report from Brecon had come through. For a second, I had the feeling they might have decided to screw me after all by writing me a damning report. The colonel read through it without his face betraying the report's contents. At least he's not laughing, I thought.

'Right,' he said breezily, clapping the green folder shut. 'They say that you are "robust", Curtis. And have initiative. You should also have made sergeant and I believe you will. How soon that happens is now up to you.'

We had more fun over the following weeks as we practised our crowd control and riot-quelling techniques. From the outset I thought that the tactics we were using were hopelessly outdated. They might have been effective in the past for contolling a bunch of mardy Victorian tarts, or some such crap, but I didn't fancy facing fifty hoolies on a Bottle-throwers' Day outing.

The current training was this: as a gang of bored soldiers from another regiment played out the part of disaffected rioters, a square of our lads would shuffle towards them with shields raised Roman legionary-style, like an arthritic tortoise. Then they'd stop and struggle to raise and unfurl a banner which bore a legend guaranteed to strike fear into the hardest rebel. It said, 'You Are An Illegal Gathering – Disperse Or We Will Fire'. The result was always immediate and conclusive: the soldiers got pelted to hell and back with stones, bin lids, bottles and old boots by the laughing rioters. Then they laid into the riot squad with great enthusiasm. It was quite amusing to watch from a distance as this great, green animal of many legs scuffled back with its tatty banner flapping sadly. After a few days of this I decided that a drastic rethink was desperately needed, if only to keep more of our men out of hospital than in it. One lad had lowered his guard after a halt to one of the exercises had been clearly called, only to be pole-axed by a real peach of a perfectly pitched cricket ball from the other regiment.

' 'Ow is 'ee!' the bowler shouted.

'None too fucking well!' came the reply.

I put a suggestion to Lieutenant Mather and he agreed that we should move to stage two of the regulation method of dealing with an unlawful assembly. This invloved the much more satisfying technique of identifying the riot ring-leaders and shooting them. As that was something that even we wouldn't do for a laugh (well, we weren't allowed to, put it that way), we got our revenge by sending a three-man snatch-squad thudding into their group. Our boys would pick out the ring-leaders, drag them out, and then beat countless colours of crap out of them.

I was pleased by the thanks I received from my platoon for instigating the tactic. We even managed to get the amateur bowler and return the compliment with an unorthodox batting technique.

I knew Ireland was going to be a much more serious affair but I still looked upon it as an adventure, and at least it wouldn't be boring.

I already had bonds with Ireland. My father's forefathers had been Irish and, raised Catholic, my spiritual grounding was there. So it was a very different feeling for me to be going there rather than the alien cultures of the Caribbean or Far East that I had visited in the past. This time I didn't feel like a visitor, or an invader, but more like a returning 'natural' coming back to help out. My sympathies were with the Catholics because of the denial of their basic constitutional right to vote through the 'no house – no vote' system. Hopefully, it would all be over soon.

The aircraft moaned in a deeper tone and I felt the descent begin. We lowered into a range of heaven-white clouds so full and blindingly white that you could believe we were about to touch the wheels down on St Peter's own landing strip. Passing through, we seemed to suspend there before we broke out beneath, slipping down to a thinner and less religious collection of lower-ranked clouds. The island below could be glimpsed with increasing clarity until it finally blasted fully into view. As the plane descended, the land filled my window until I was taken aback by the sheer beauty of it all. It seemed a brighter green than any other land I had ever seen.

The VC10's drop began to steepen and the land sharpened beneath me, revealing details of grey stone walls that divided the land into a large patchwork-quilt of fields with tiny stone houses trying to connect to the sky with ribbons of chimney smoke. It looked so tranquil that I almost doubted there was a reason for us to be there. But I knew that once we touched down a very different reality would hit me.

2

TOUCH DOWN

As the VC10's engines wound down from a howl to a heavy rumble, my unit disembarked. After witnessing the beauty of the island from above I was disappointed to find the airport much like any other I'd been in across the world: same playing-field of tarmac edged with the light-filled blocks of the terminus.

It was a cloudy but bright spring day which we didn't have the chance to appreciate before we were thrown in the back of a truck and driven away to the airport barracks by armed guards. The truck rocked along on its regulation, army-issue suspension – i.e. none – making every pot-hole feel like a landmine. The green side- and back-flaps were pulled down which meant we were travelling blind. Through the flap-cracks shafts of sunlight flashed in the gloom like on/off neon strips.

As I bounced on the bench seat, I looked around at the others, all Yorkshire lads like me and part of the northern-based Green Howards: 'Tapper' Wilson, so called because the only fags he smoked were everyone else's; Paul Austin, a danger to himself, let alone the IRA; Ken 'Blakesy' Blake, a hard-as-nails chain-smoker that measured time in fags; 'John-Boy' Matthews, so fresh faced he shaved once in a blue moon, hence being named after the son from *The Waltons*; Kev 'Socks' Crosier, because he washed them about as often as the Pope visited a brothel; Tom 'Nigger' Wallace, the permanently tanned self-appointed playboy of the group; and lastly my 2 IC (second in command), Stan Overend.

Jesus, I thought, 'Tapper', 'Nigger', 'Socks'; I hope we're better at soldiering than we are at thinking up nicknames. The army's not renowned for its originality when handing out nicknames. Any weakness, eccentricity or, preferably, major flaw is immediately jumped on. Through some grace of God I'd managed to avoid being saddled with one. And once you've got your given

21

name you'd better get used to it because only death, discharge or an act of God will rid you of it. I knew one poor bugger that had been out of the forces for years and thought he'd safely left it all behind until an old pal ran into him on the high street. Unfortunately he was with his new wife and equally unfortunately he'd had a past reputation in his unit for having a dicky stomach. Imagine him stood there while some old army buddy called him 'Crapper'.

A side-flap snapped in the wind and flickered a stripe of light down John-Boy's face as he murdered some chewing-gum, making him look more nervous than he probably was. Blakesy's fag-end flared up in the dark as he dragged the last life out of it and then immediately lit a fresh one off the dying tip. Tapper leaned across and shouted over the roaring axle beneath us, 'Got a smoke, Blakesy?'

Blakesy caught my eyes and smiled with his own. 'Yeah, thanks.' We all looked at Tapper who didn't reply with the usual, 'I meant give me one you tight bastard,' as you would with most blokes, because you had to be sure Blakesy was in the mood for such backchat. Otherwise he might give you one all right, right in the neck. Tapper sat back and Blakesy pulled one out of the pack with his teeth and threw it across the truck.

'Cheers, mate,' Tapper piped.

'Tapper,' Blakesy said, leaning forward himself now to be heard, 'you do know smoking's bad for you?'

'Yeah, well, I'll take my chances with cancer.'

'Screw cancer, I meant that if I run out of fags before the barracks I'm gonna fucking fill you in!'

Our laughter was cut short by the squeak of the brakes.

'Two cigs!' Blakesy shouted, meaning the journey had taken about five minutes.

We clambered out and entered the airport barracks to retrieve our weapons. Whenever we crossed borders or were transferred to another country, the arms would be sent separately. We unwrapped our stuff: SLRs, rounds, CS gas and rubber bullets. Kev tore open the packaging and then piped up, 'Something's missing, Sarge.' The duty officer approached. Stan continued, 'I distinctly remember wrapping ten thousand pounds in cash before we left Germany.'

'Bit of a comedian are we, son? Well don't give up your day job. Which reminds me – get back on the fucking truck!'

'Nice one, Socks,' I whispered as we filed out.

The journey into Belfast itself was longer, nearly a full pack of twenty according to Blakesy, including Tapper's 'begs'. The back-flap was finally yanked open to a square of sunlight that made us all blink as we jumped out. The trapped cloud of Blakesy's fag-smoke twirled skyward. Our boots rang off the stone of Howard Street. This was just off the Falls Road, a predominantly Catholic area of Belfast. Row upon row of terrace houses ran alongside and away from us. I thought we'd landed in Coronation Street. The houses, even for cramped, arse-to-arse terraces, were tiny.

'It's like bloody Toytown!'

The clatter of the others faded into the background around me and suddenly I was struck by something that would haunt me for years – an incredible, surging feeling of déjà vu. Even though I'd never been to Ireland before, in this moment it felt like a homecoming. It was a strange mixture, of newness and yet something warmingly familiar. With my grandma being a classic, flame-haired Irish Catholic, I was used to the accent and tales of the old country, but nothing that prepared me for this.

I remembered how I used to go down to visit her every Tuesday; always Tuesday because it was pension day and, necky little sod that I was, I knew she'd slip me half-a-crown, and it was here that I lay on the floor and watched an old black-and-white film that was also to stay with me down the years. It was called *The Informer* and told the story of a young Catholic whose life is changed one day when he sees two signs: one says 'WANTED! INFORMATION ON IRA – £20 REWARD!' and the other, 'YOUR NEW LIFE IN AMERICA – £20 PASSAGE!'. He made the obvious connection, grassed up some gunman and, after the Black and Tans had done the killing, received his money to start a new life. But he couldn't go to America, forever haunted by the guilt of what he'd done.

'Corporal Curtis! What are you waiting for, a twenty-one-gun salute? Move it!'

I turned back to the group thinking a strange thing, that no matter how bad it got here, I would always be protected; as if there was an outside spirit watching over me. I could almost hear Johnny Jones's cry from back on the training ground: 'What is your secret, Curtis? You seem to think you're bloody bullet-proof!'

Don't get too caught up in this idea of divine intervention Nicky boy, I thought, you're just as liable to get slotted as the next man.

Though I'd been raised a Catholic, I'd committed the mortal sin of not going to Mass for a good few years, and my last confession had been breaking old Mrs Stolley's window with a football and blaming it on my pal Derek. Little did I know that my time here would keep a good Catholic boy in confession for the whole of the bloody football season.

There being no army barracks in Belfast, of course, we were stationed in an old, commandeered mill on Howard Street, just off the Falls Road. The high perimeter walls were dotted with patrol guards cradling their rifles like babies. Inside, the mill was a vast aircraft hangar of a building converted into barracks; subdivided into rooms, offices, and dormitories lined with beds and 'thunderboxes', as we called the portable toilets. Every week the 'sludge gulper' (a waste-disposal wagon) would come to suck out the muck.

We threw our stuff on our bunks and occupied ourselves with a few of the four s's – shave, shit, shower and shoeshine.

While we had been back in Germany word had come through about the situation over here: the increasing number of riots kicking off and so on, and we'd all checked out the news reports when we realized we could be sent over. I remembered one thing in particular by an Ulster MP called Bernadette Devlin when she said, 'If British troops are sent in I should not like to be either the mother or sister of an unfortunate soldier stationed there.' Well, we didn't feel too unfortunate at the moment.

Out of the lads there, only Paul Austin shared any Irish ancestry with me. I watched him unpack his kit in his usual slow, bumbling manner and thought, I'm gonna have to watch out for you, m'lad, if things get hot. We were all in our early twenties, apart from Blakesy who'd just touched thirty. Having been around a bit, he was a solid, steadying influence on some of the others: a good lad to have on your team.

To the others this was just another soldiering job – get your head down and get on with it – but to me it felt like something more. I was aware of the history of the present situation: the discrimination that the Catholics lived with under Protestant rule; their being denied one man, one vote, the lack of freedom of speech and assembly and all the political bullshit that always goes along with the screwing up of people's lives. It was the kind of situation I'd seen in other countries that led ordinary people to snap. It's universal. But this was so much closer to home, not just literally but in the fact that I'd felt good about having a chance to help people who I felt some kinship with.

We were here as impartial peacekeepers. The Northern Ireland police (the RUC) and the B-Specials were viewed with hatred and distrust by the Catholics. They didn't trust either organization to protect them from Protestant attacks. Little over a year earlier the first Catholic civil rights marches through Derry's Bogside had degenerated into fighting, with the RUC and B-Specials laying into the marchers. This was when CS gas was used for the first time in the UK. When the first of our lads over there were spotted by the Catholics they were actually cheered. After one particular riot which the army helped to quell, graffiti was seen the next day proclaiming 'IRA – Irish Ran Away', because they hadn't protected the Catholic protesters. And only six months ago, in the Protestant Shankill Road, the army had battled with Loyalists who waved the Union Jack at the same time as they were screaming for us to get back to Britain!

I felt it was wrong that basic rights were being denied to one section of the community – the Catholics – by another, purely because of religious differences. It seemed crazy to me; this was 1970 not 1570.

Things had only recently started to get out of hand. Though most people still hoped for a political solution, frustrations were building. That first major riot in the Bogside had followed the usual scenario of police cars and windows being shattered and battered, and milk bottles being turned into petrol bombs. Hopefully we could help to keep a lid on it until some sense prevailed.

I snapped out of it as Blakesy chucked another of his empty, crumpled fag packets at Tom Wallace as he preened in front of a wall mirror. 'You better stick your head out of the window to top up your tan, Nigger,' Blakesy said. 'Or we'll have to start calling you "Whitey"!'

We won't be getting any R and R for a good few weeks, I thought. So we'd better start to get used to it.

Our job was to police the area and try to keep the two warring communities apart. In Belfast this was particularly difficult as the Catholics and Protestants lived back-to-back, within shouting distance of each other. The RUC couldn't police certain areas, or weren't allowed to without getting every colour of crap kicked out of them. We settled into a routine: one day patrolling, the next on back-up for the units on patrol and then the third day on guard duty back at the mill.

My friendship with our platoon commander from Minden, Chris Mather, strengthened. Particularly when we were out on patrol. That's when you really get to know someone. Out in the field can be a testing time and it lays bare the strengths and weaknesses of a character.

I'd long since changed my opinion of Chris from that first time I'd seen him on the parade ground in Germany, when I'd thought, Oh here we go, another Rupert who thinks he's David bloody Niven. With the squaddies being solidly working class and the offi-cers, more often than not, university chaps with a fast track to the top-flight positions, there was a natural animosity. We enjoyed taking the piss out of them (privately, of course) as book-learned but know-nothing Ruperts, and they enjoyed us enacting their battle plans.

Mather was one of them, but he also managed to be one of us. We hit it off almost immediately and became friends despite the differences between us. I soon learned he was as hard as nails and the squad's ex-champion middleweight, which is where he received what I called his 'posh' broken nose – a 'war' wound inflicted under the Marquess of Queensberry's rules rather than during a pub brawl. The major difference between us was religion, or Chris's lack of any. The legacy of my Catholicism was the belief in an ever-watchful God. As far as Chris was concerned, he was only watched over by the commanders.

It felt strange at first, patrolling British streets kitted out in uniform – webbing, helmet, SLR in hand – and reaction to us from the locals was divided. Most of them welcomed our presence as a buffer between them and the Prods and the RUC. We'd be handed bags of sandwiches or someone would pop out from a doorway and tell us to go round the back of the house, where we'd find a tray of biscuits and cups of tea on the dustbin waiting for us. I think to some of the mothers with sons of their own, we looked like nothing more than babies ourselves. 'See him?' one old dear said to me as she pointed at John-Boy. 'Is he really old enough to hold that weapon?' Sometimes we'd kick a ball about the streets with the kids there. Many of the people were worried about being too open about welcoming us because of fear of reprisals from the ones that held another view of our presence. These were the pure Republicans. To them, we were just another arm of the British and Northern Ireland governments, over there to do nothing but prevent their quest for equality. We were spat on and shouted at as we passed.

One incident in particular made me realize what we might be dealing with, not just from the locals but our own command. Out on patrol we turned into a street, all pretty casual until a guy came out of one of the houses swearing the air blue and waving a Union Jack. He started stomping and spitting on it. A few local lads sitting on a wall looked up, shifted and made to come over. Out of the corner of my eye I saw Blakesy turn, Tapper and John-Boy stiffen and Paul Austin move on up to join us.

'He's got a wasp up his arse,' I said, nodding at this guy who was now practically tap-dancing with rage.

'Don't you mean a bee in his bonnet?' Tapper said, moving alongside me.

'I know what I mean. He's not wearing a fucking bonnet. He looks like he's had a sting on the ring. I'm calling through. Austin, get your arse up here!' Austin, our radio man, lumbered up and turned his back to me so I could get at the receiver. I radioed through to our company commander, Major James Rocket, or 'Daddy' Rocket as he was known.

'Bit of a barney brewing here, sir,' I said without having to explain much further because of the god-almighty row in the background. I filled in a few details for the major: flag, lads, threats, wasp up arse and so on. As I replaced the handset I must have looked a little puzzled because Stan moved over to me. 'What did the old man say?'

'He said, and I quote,' I paused to adopt my best BBC English, ' "Approach the chap, inform him of his bad manners and relieve him of the flag."'

They all snorted: 'Where does he think we are, at a frigging dinner dance?' I half toyed with the idea of going up to the guy and actually saying, 'I must inform you of your bad manners, sir,' just to see the look on his face. It would have probably stopped him in his tracks. But then I glanced over Kev's shoulder at the youths hanging back over the road, looking to each other and back over at us, getting jittery with their own anticipation of what they might do. Oh, screw this, I thought, and walked up to the flag-dancing Fred Astaire. He backed off and called me a Brit bastard, the Belfast bark added extra bite to the last word. I bent and picked up the flag, and it was over.

It seemed nothing then, and we laughed about it as we walked on, but I realized how quickly that 'nothing' could turn into a pretty bloody big 'something': different time, different street, a few more bored or aggrieved lads that decided to join in . . . before you know it the stone-throwers are out and your tin hat's ringing like a bell. And the major, nice guy though he was (hence the nickname 'Daddy'), obviously had no inkling of the realities of confrontation. It planted the first seeds of disquiet within me as I started to think of how nasty things here could really get and how much we might have to rely on our own wits to get out.

The next night, though, we weren't concerned with surviving anything more than one of the discos that we occasionally threw at the mill. As usual Mather and I went up to the nearby Victoria Hospital and politely informed the matron that we would like to invite some of her lovely nurses along to our 'do', and as usual we chose the best-looking ones we could find, not wanting to disappoint the lads. The many nooks and crannies of the mill, particularly with the lights out, provided ample opportunity for cementing Anglo-Irish relations. Probably spawning a few as well.

Back out on patrol, the little goodwill we had from the locals was eroding in face of increasing violence. Riots were exploding with predictable regularity. Friday afternoons quickly became the favourite time for the kick-off. This was the traditional time for the Irish to hit the bottle, starting the weekend early. The local lads, bevvied up with beer, their engines revving with aggression at the sight of us, would congregate at a street end and lob samples of Irish stone, house-bricks and timber for us to dodge. Paul Austin, not the most agile of our unit, probably took more on his head than George Best did during a whole season.

Things were pretty lively but not too heavy; we'd bop a few of them on the head and they'd do the same to us. This aggro was almost recreational, something exciting to do for the mostly piss-poor and shit-bored unemployed youths that we were facing-off with every weekend and something exciting for us, too. Most soldiers never get a whiff of any action, so when you do you're naturally eager to get in there when it starts. Then we'd all retire, them and us, and, like cowboys round a campfire, exchange stories of our latest battles.

The school holidays came around and we were billeted at an empty school a few hundred yards down the road. A torrential rainfall came down over the next two days, real stair-rods, and the surrounding streets became flooded. They were now knee-deep rivers of dirty water. We moved out to help with the clearing-up operation and to rescue people stranded in their homes. As we waded slowly down the street it was like we were on manoeuvres in an urban jungle, tropical river and all.

An upstairs window flew open and an old woman stuck her head out screaming blue murder, 'Help me! Help me, I'm trapped!' I ordered Kev Crosier to get her down before her screaming started another bloody riot, although in these conditions the petrol bombs would be nothing more than damp squibs that would plop into the water and sink without trace.

Kev dropped a ladder against the house and shimmied up to our cries from below of, 'Go on, Socks! Give her the fireman's lift!' He grabbed her. Then, as the ladder wobbled and he put his hand out to the drainpipe for balance, there was an almighty bang. What we didn't know was that the flood waters had shorted the electrics and somehow made the drainpipe a live wire. We all shouted, 'Fuck me!' as the volts threw Crosier away from the wall, dragging this old dear out of the window with him. She seemed to sail down in slow motion, her skirts blown up around her startled face, and they both belly-flopped into the water with a slap. She staggered to her feet, looking like a drowned rat and crying her eyes out, as if she wasn't wet enough already. 'Jeysus! Jeysus!' she kept saying. Kev just sat there like a prize coconut knocked off its shy while we all fell about.

'Good work, Private Crosier,' I shouted. 'That's what I call an efficient manoeuvre!'

No sooner had we helped out in some way than we'd be liable immediately to get bottled again for our pains. Soon after, on one boring Monday afternoon, we saw a crowd of local women marching down the street towards us in some kind of protest. We couldn't work out what was going to happen.

'They probably heard about Crosier,' I said. 'Trying to break into that old bird's window for a leg over.' We all laughed but we were wondering if this was a set-up for something less funny coming from behind them; something milk-bottle shaped with a flaming rag in the top. Our platoon sergeant, John Tombs, daft bat that he was, ordered us all to get out in our riot gear and approach. So there we were, tooled-up to the back teeth with shields and batons, walking towards them while they walked towards us. The meeting point was fast approaching and I was thinking, Well, what the chuff happens now? As soon as we'd hit the street the unit came under my command. Tombs was five hundred yards back and he'd put me right in the shit. This was my first real test of command and I was in a ridiculous position. Do we arrest them? Do we let them walk through? If they hit us do we bop 'em back? This is crazy.

Fortunately, our commander, Colonel Eccles, looked out of one of the school windows in the nick of time and saw this strange scene. He leaned out and screamed, 'Tombs! Get those men back! Now!'

We filed back like a bunch of idiots and the women burst into the Irish anthem at full voice.

'We'll put that one down to a home win then,' I said to the others.

I tried not to make any mistakes, and if I did to learn from them; or from the mistakes others had made. Not everyone had the same idea. Some just didn't know when to take advice. Invariably these were the men of a higher rank, because if a guy was below you in rank you didn't waste time 'suggesting' he should do something, you just told him to do it. 'When I say jump, you say how high?' was the general philosophy. When it came to an officer above you, the most you could do was tactfully to make a suggestion.

I found myself in this position a week later and, because of what ensued, for once I was glad my advice hadn't been taken. We left the mill gates and within a hundred yards ran slap-bang into another crowd of women holding a protest. There must have been nearly two hundred of them. They were a surprisingly formidable sight. From what I knew, I thought I'd rather face an angry Englishman than a riled-up Irishwoman. They were all in full-blooded voice, singing Irish anthems.

Over my shoulder, I heard Nigger say, 'That's all we need. A couple of hundred Irish birds on their period.'

'Put a lid on it, smartarse!' I said, turning back to him. 'We've got to deal with this, remember? I might just send you in first.' He looked like he relished the idea about as much as I did. We went back into the mill and togged up in riot gear just in case, then returned to the crowd. I peeled off and approached them, making a bee-line for who I thought was one of the leaders. The singing continued. It actually seemed to get stronger as I walked over. I only managed to say a few words before they informed me I should fuck off back to England quote 'you Brit bastard', unquote. Then the first of a volley of bottles and bricks pelted down on top of me as I retreated with as much dignity as I could muster, which was none at all.

I scanned the lads' faces for Nigger's. I thought, If I detect even a *hint* of a smile from him, I'm gonna bollock him something shocking when we get back to base. He knew this and he looked back at me blankly. Yeah, I thought, you always were a smart bastard.

By this time the singing and shouting, not to mention the other locals who'd come out to spectate, had drawn Major Dixon from behind his desk and out into the street.

'What's going on here, Corporal. Trouble?'

Oh, here we go, I thought. 'Err . . . could say that, sir. Nothing we can't handle. Could be a riot brewing if we don't nip it.'

'Have you attempted to negotiate with them, Corporal?'

I thought, Yeah, if you count a few words, a 'fuck off' and a bottle on the head as 'negotiation'. 'Yes, sir,' I replied. 'They're not having any of it, sir.'

'Okay, Corporal. Let me try.'

'I don't think that's a good idea, sir.'

'Nonsense. We don't want this to escalate, now do we?'

'No, sir. But I think you'd better take my helmet.' I moved to take it off but he waved me away. 'No, really, sir. I think you'd better take it.' He strode off, leaving me behind holding the helmet in my outstretched hand. I watched him cross the ground between them and us, marching over with all the confidence of General Custer and with about the same amount of savvy.

We held our breath as he made it to the front line and exchanged a few words with the same woman I'd approached. They talked. Nothing happened. We all looked around at each other in amazement. Maybe the old bugger's pulled it off, I thought. Amazing the weight a few pips and stripes can carry. I didn't have these women down as the type to be impressed by a man in uniform.

Finally, he turned away and started back. The first brick hit him smack on the back of the head and felled him like a tree. The woman at the front punched the air at her own accuracy. Funnily enough, right then I felt I had more in common with her than him. Then a storm of bricks and bottles came out of the crowd.

'*Fucking* hell!' We stood rooted to the spot for a second, then dashed in as Dixon's flat-out body began to get covered in debris. Three of us lifted him as the others charged the mob to keep them back. I'd dropped my helmet in the rush and felt a brick flick the top of my ear as it whizzed by. Major Dixon's body sagged dead-weight between us, his left foot bobbing along the ground as we dragged him away.

Behind, I could hear the women shouting, mocking some of what he had obviously said to them: 'You fucking "disperse", you fucking old fart!' and 'How's that for "escalation", yer bastard!'

By the time we got him inside the mill the hair on the back of his head was wet and matted with blood, like someone had cracked a box of raw eggs on him. He was just starting to come around as he was whisked off to hospital. I heard later he needed a dozen stitches.

After that he wore a helmet.

The riots swung between the dangerous and the farcical. A guy called Nicos Michaelidos temporarily joined us. Of course, he was named 'Nick the Greek'. His parent company the Prince of Wales Regiment had just been posted out to Cyprus but he couldn't go because of his Greek background. Conflict of interest. So he was sent over to Northern Ireland and ended up with us. Trouble is, he had had no preparatory training. He just came in cold and tried to wing it.

Which he did quite well until we walked into a riot one day. It turned nasty enough for us to pull on our masks and fire CS gas into the crowd to make them disperse. It always did the job. The stuff stripped your throat raw and made you feel that your lungs were being rubbed with sheets of sandpaper.

The first of the gas was starting to bite when I felt a tap on my shoulder and turned to see Nicos in just his beret, turning green at the gills. He was gesturing wildly to me that he didn't have a mask. Through mine, I shouted to him, 'What the fuck do you want me to do?' but the noise around us was too loud for him to hear – not that I was telling him anything useful. Then the gas really bit into him and he turned and ran off, coughing his guts up. Welcome to Northern Ireland.

Next time he wore his mask, but then forgot to stay within shouting distance and as I bellowed orders at him to come back, he ran off down the street, deaf to my calls, chasing rioters by himself. Luckily he ran into another patrol, eventually, and returned safely with them.

Our intentions of by-the-book behaviour when it came to rioting didn't last very long, especially when we worked out the rioters were going by a completely different book – *DIY Death and Disorder*, probably. Shouting out to them, 'You are an illegal assembly – disperse or we will use tear gas!' had about the same effect as shouting out the recipe for sponge pudding. In fact, they probably would have taken more notice of that.

One particular time we rushed a crowd to break them up. It wasn't too big but was vicious. Little running battles were kicking off. Most of the street doors were open, with people spectating: just stood there, gawping, leaning against the door jamb shouting abuse and flicking V-signs. They all wanted to see a Brit fall. At one point a frying pan flew out of God-knows-where and banged off my shoulder.

Chris spotted what he said was one of the 'chief goaders' in a doorway. We moved from our usual block formation into an arrow shape (this was Chris's idea; an adaptation of the Roman legionaries' 'wedge') and advanced with shields held high. The bottles bounced off and we stormed the target's front door as he disappeared inside. Unfortunately, we forgot to break formation, ran full strength into the doorway and got jammed there. It was like something out of bloody Laurel and Hardy. We pushed and pulled ourselves free, practically falling inside the house to find Blake already tussling with the guy, who was holding a lampstand. As he drew his arm back to hit Blake, he accidentally bopped Tapper as he came up behind. We fell about around the furniture until we managed to drag the bugger out into the street. There stood Chris. Shaking his head he said, 'No. I meant *that* door . . .'

But the little amusements would wither away as the danger increased. The first deaths were nearing.

The battles between Protestants and Catholics were increasing. They were running each other out of their homes in the areas where the two met. I also detected an increasingly organized nature to the riots we were facing by those who planned them. Orders were obviously being relayed to the mobs by their commanders, pretty much in the way we got orders from ours. The RUC was unable to cope with this groundswell chaos and their job in the no-go areas where it originated was near impossible. Belfast was fracturing into ghettos and the army was gradually being forced to take over as the force of law and order.

On the edge of the violence, just audible above the shouts and the shitola, I was aware of politicians making noises in search of a peaceful settlement but it sounded like nothing more than the faint and faraway honking of geese. And do you know how much use a goose is on a battlefield? We used them as sandbags.

In June 1970 the British general election saw Harold Wilson pack up his pipe and slippers as Labour fell to the Conservatives under the leadership of their chief goose, Ted Heath. The relative restraint that Wilson showed in using the army in Northern Ireland gave way to a different, more involved approach by the Tories. Within days of the election we found ourselves part of a massive operation.

A large arms cache was found on the Lower Falls and General Freeland decided that enough was enough and ordered a three-day curfew to be imposed on the Falls Road. When orders came through we realized just how big an op it was going to be. The guts of 3,000 troops were to go into the cordoned-off area and search for weapons.

The next Friday afternoon we moved in on the ground while helicopters hovered and glowered above us. Even I found the sound of those things scary, and they were on my side. Through loudspeakers the choppers barked out orders for the residents to stay in their homes at all times. It was the biggest manoeuvre I'd yet been involved in. Even though each unit was only aware of what was going on immediately around them, you could feel the presence of all the ground forces moving in.

I moved my unit through the small streets. They seemed already clotted with tension. Even above the clatter of chopper blades I could hear the din of shouting and banging all around us. It echoed over the rooftops, making it seem like the whole of Belfast was involved in a massive, screaming argument. The stay-inside rule for residents was to be adhered to and enforced rigidly. If a guy popped his head out at the wrong time, it was whacked and pushed back in. I looked around and saw Blakesy on the other side of the street doing just that to a guy trying to leave his house. Blake bopped him and the bloke started protesting that he was only going out for some fags. Blake, being the biggest Fag Ash Harry of all time, probably understood this craving more than most, but orders were orders.

I heard him shout, 'Smoke a bloody chair leg or summat! I don't give a fuck – just get back in the bloody house!'

As the light began to drop, the rioting kicked off big-time. I didn't think there had been room for it to shift up a gear, but it did. Squaddies came out nursing lumpy heads and limping from cracked shins where bricks had skipped under their shields. Some of the shields were split in two. Or I'd see the odd soldier being helped away as his head smouldered like a snuffed candle where the flames from a petrol bomb had just been patted out. We spent the whole night buried in chaos, trying to quell it, or manage it; at the best survive it, at the worst avoid it. For the first time we came under sniper fire. They'd found another gear.

At first light we hit the houses in quick succession, clattering up tiny staircases that made you feel like a giant; the rush of adrenalin pumping you double-size as the steps were taken two at a time. We turned over beds, and wardrobes. The homeowners reacted with anything from sullen defiance to outright screaming fits of indignation. We went through them all ruthlessly and methodically, as we had to. As we were trained to.

I caught the whiff of the first CS gas pellets breaking open; heard the dull *buff* of petrol bombs and the crack and tinkle of breaking glass that would last the rest of the day; a wail of voices over the bark of dogs and orders.

As things progressed we knew that we'd fall out of the doorway of one house only to see fighting in the street outside another. A guy still in his pyjamas came out cursing, wielding a lamp and whacked Stan across the head. Stan dodged the next one and decked the bloke with his rifle butt. I knew full well that a lot of the lads were taking this opportunity to vent their anger over things already done. Heads were being cracked and houses trashed from top to bottom. Everything in the houses became a mass of rubble but, out of the blur, little, sharp details still cut through: school photos; smiley family pictures (cracked); trinkets and crucifixes (snapped); kids crying; crunching on the glass of the Pope's picture; unfinished meals and bad wallpaper; coloured toys and TV noise and radio crackle; painted plates; shoes; a body in the hall, flattened against the wall.

The home is a very private place. You'd even choose to die there, if you could. I knew it wasn't just to an Englishman that it was a castle but to an Irishman as well. This is when I did feel like we'd invaded.

I curbed the lads in my unit, bollocking anyone that got too far out of line, and tried to prevent any of the wholesale destruction that I knew was going on around the streets. Fear and recrimination: I understood both and liked neither.

I could do little about the rest of the squads. This is sometimes how human beings behave, I thought as I stood out in the street, surrounded by it all. And soldiers are human beings, too, with all the good and bad that implies.

I turned and saw a lance-corporal searching three men against a wall. When he started laying into them I ran over and stopped him.

'They're carrying live ammo, Corporal!' he said.

I looked at his outstretched hand. What he thought were live rounds were just empty CS gas cases that the men, for reasons best known to themselves, had picked up and pocketed.

'These are dead cases you daft bastard! You should know the difference! Let them go.'

We got news that one of the armoured personnel carriers (or PIGs as everyone called them because of their snout-shaped bonnets) had run over a local lad and killed him. All hell was breaking loose. These people were devout Catholics and I thought to myself, Where is their God now? Then I realized that for the first time I could remember, I had thought of God as being someone else's concern rather than mine.

The curfew remained in force over the whole weekend. We stayed on the streets throughout night and day, unable to sleep as we were on continuous patrol. At one point I saw a squaddie down on his haunches, resting his gun butt on his ammo pouch to take the weight. He rocked back and forth as he nodded off until he finally lost it and keeled back straight through a shop window. This did quite a good job of waking him up.

Things were turning really nasty. As the curfew continued, the residents were getting increasingly angry about being trapped in their own homes. We were getting more tired and more likely to snap. Eventually an appeal came out of the area to let the women and children come out for provisions. After some deliberation, the go-ahead was given and the women filed out, pushing a squeaky-wheeled convoy of prams. We had no female WRACs here (who were the only ones authorized to search women) and I knew some of the prams were going out with guns hidden under the babies.

By the last morning we were all completely knackered and aching for our bunks. By this time they'd feel like fur-lined waterbeds.

In the days that followed, the arms and explosives we'd found, which wasn't a great deal, unsurprisingly, were laid out for all to see and the media to report. Still, I'd seen the hatred in the faces of the people and I couldn't keep the lid on a constant, nagging feeling I had that something more than houses and Provo gun dens had been destroyed over the weekend.

3

THE OBEDIENT DEAD

The developing situation in Belfast wasn't our immediate concern any more, as only days later we returned to camp in Germany on leave. Almost immediately we received some devastating news. Sergeant Collier approached, grim faced.

'Sorry lads, I've just heard that Leeds lost to Arsenal.'

The Green Howards, being a northern regiment, and most of us Leeds supporters, let out a collective moan punctuated by cries of 'southern bastards'. This meant Arsenal took the Championship from us.

'Oh, and also,' the sarge added, almost as an afterthought, 'the IRA set off a bomb at Springfield police station.'

We were still too upset about Leeds to give a tinker's toss about this other news. The four months' leave ahead of us seemed like for ever.

My second descent through the clouds came round soon enough, though. This time the Emerald Isle had lost some of its shine for me. I knew it would be only minutes before that green turned to grey.

We were now stationed in a mill on the corner of Flax Street where it met the Crumlin Road. This was in the Ardoyne, the predominantly Catholic enclave in the very heart of Belfast.

The mill was in one of the worst areas of what was, by now, an altogether pretty bad scene. Thinking about our move from the previous mill to this one, the words 'frying pan' and 'fire' came to mind. Far from improving, or even stabilizing, matters had deteriorated. Guns were now more frequently being used against us during rioting.

The next morning I was taken out on the streets by the section commander of the light infantry that we were relieving. He was to show me the ropes, and how to avoid getting accidentally hanged by them.

We walked the tangle of narrow streets and terraces. He pointed out likely ambush points and escape routes. Past the Holy Cross Primary School and down Herbert Street, we came to a narrow passage. This led from the area we were in, the Old Ardoyne, to what was known as the New Ardoyne. Here the streets breathed a little wider. The houses were still packed in rows like giant dominoes but they had the luxury of small gardens out front. These at least offered some chance of cover if you were pinned down. Back in the old part, once a door was slammed on you, your arse was hanging out in the street. You could only squeeze half of your body flat into the shallow doorways.

We walked past the bus depot, then two streets up crossed Farringdon Gardens where the Protestant area of the Ardoyne begins. Safer ground.

All the time he pointed out known faces, differentiating between local likely lads, troublemakers, and the more important hard core: these were known members of the Provisional IRA. One man in particular struck me, and not just because of the extra edge in the commander's voice as he motioned towards him. It was when we were returning to the mill, near to the Crumlin Road, as we passed the Frank Kelly Club. The guy was just coming out of the club and crossing the road in front of us. He was a small, barrel-chested bloke with a pitted face.

'That's Martin Meehan. IRA staff captain. Big-time bastard.'

I clocked him and logged it. I rarely forgot a face especially one that looked like Meehan's.

We had cause to remember a lot of ugly faces. They were probably visions of beauty to their mothers back at home, but out in the street in the middle of a screaming riot they lost some of their charm.

I understood their frustrations and the fact that we were the easiest and most visible target to vent them on, but the trouble was I could see we were being gradually pushed into responses that made us feel at war with the Catholics. However sympathetic I was to their predicament, the natural response to being attacked – especially for a soldier – is to fight back.

We were constantly thinking up ways to outsmart each other. The water-cannons that we brought in proved ineffective – some bottle-thrower would be knocked on his arse but get back up and move just out of range before he started swinging his arm again. And in the long, hot summer of 1970 their only effect was to encourage kids to come outside for a cool soaking down. What with the sun and all the water we supplied, every riot would end with a little rainbow in the street, arcing over broken glass and brick dust.

So the next bright idea was to fill the cannons with blue dye, blast the guilty and then spend the rest of the week arresting anyone walking the streets stained up to the eyeballs. But, the spray being so indiscriminate, every man and his dog would get blasted. The next day uniformed squaddies would stop off-duty ones who had been hit and hadn't been able to wash the bloody stuff off; Old Mother Reilly from No. 27 would get a faceful as she poked her head out for a nosy; innocent bystanders on their way to the shops would go home looking like blue-arsed baboons. The Ardoyne ended up with more blue faces than the North Pole.

The directives from High Command seemed increasingly like a joke to me. The Rules of Engagement we were supposed to follow were laid out in a little yellow cardboard booklet we were all issued with. We were supposed to cry 'Halt!', shout a warning 'as loud as possible, preferably by loud-hailer, to anyone not doing so', and then 'Never use more than *minimum* force necessary to enable you to carry out your duties'.

Unfortunately, the little yellow book of rules sent out to the rioters and the IRA must have got lost in the post because they decided to play by their own rules. And after headbutting one too many house-bricks, the general consensus in my unit, mostly down to me, was 'Bollocks to this'. Chris and I decided to come up with our own plans for getting out of here alive.

It became obvious that the riots were now less spontaneous outbursts of anger and more orchestrated attacks on us. I realized that the bottle- and stone-throwing was now just a 'come-on' to get us out to play: the foreplay before the snipers came out to screw us. One day I decided I'd had enough and came up with a new plan of action. I thought, Well, why don't we cut through the crap of the first stages and get the big boys out into the open as soon as possible. Get it over and done with and see who's left standing. One of the directives of the new Curtis Rules of Engagement was, during night-time battles, to shoot out the streetlights. This got the pawns off the board and the bigger pieces with the guns into play. The trouble was, we couldn't use our own rifles because their sound was instantly recognizable across the whole of Belfast. And if the commanders at HQ heard it, which they would, then we'd have to radio in and report a contact. So Chris and I bought our own handguns: a Spanish Star pistol for me and an American Smith & Wesson for Chris. He really treasured that gun; he'd turn it over in his hand, saying, 'Isn't it a beauty?' Like many of the guys who carried hand-guns, he adapted it by knocking off the grip on the right-hand side of the butt. This meant it sat more snugly in the palm.

Using our own pistols to shoot out the lights, however, led to another, unforeseen, problem. One time it caused us to shoot at each other. I had banged out a few streetlights, unaware that another army unit was near-by. They heard the crack, realized it wasn't the sound of an army-issue round and assumed it was IRA gunmen. They fired on us and, not realizing who they were, we did the same to them; in the heat of the attack we couldn't stop and listen to their gunsound – we just immediately fired back.

In the middle of this I tried to contact any other unit for back-up. Inevitably I got through to the unit that was firing on us, which happened to be 1 Para. After a brief exchange of information – including a lot of 'fuck offs', 'daft bastards' and jokes about one being as bad a shot as the other – we finally established that they were at one end of the street, we were at the other and there was no bugger between us. We met up in the middle of the street and, after cursing each other, agreed that it was lucky we hadn't been on top form or someone would be dead. They have a term for when you're fired on by your own; they call it 'friendly fire'. But when you're on the receiving end of it, it feels about as friendly as anything that's come from your enemy.

Part of this 1 Para outfit was a Greek lad I knew called Georgio. I recognized him immediately as he approached. A foot shorter than everyone else but twice as hard, he bounced on his feet like a boxer. Months later I'd hear that one day he went out dressed in civvies with a shotgun inside his jacket lining. He pulled the perfect bank job: got in, got the money, got out. And then he ran right into an army patrol and got eight years.

Another ploy that worked for me was to shoot down roof-tiles on to the rioters. None of this was exactly standard procedure as laid out for us, but I decided I'd rather risk a bollocking back at base from a Rupert than get one in the neck out on the street during a protracted engagement. Graveyards are full of the obedient dead, I thought. I'd rather be a disobedient breather.

The roof-tiles ploy came into use not long after when we were out on patrol.

At the foot of Brompton Park a half-brick appeared in the air above me and whizzed over my helmet. I winced as, behind me, I heard the familiar clank of brick-on-head. Without turning round, I said, 'Austin?'

'Sir?' He sounded pained.

'You can dodge if you want, lad. What are you aiming for – a world headache record?'

'Didn't see it, Corporal!'

The raggedy-arsed kid that had thrown it can't have been more than twelve. He punched the air laughing: 'Yer British fuckers! Fuck off!' His face dropped and he spun round and ran as we ran at him. House doors slammed in succession ahead of us as the spectators fled indoors. The cheering crowd shifted but didn't disperse as usual. This is going to be different, I thought, and as we hit the halfway point of the street the first volley of petrol bombs rose out of the back of the mob and shattered in front of us. The bottles boomed open and balloons of flame mushroomed up and then splashed out flat, skittering along the street towards us. We flattened against the houses to a loud cheer from the crowd. A body hit the wall behind me and I turned to see Nigger doing a war dance, stamping out flames on his toe-caps.

'You know that nurse you shagged the other night?' I said.

'Yeah?' He was breathing heavily.

'You might be getting to see her again sooner than you think the way this is going.'

He looked at me and we both stared at his smoking boots.

'And those fuckers are gonna take some polishing up,' I said.

'Maybe we should approach them and inform them of their bad manners,' he suggested.

Through the fire, I looked at the mob of red screaming faces wobbling in the heat haze. The stench of fumes made me light-headed, but through the fire I noticed something. Although the front of the crowd was still bouncing with aggression – lobbing bricks and giving V-signs – there was a small pocket of calm at the back. A few noticeably older guys were exchanging words and nods and surveying the scene with some detachment. Something was relayed from the back and the mob, which had now swelled to over a hundred, started to advance. There was a sudden loud crack. I looked around but we were all still there. This was a trick of the rioters: to set off bangers in imitation of gunshots in order to scare us or get us to react. There were only eight of us and we'd learned as quickly as they had how warning shots over the head soon lose their power to shock. I sank the SLR into my shoulder and felt it buck as I sprayed a whole row of rooftops above the first advancing lines. The bullets hammered the slates apart and sent them spinning and smashing on to the people below. They scattered and backed off. It was unorthodox, but it sure as hell worked.

'Austin! Get the radio up here now! We're not gonna be back for tea tonight.' I radioed through and explained that this one was well organized. Within minutes, the back-up patrol had fired out of the mill, all tooled up with batons, visored helmets and the six-and-a-half-foot transparent shields used to form a wall. By the time we'd been back to the mill to fetch our own and returned, the crowd had swelled to four hundred rioters while two cars engulfed in flames formed a barricade. The flames grew brighter as the sun went down.

Chris, being our platoon commander, was surveying the scene.

'Those three at the front are orchestrating the rest around them. Take a snatch squad out there to put the shit up them and drag them in.'

At that point a guy who, I must admit, must have had some balls, found the bravado to advance the extra ten yards needed to fling a petrol bomb close enough to hit us. The bottle seemed to disappear in the dark and then suddenly it zipped out of the flames of the barricade and split open on the wall of shields. The shields danced back and split as a fire extinguisher was brought forward to douse the flames. One lad hopped around with his shins on fire until a fire blanket was wrapped around them. I heard a muffled cheer through the crackle and spit of the burning cars.

Blakesy, Tapper and I swapped our larger shields for smaller portable ones, pulled out a baton each and got in position. This is what we'd trained for. The street was partially blocked by the cars but the open part was filling with the advancing mob. A rain of bricks clanked down on the helmets in front of us. One chunk ricocheted under a visor and split the lad's chin open. As he was passed back through the ranks we advanced like a Roman battle squad. I could see one ring-leader beckoning us on with one hand, a bottle topped with a flaming rag held in the other. Now! The shields split. We belted through and out. The crowd spread. Most of them ran. A quick volley of bricks hit us from those who dared to stand a second. Blood banged in my ears. Tapper shouted, 'Shit!' as a brick hit. He stumbled and nearly fell, then caught up with a guy who turned and instinctively headbutted him; the rioter knocked himself clean out on the helmet! The ring-leader spun to me, raised his arm, then tripped backwards and fell. The bottle landed intact and spun, flickering. I leaped over it and cracked him in the face with the arm shield as he rose. His nose liquidized against the hard plastic. I grabbed his shirt, which ripped open to the waist as he tore away and ran, bounced off a wall and disappeared. A whole crate of petrol bombs landed in the street and blew. I caught sight of people hanging like monkeys on the house roofs, lining up more.

We staggered back breathless, Tapper dragging his unconscious charge by the ankle. Blakesy was still out there, just behind us, kicking a guy in the balls as another car was driven at speed at one of those already on fire, shunting it closer to us. Sparks blew off from the impact before the new car hit a lamppost and groaned. We all got back as a cheer erupted from behind the flames.

I heard the dull *buff* of the first rubber bullets going out as we were swallowed back into the parted shields.

'This stupid sod butted me!' Tapper said, almost laughing. His cracked visor danced with the reflected flames of the barricade, making his face seem on fire. Harry Headbutt was starting to come round as he was dragged away.

'I can't believe that bottle didn't blow,' I said.

'Someone smiled down on you and that bastard that dropped it, Curtis,' a voice said. I looked up from down on my haunches to see Chris. He turned as another round of rubber bullets went out into the night. They were fired by fat-barrelled Fed guns, so called because they'd been bought from the American Federal Guard, who had used them on black civil rights marchers in the States. I remembered what I had thought when I read about that: America – a supposedly civilized Western democracy, on the verge of a civil war – how could that happen in this day and age? The irony struck me: here we were facing the same thing in our own back yard.

'So much for withdraw and observe,' I said to Chris, referring to the now long-defunct procedure we were supposed to follow.

'Yeah, well sod that,' he said. 'If they want a fight . . .'

A PIG rumbled up behind us. As we parted, it sped through and smashed the burning cars away like toys. The shower of orange sparks looked almost bonfire-pretty.

We followed through, picking up anyone we could catch and throwing them in the back of another PIG. As we reached the end of the street, most of the crowd had fled, leaving behind the dropped evidence of the attack: piles of bricks and bottles mingling

with the spent rubber bullets. I saw one rioter on the ground holding his face. Blood ran through his fingers.

I noticed Nigger against a wall in conversation with a civilian.
He didn't look like a local in his obviously expensive leather jacket
and patent loafers. He was scribbling in a notepad as another guy
in a heavily pocketed bodywarmer took photographs. Nigger
finally sauntered over, looking smug with himself.

'What were you telling them?' I asked, 'That you're the playboy
of the British army or summat? Chief nurse shagger?'

'Funny you should say that,' he said as he turned to throw an
exaggerated salute as the two moved off. 'You're not gonna believe
this, but they're journalists from *Playboy* magazine!'

'Get stuffed.'

'Straight up! I told them that the Irish women love it when a riot
kicks off 'cos afterwards they go round picking up all the rubber
bullets so they can use them as dildos! And he fucking believed
me!'

He had a point. They did look similar. If they'd been modelled
on a horse's, that is. True enough, a month later Wallace would
come running into the mill waving the latest copy of *Playboy* with
the photo taken there against the wall, quote and all. We pointed
out how he'd probably scuppered his chances with any Irish bird.
He said no God-fearing Irish girl would ever see a copy of a porn
mag, or dare admit to it if she had.

It wasn't all head-the-bottle battles, though. A good deal of
soldiering is downright boring. We had to learn to cope with that,
too. Although I didn't have to be a rocket scientist to be able to see
that these stretches of boredom we had now were going to get
shorter and shorter over the coming months. There was something
in the air other than petrol bombs.

For the time being we made the most of the calm. One of my
unit's regular diversions came about during a particularly uneventful night patrol. The place where I'd had Martin Meehan pointed
out to me – the Frank Kelly Club – was an illegal drinking joint. It
was one of many. The locals were frightened of drinking anywhere
but on safe home turf in the Ardoyne, so they began opening places
like this. Both us and the police let them get on with it. The general
thinking was that at least we knew where they were.

All they did was throw a few tables and chairs in a room, knock
together a makeshift bar, buy in the beer and they were up and
running. It took more than the threat of a civil war to keep an

Irishman from his drink. This was good for us because whilst patrolling the area we found that the beer was kept around the back of the club in an outhouse. The smallest lad in the unit would clamber in, pass back a crate of beer and then we'd sit in the alley yard having a fag and a bottle of Guinness. To begin with we weren't properly prepared and so, as I was known for my small talent of removing beer caps with my teeth, this duty fell to me. As it became a regular fixture, for the sake of my teeth, someone always brought a Swiss army knife with a bottle opener. But we only had one each and always returned the empties. We thought that was fair enough. We would never have got a drink there any other way.

I guess it was when they started listening in to army radio frequencies that they must have been tipped off as to why 22 Alpha patrols coincided with crates of Guinness going missing.

Pretty soon, though, we had plenty else to keep us amused.

We were now, without doubt, the enemy. The tea and biscuits left out on dustbins were long forgotten. They were now more likely to be booby-trapped to explosives in the bin.

Increasingly, as the situation deteriorated, dirty tricks were being employed by both sides to counteract each other's. For example, a couple of inches would be chopped off the length of the rubber bullets to enable two or three charges, instead of the usual one, to be inserted, along with nuts and bolts.

There was a conflict here I felt strongly: not just in the streets, but inside me. I was doing the job I'd trained for and knew it was something I was good at (soldiering had always come naturally to me) but our position had changed. You can only be pushed on to the back foot for so long before you have to attack. Ideas of impartiality can be easily eroded by the far more immediate reality of a brick in the face. With the Catholic community having more to fight for and therefore more to lose, I found myself in the dilemma of understanding them and yet, at the same time, increasingly horrified by their methods. A soldier cannot afford to question too much. There's duty, and duty is everything. Duty is drilled into you from day one. Although I no longer prayed and hadn't done so since I was a kid, Catholicism was still at the heart of me. It was another duty, I suppose: the duty of faith; the faith that God was always there with a hand in things, rewarding rights and punishing wrongs. They say the bad sleep easy because they have no conscience about what they've done, but the priests of my child-

46

hood conjured up the patient flames of hell so vividly that I knew differently. That 'easy' sleep only lasted for a lifetime; divine retribution began after death. And that's another saying that haunted me – you're a long time dead.

I hoped I could make some sense in the space between holy orders and military ones. I was trying to do what I felt was right and what was needed to be done, but nothing more, nothing unnecessary. I tried to curb the excesses I knew it was all too easy to slip into.

One time we banged through a front door on a house raid. This time the riot had ended in an exchange of gunfire and I'd seen a guy dash off into a nearby house. As I hit the narrow stairs, running, I could hear my lads down below, hyped up and alert, searching the place to the screams of the family. With the tip of the barrel I rammed open the door that faced me and ran in. What I saw stopped me dead. Two faces looked up at me, both shining. The lad was lying in bed with the blankets to his chin. His face was grey, the flesh waxy and wet with sweat. He looked at me, barely focusing, his eyes smoked over. What I assumed was his mother, or maybe even a much older sister from a typically large Catholic family, was knelt by the bed holding his hand. Her face was wet too. He'd obviously been shot. He looked like he didn't have long to go. What use would it be to tell anyone? To arrest them? Bad enough to lose a son. I said, 'You don't need any more troubles do you?' and left. Another time, a black taxi screeched to a halt on the other side of a street and two men and a women fell out carrying a third man. He looked in a bad way. I'd already heard the noise of a riot kicking off a few streets away. This guy had obviously been involved and been hit. When I approached they all protested that he was just ill and needed to be given treatment. I looked at him again and he really did look like he was on his last legs. I let them go to do whatever they needed to do. Probably just give him the last rites from the looks of things. I was letting people off when other squaddies would have kicked them stupid. These incidents weren't the only times I turned a blind eye, but they were close to being the last.

In the ghettos of Northern Ireland, and particularly Belfast, all the frustrations had given birth to a terrible anger – fear and distrust were the midwives. This in turn laid the foundation for what was now emerging as an increasingly organized Provisional IRA. The petrol bombs became nail bombs, tin cans jammed with explosives, nuts, bolts and nails.

One patrol found us merging with another unit. We made to go down the alleyway at the end of Herbert Street. Fortunately for me, and unusually, I wasn't at the head. The other unit's corporal advanced first. No one saw the trip-wire strung across the path as he moved down it. The alley rocked with an explosion. He hit the wall and dropped. A nail bomb had taken his leg off at the knee. We ran in and dragged him out, leaving his boot behind with the foot still in it. His whole right side was porcupined with nail heads. As his unit tended to him and waited for back-up we carried on through to the riot that was starting at the other end of the alley. John-Boy swore as he tripped over the severed limb.

In the middle of the riot's chaos I saw someone about to throw what looked like another nail bomb. I quickly shouldered my rifle and loosed one off at him. It missed. He spun and fled. I turned around and realized that I was stranded down the middle of the street with Austin. The rest of the unit was some way back. We both flattened ourselves into the nearest doorways. Everything had suddenly gone quiet. Everyone had fled. We were about to find out why. Tapper was shouting at me and pointing at something in front of us. Austin and I looked at each other, shrugged, stepped out of the doorways and peaked into the gutter. The nail bomb lay there scowling. It had obviously been dropped and then rolled over the street to say hello. They don't tick, of course, but my brain seemed to hear it. It was one of the large cans and the bastards hadn't even bothered to rip the label off. More than baked beans inside, that was for sure.

Austin and I suddenly panicked to life and turned to run. Heading in opposite directions, we ran slap-bang into each other and fell on our arses. We jumped up, cursed and sprinted off to opposite ends of the street. Seconds later the bomb blew apart – deep and low in sound, flying metal high – just as we both hit the deck. I glanced round the corner and saw the doors we'd been up against were now black with bubbling paint and gouged open with needles of metal. They looked like vertical beds of nails. I looked to the far end of the street and saw Austin's goggle-eyed face staring back at me.

Guns were now also out in force and being used. We had to adapt to the crack of rifles as well as petrol bombs. Our patrols became more fraught. A sniper's bullet could take your leg off at the knee and that was if you were lucky and didn't get one in the face.

At night we'd come out of an almost completely black back alley, lit only by the moon's light on roof slates, to what seemed like the virtual daylight of orange steetlamps. I'd count the boys across as they zipped over the road: Tapper, Stan, John-Boy, Blakesy, Nigger, Socks and then last, and unfortunately least, Austin. I'd hit the wall on the other side and find him against my shoulder panting like an asthmatic in a wind-tunnel.

'Calm down, Austin. Bloody hell, we haven't even been fired on yet,' I said to him. 'Tapper! Get a fag off Blakesy for Austin.' I heard a mumble from the front as Blakesy said something not dissimilar to fuck off.

'I don't smoke, Corporal,' Austin said.

'Well, maybe you should bloody start.'

One night we continued the patrol until we found ourselves halfway down another God-forsaken black hole of an alleyway. Suddenly I noticed some movement no more than three feet away against the wall. I raised my hand and everyone froze. I could hear the squelch of Johnny's gum increase in speed. Our eyes widened in the moonlight as we realized that Johnny's gum wasn't the only thing squelching. One dark body was lunging into another against the wall; it was some local lad shafting his bird. I gave a wave and we all filed past silently. The couple didn't even miss a beat as we passed. Curiously, not one of us mentioned it again. Until we got back to the mill when Tapper felt compelled to break the silence and ask why we didn't do anything; they could have been concealing weapons or anything, he said.

'From what I could see,' I said, 'that guy's weapon was far from concealed. Anyway, even in the middle of a war I think there are some things that should still be respected. And a bloke getting his end away is one of them.'

To no one's surprise, Nigger, Mr Playboy centrefold himself, immediately agreed.

It was Nigger who invented a scam of his own shortly after-wards. Every three days our turn would come to go out on vehicle checkpoint patrol. We'd take out two PIGs and angle them across a road we'd chosen. Behind them we'd lay a Caltrap at the side of the road. This was a wire rope of spikes that could be pulled under the tyres of anyone that was mental enough to try to run through us. And they'd only risk doing that if their car was loaded. It very rarely happened; the VCPs were pretty boring duty. The chances of pulling someone with a boot full of weapons or explosives were slim but it kept them on their toes. Better to make transportation of arms as difficult as possible. Nigger took to lightening the boredom in his own particular fashion.

The first time he did it I'd wondered why he'd volunteered so readily to search the next car. It came along. It stopped (not much choice really). Nigger went through the usual routine: 'Can I see your ID, sir'; 'Mind if I search the car, sir'. After he'd looked in the boot he slammed the lid, tapped it twice to signal the driver and then shouted to me, 'OK, Corporal. It's clean!'

The driver pulled away, probably too nervous and relieved to look in his rearview mirror and notice that at Nigger's feet was the toolbox he'd lifted out of the boot of the car.

'You sly bastard,' I said as I walked over. The other lads did the same, all laughing. 'How long have you been planning that?'

'Oh, you know me – think on me feet,' he said, grinning as the others formed a scrum and started delving into the metal box.

I said, 'Yeah, right, Nigger. I bet you've got a chuffing buyer lined up for it already!' He just smiled back. I didn't mind him messing around with his little scams but he knew he was on his own if an officer got wind of it.

Actually, because of it, we now started to look forward to the VCPs and seeing just how many toolboxes Nigger could 'liberate', as he put it. He got the routine down to a fine art. They never suspected a thing as they drove off, leaving Nigger with a Cheshire Cat grin slapped across his mush.

'Normally I wouldn't touch other men's tools,' was his usual line, 'but this is business.' In time we lost count of how many he got but we enjoyed the thought that he might have done it to two fellas who knew each other. We imagined them comparing stories: 'Jesus! Did that happen to you, too? My fucking toolbox has gone missing as well!'

More time locked in conflict seemed to bring new resolutions from all of us: the IRA, the Loyalist equivalent, the UFF, and the army. Trouble was we all resolved to do nothing more than try to fuck each other off even more royally than we'd been doing already.

The Belfast brigade commander, Frank Kitson, visited the mill on a morale-boosting visit. He stood on a fire-escape platform as we all assembled below. He had the superior look and manner of one of the old-boy network, straight out of the gentleman's club and still lamenting the passing of the empire. As I listened to him I thought it was either the most foolish or the most optimistic speech I'd ever heard.

'You, the Green Howards, are fighting the brunt of the IRA, but within six weeks we'll have them beat.'

Shortly after, and still just fresh into the new year of 1971, Gunner Robert Curtis became the first British soldier to be killed in Northern Ireland for nearly fifty years when he died in the spray of Provo machine-gunfire. This affected us all, of course, but it was doubly sad for me because I'd trained Curtis. The fact that we shared a surname made me think how we could have been brothers. As it was known that I'd trained in Brecon under the SAS and now also had front-line experience of being on the streets, I was chosen to train some of the new recruits who were being flown in. I couldn't believe just how green they were. Robert Curtis had been one of them.

The next day the Northern Ireland prime minister, James Chichester-Clarke, appeared on television and announced: 'Northern Ireland is at war with the Irish Republican Army Provisionals.'

Like we needed telling.

4

TRIPPING THE BLIND

My leave came around again and I went back home to Yorkshire. I felt strangely blank and couldn't manage much more than pleasantries with Mum and Dad. The conflict wasn't mentioned even with him. An ex-soldier himself, he probably understood more than he let on. He was never big on soul-bearing and I was the same. It was how he'd been raised and how he'd raised me. Mum tried to chatter things along to something that would lighten the mood but she'd grown up with the silences of men who didn't express their hurt, so she didn't push it. Mining villages are built on deep holes that have been dug by men who learned to be as hard as the seams they travelled down to every morning.

This short time at home felt strangely temporary, even more fleeting than the few days it actually was. It felt like a very brief interruption of real life.

And real life began as soon as I returned to Belfast. The usual: equal spells of violence and boredom. We had a name for it: we said we were fighting the two-hour war. A couple of hours of getting the crap kicked out of us or us doing the same to them, and then out for a drink in a local bar. It still felt safe enough to do this, despite everything.

The Catholics and Prods didn't take time off from each other, however. Out on patrol in the New Ardoyne we came across hundreds of local Protestants leaving their homes. They were laden down with as much as they could carry or transport. This was one of the so-called 'interface' areas: a flash-point where Catholic and Protestant communities met. The Prods said they'd grown so sick of Catholic intimidation that they'd finally decided to leave. The houses stood empty, many with their doors open, and dropped belongings lay about the street. Before long most of them returned. I saw one guy on his doorstep stuffing newspaper under the door.

'What's going on here?'

He looked up at me. 'You don't think we're leaving anything for those Taig bastards to take do yer? We're torching the lot.' He was struggling to light the paper. It finally took and then quickly burned out against the wood, leaving it black and blistered. I looked around. There were eight of us in the unit and hundreds of them. We couldn't stop this if we wanted to. Common sense suggested one thing.

'Why don't you just turn on the gas first?' I said.

He looked up at me and smiled, 'Fuckin' genius!' The idea was relayed round the streets and within minutes the hissing of gas bottles and the smell of rotten eggs filled the air. Any low-flying bird in the area would have fluttered to earth, unconscious before it hit the ground. An end house was chosen and torched first, and that was all it needed. It blew apart like a dolls' house dropped on a landmine. We all jumped back, ducking, and ran, shocked by the ferocity of the blast. Glass and debris rained down and didn't stop before the next one went. And the next. Every house followed in succession as the ignited gas rolled down the street like a wave of God's own anger; like a massive row of fire-crackers. The walls bucked out and dropped. I saw a front door blow off its hinges and sail high into the air on a fifty-foot rope of fire. It fell on the roof of a house two streets away and, still on fire, slid down and jammed in the guttering.

We stood back to watch the rest of the show. The sky was filled with so much black ash I thought every sparrow in Belfast had taken off.

I thought I had better keep it between me and the unit about my helpful words of advice.

Urban warfare is unlike any other kind. By its very nature of being fought on streets, down alleys and from inside and behind houses, it doesn't afford you the luxury of the large spaces and greater time that were a feature of conventional battlefields. Initially we were like a football team playing away from home and out of our league. To labour the football analogy, not only had the goalposts been moved but the playing field wasn't even level. We were at the bottom of the slope and everything naturally came our way. Sometimes an incident would give you an insight into the resourcefulness of the terrorists we were facing.

One time, we were out on night patrol. I was looking for gunmen through the Starlight scope on my rifle. The Starlight was a night-scope developed by the Yanks for use in Vietnam. It magnified every available glimmer of light and intensified it into a green image. It made even the most harmless scene seem charmless, sick and eerie.

As I was scoping the street, I saw a gunman dart across it and disappear into a house. I stared intently at the door, fixing in my mind exactly which one it was in the row. Then I was up and after him. I booted the door open and an old guy and his wife looked back at me from their sofa. Neither looked particularly surprised. I shouted, 'Where's the gunman?' but they just ignored me and calmly turned back to the telly. I ran to the back door – it was bolted from the inside. He must be upstairs. I took the stairs two at a time, kicked open the door facing me which was already ajar and sprayed some rounds inside for good measure. Through the smoke I saw nothing, not even an open window. A quick search revealed the other rooms were empty too. Well where the hell is he, I thought, under the old woman's skirts? I was just about to go back downstairs when I suddenly noticed a chair on the landing. I looked up and saw a loft. The cover was dislodged. He must have jumped up. I stood on the chair and gingerly slid the cover back with my gun barrel. I peeped up and over once, then twice, and then the third time chanced a glance around. Though it was completely black I could see a point of light. It looked miles away. I thought, Jesus, just how big are these lofts? Sensing that no one was up here and I wasn't going to get my head blown off, I let my eyes adapt to the dark. Then it all became clear. The light I could see wasn't in this loft, it was coming from one at the end of the street, ten houses away. I was looking down at it through a series of holes that had been made in each of the connecting walls, making an escape route from one loft to another. He'd had the choice of dropping down into any one of the houses and then slipping out the back. He'd be long gone by now. Sneaky bastards, I thought to myself. But I grudgingly had to admit that the idea had a kind of genius to it.

A few days later three deaths changed everything and everyone, Chris Mather and myself especially. There was nothing remotely inventive about this action. It was just a stone-hearted, cold-blooded atrocity of the lowest order. Nothing more, nothing less.

Three off-duty soldiers were out drinking in a local bar. Despite everything, we still felt safe doing this if we knew the area well enough. They were befriended by a couple of local girls and their three male friends, who treated them all to drinks throughout the evening. The soldiers left with their new pals at the end of the night with the promise of a party. Halfway up a dirt track on the way to a farmhouse, the three soldiers felt the pressure of all those beers and got out for a slash. Standing at the side of track, bottled beer still in one hand, dick in the other, each was then shot in the back of the head. Like three blind mice, they never knew what hit them. At least that was the only consolation you could cling to: it happened so unexpectedly that they never knew.

They were the first off-duties to be murdered. All merry hell broke loose. The outrage felt by everyone except the Provos responsible was unanimous. This was a horrific turn for the worse, but so disgusted were we at the manner of these lads' deaths that we didn't want to turn things back to how they were, just to get back at those responsible. I tried not to replay how the scene must have been: turning from the innocence of a drunken night out – with all the laughs and daftness that goes with it – to three faces blown off in the cold and dark. I tried not to, but I couldn't stop myself. To die like that. Not in the heat of battle where you accept and sometimes even expect it, but on a bloody night out! I couldn't stop thinking about it. And nor could Chris. We sat down and made a pact to do whatever it took to find the three killers.

The soldiers were all Scottish Protestants: two brothers and a cousin. Their deaths became a defining moment in the Troubles up to that point. Catholics and Protestants polarized even further and with the lads being Protestant, support for the emerging Loyalist paramilitaries grew, their membership increasing. Even the most liberal of Protestant sympathies to Catholic cries for equality were destroyed that night. Over the following days I felt a very real sense of the whole conflict shifting and sliding into even greater ugliness.

Chris and I decided there and then that we wanted to be in the thick of it. It seemed to affect Chris even more than me. I could see how consumed he was with the desire for revenge.

Forty detectives from Scotland Yard came over from the mainland to investigate the killings and, through our network of informers, try to name the three responsible.

The murders also played a part in bringing into force another major development. It made it far easier for the government to sanction something that had been planned for months, but delayed because of strong objections – internment.

Internment was the practice of imprisoning someone without trial on the suspicion of terrorist involvement. Proof was needed, but only to the extent of justifying their arrest. In this situation we couldn't hang around to wait for a court to validate the arrests with convictions, which were hard to come by anyway. We'd pull someone in that we knew damn well was up to his neck in it but when he got in the dock he'd lie like it was going out of fashion, backed up by another bunch of liars that gave him alibis. So we learned to do the same. Then both sides' lies would be presented by another bunch of lying bastards (the barristers) and the judges would decide who'd lied the best. When someone once famously said that truth is the first casualty of war, he, at least, wasn't lying.

Another reason for bringing in internment was the fact that, although there were now fewer riots, they were much more intense. Fully fledged gunbattles were almost the norm. The realization of how much had been thrown to the wind came one day when we went out on patrol in a PIG. As usual we sat on the bench seats with the back doors open, scanning doorways and rooftops for snipers. A flick of movement caught my eye and a guy fell out of a house behind us, raising a gun from the barrel-down position. It was a Thompson sub-machine-gun, like those used by American gangsters in old movies with the big, round ammo mag beneath it. Everything seemed to click down into slow-motion: him raising the barrel and grimacing as he prepared for the bark; me and Tapper at the back, reaching for the doors; the bullets kicking up the street as he fired too soon and too low; the little white tufts of dust from the approaching bullets; and then *slam*! Back into quick-time action, we banged the doors shut, our hands still on the handle as the rounds hit. We jumped back and a row of bullets thunked into the doors, leaving a stitch of thumb-dents. The PIG roared off round the corner and we immediately piled out and ran back to squat at the street end. No time even to appreciate how lucky we were. I glanced back and saw that the bullets had pierced the lower skirt of the PIG, which was single-sheet metal, but only managed to dent the armour-plated doors.

Incidents like this added fuel to the fire of opinion that reckoned the gunmen were about to take over. As always, the Green Howards were in the thick of it. But no matter how heavy it got we always made light of it when we got back to our bunks. Otherwise we'd all just end up putting the shit up each other and you can't afford to dwell on what could have been or what might be. The ifs and maybes of life can kill you, too.

The morning after the attack on the PIG, we were back out patrolling in the same vehicle. When we reached what we considered a safe enough area we pulled over for a rest. A unit of marine commandos was doing the same just over the road. Their commander strode across to us. He was tall and imposing and wore the mantle of his authority with the easy manner of a natural officer. I saw him eyeing up the dents in the doors and the bullet-holes in the skirt. I described the attack to him and he looked at me intently as I did, nodding slowly. I noticed he had a distinctive blue-grey eye-colour.

'You were quite lucky that time, Corporal,' he said. 'I hope your luck holds out. Keep up the good work and don't let the bastards grind you down.'

The day for Operation Demetrius, as the internment operation had been named, drew closer. Talking to Major Rocket, I learned that he and the command were puzzled as to why many of the women of the Ardoyne had taken to hanging out on street corners until the small hours of the morning, chatting and smoking. It seemed obvious to me – what my dad called 'common bloody sense, lad' – the women were look-outs. Several trial runs of the procedure we'd gone through for internment, combined with the preparation of three major holding areas for the arrested, meant you didn't need to be Einstein to work out what was coming. Daddy Rocket said he'd pass on my views to Brigadier Frank Kitson that same night when they were due to have a meeting. Old Daddy came to see me the next day to inform me that Kitson agreed with me. Well, halle-bloody-lujah, I thought. At least we won't get full blame if it all doesn't go exactly to plan.

Come the time, we only managed a couple of hours' kip before we got up to prepare for the raid. We went in at four in the morning. Outside it was pitch black. Each one of us had been given a 'P' card. These were ID cards with the names and addresses of the men we were to lift. Only rarely did the card carry a photograph.

Over the next few hours the best part of 4,000 troops kicked in doors and dragged off nearly 500 suspects. Chris Mather led our section and I saw the fervour in him as he threw men in the back of the PIG. He obviously hoped three of the arrested men might turn out to be the killers of the three off-duty squaddies.

We entered one house after a guy called Daniel Flynn. The 'P' card had no photo, only his name. The Flynns, a typically large Irish family, were all at home; all eleven of them. The full football team. Any one of the six brothers could have been Danny boy, so I was forced to ask him to identify himself.

'I'm Danny Flynn,' one of them said. As I moved towards him one of the others stood and said, 'I'm Danny Flynn!' And then another and another until all of them were glaring at me and claiming to be our suspect. It was like the scene in *Spartacus* when the Romans ask him to identify himself and all the slaves rise, saying, 'I'm Spartacus!'

I scanned their faces, looking for a tell-tale sign of the real one and saw nothing but cold loathing and defiance. Oh, sod this, I thought, we could be here all day.

'If you all want to play Kirk Douglas, I'll take the whole bloody lot of you,' I said. No one moved. 'Right, take the whole fucking lot of them out!'

As they filed out and I handed them over to the receiving company due to transport them, the company's officer looked at me and pompously announced, 'I don't want all of them, Corporal. Just our man.' Great, this was all I needed, some wanker trying to humiliate me. I explained the situation. The officer took the 'P' card from me, read it and then addressed the assembled Flynn menfolk.

'OK, which one of you chaps is Daniel Flynn?' The whole of the *Spartacus* scene was replayed in full. The officer paused, realizing he could do no more than I'd already done. My unit all looked at him expectantly and I could tell he could feel our eyes on his back. The officer offered me the 'P' card with his outstretched arm without even looking at me and said, 'Right. Take them all.' Blakesy caught my eyes and rolled his.

We transported our arrests to an old Second World War airfield at Long Kesh, north of Belfast. Then we made our way back to the mill, passing through the New Ardoyne, the scene of the earlier house burnings, and walked down towards the Crumlin Road, which would lead us back to base. The path we followed was a ridge that looked down into the whole of the Ardoyne area, and it was like looking down into hell itself.

The worse rioting I'd ever seen had exploded immediately after the arrests and our withdrawal. I saw a massive arena of chaos, ringed by barricades of burning cars and furniture which enclosed the whole of the Ardoyne, completely shutting it off. No one getting out, no one getting in; a dozen Bonfire Nights all come at once. It might have looked like a huge celebration if it hadn't been for the sound of gunfire ringing out across the city. And the shouting. And the fireflies of petrol bombs smashing open again and again. There was an unholy banshee cry from women out in the streets as they whistled and banged dustbin lids to warn the men of further patrols arriving. Gunfire was aimed into the ring from Protestants in their positions on the outside.

'Keep tight together,' Chris said to us. 'We know our way back from here.'

I turned to him and he looked tense. His eyes were ablaze with more than just the reflected flames from down below. We both knew this was something that wasn't going to burn out quickly. This one was going to last.

'Hardly seems any point in going back to the mill,' I said. 'We're gonna be back out again soon enough.'

'Yes, I know. I'm not planning on us staying. We're going back to get tooled up and then straight back out.'

Half an hour later we left the mill and hit the far end of Jamaica Street, just off Flax Street, which led back to the mill. We commandeered the end house as a look-out point and stationed ourselves there. Smoking barricades clogged almost every street around us.

I positioned Blakesy, Austin and John-Boy at upstairs windows and the rest on the ground floor. The family of the house, Protestants, retreated to the safety of the back kitchen and supplied us with cups of tea. Funny how even when we were in the middle of a battlefield, it was never very long before a kettle went on.

We sat it out for a while. It's not exactly a calm you feel before the storm, more a queasy mixture of tension and boredom. If something was going to happen, you just wanted it to happen and get it over and done with. The apprehension you felt before was worse than anything you felt during, mostly because when you were in the middle of it you didn't have time to feel anything. Fear came afterwards, if you were lucky enough to be still standing.

Chris paced up and down and it came as no surprise to me when he said, 'I'm going in.' He bolted downstairs and out of the door with Stan on command to follow. With poor Stan in tow, Chris leaped the barricade. He was known for his fearless forays into no-go zones and dangerous areas. I watched him zig-zag deeper into the Ardoyne and disappear. I felt a sudden surge of emotion for him – a mixture of pride and fear. Funny thing is, when I did worry, I'd always worry more about someone else than myself. I guess, like everyone else, I thought I was different; that I'd never be the one.

My thoughts ended abruptly when a volley of sniper bullets hit the side of the house and the bedroom window blew in. We returned fire, dodging between the windows and the walls. My shoulder was covered in shards of glass. I heard firing down below and quickly glanced out to see Tapper outside by the front door, sheltering behind a dustbin. I couldn't believe it. I thought, What *is* he doing? Does he really think that old tin bin's going to offer him any protection?

'Tapper! You daft bastard! Get back inside!' My shout was cut short by another burst of fire. Bullets thunked into the bin. I heard the lid clatter to the ground and then the bang of Tapper falling back into the house. The dead dustbin rolled out into the gutter. I was still pressed flat back against the wall when I heard Tapper shout from downstairs, 'I'm OK!'

'Lucky bastard,' I whispered.

'You think that's lucky, Corporal?'

I turned to see Austin on the other side of the window holding something out in front of him. It was his beret. He balanced it on two of his outstretched fingers and the tip of each one poked through a bullet-hole, one at the front, one at the back. He always wore his beret high and the bullet had passed through the gap, neatly perforating it on the way. His big, gormless face looked back at me and we both turned simultaneously and traced the line the bullet must have taken across the room. A framed picture of Christ lay on the carpet in smashed glass. Above it was a neatly drilled hole in the wallpaper where it had hung.

'God's just died for your sins, Austin. Now try to keep your fat head down!'

Nigger popped his head round the door, took in the scene and said, 'You jammy bastard!' just as the radio on Austin's back crackled with static and jolted him back to life. It was Chris. He'd taken over a house further up the street. The two old dears that lived in it were tied up on the floor as all holy hell exploded around them.

'I can see the gunmen!' he shouted and the lonely echo down the line made him sound miles away. But I could tell from the excited edge in his voice that wherever he was, it was exactly where he wanted to be. 'There's nearly twenty of the bastards! They're in the school at the top of the street.' I heard some rounds pop off outside and the same sound, but muffled, come down the line. Then a burst of return fire from Chris and Stan. Then static and silence. We pinpointed where they were, leaped back to the windows and blasted off a concentrated reply. The sound echoed away, dying down with the smoke. There was silence now, broken only by a solitary crack from up the street. Then nothing. We waited.

The firefight continued through the rest of the day and then sporadically through the night. As dawn began to break, sending grey light down, some slight and then suddenly active movement caught my eye. I peeked round the window's edge and saw the dull, red berets of a unit of paras skirmishing up the street. They were going in to give cover for the clearing of the debris. I was in two minds whether to acknowledge them and let them know we were here, but then decided I didn't want to get mistaken for a sniper and shot. I let them pass.

Soon enough the cracka-cracka of fresh gunfire split the air. We bounced up and returned the compliment to them as breakfast. The gunfire from the school died immediately. We sat it out for a minute. The rumble of engines that we'd detected a few minutes before now grew in volume and an armoured Saracen suddenly roared around the corner. It drove at the barricade, smashed straight through and carried on. We ran out and followed.

By the time we got to the school most of those inside had fled. Chris and Stan were in the street. We covered the school and each other until we thought it was safe to go in. The body of one of the gunmen was dragged out and laid on the pavement. His face was sheet-white and streaked red. A bullet had caught him just under the hairline and flipped back the top of his skull like a wig in the wind. Just like a flip-top bin lid. His eyes, mouth and brain were all wide open to the sky: another one completely startled by his own death.

We figured out that from the gunman's position and the way the bullet had hit him, it was one of our lads downstairs in the house that had got him. Ironically enough, probably Tapper.

That night there was an eight-gallon barrel put behind the bar for us. Getting a gunman was a rare and difficult thing. In the middle of the pitch-black night all you'd hear was the crack-crack-crack of gunshots. The proverbial needle in a haystack was like a javelin compared to trying to ID a sniper, let alone drop him. So celebrations were in order.

After the gunbattle, the rioting continued for twenty-four hours. The fires finally cooled but they were all that did. Both Catholics and Protestants fled to safer areas as they ran each other out of their homes.

Back out on patrol we found ourselves in the narrow alley at the end of Herbert Street that led from the Old Ardoyne to the New. This was where I'd walked down a few months back with the former section commander as he showed me around. We were now surrounded and pinned down by rioters and, short of shooting our way out, I could only see one option. In desperation, I ordered the whole unit to pile into a PIG that was patrolling near by. We fell on it and jumped inside like it was the last lifeboat off the *Titanic*. With the PIG's crew already inside and our unit on top, we numbered sixteen – all squashed into a wagon that was only supposed to take eight. As the lid clunked down, the rioters swarmed all over the vehicle, banging the hell out of it. They snapped the aerial off, preventing us from calling for back-up. The driver got panicky. Not surprising, really, as he had my foot stuck in his left ear, Kev Crosier practically sitting in his lap and all of us screaming blue-murder at him. The vehicle rocked. And then it stalled, twice. Then it wouldn't start at all.

'Use the chuffing choke for Christ's sake!' I shouted. I had visions of them carpeting it with petrol bombs and roasting us inside for dinner. Blakesy burst out laughing at the absurdity of it all.

Someone shouted at the driver, 'Get this bag of shite started or you're the first one out!' Finally, it coughed to life and we kanga-rooed down the street like a clown's car in a circus ring.

The gardens of the New Ardoyne houses provided another funny incident. The laughing only usually began after you'd got out of trouble and were back in barracks. That's when you could afford to see the funny side and play up your own bravado. This time, though, we couldn't help creasing up there and then.

Out on patrol we heard a crack. It could have been a gun or just one of the fire-crackers that they sometimes let off to goad us into reacting. A unit of paras was ahead of us and one of them kicked a fence down and took cover in the garden. No sooner had he crouched there than this big Irishwoman bounded out of the house, finger-wagging and calling down every wrath of God on him for destroying her fence. We were some way back, watching and laugh-ing as he tried to shush her, but she wasn't having it.

'Eh, you! You bloody hooligan! Get out of my garden yer British bastard!'

'Shut up! Get back in your house!' he said, trying to muster enough authority to get the old bird out of the way, for her own safety as well as his.

'*You* shut the fuck up, you hairy-arsed eejit!' She didn't miss a beat or take a breath and her screaming rose in pitch. Now, the paratroopers aren't known for having the most difficult-to-light fuses and when her slipper hit the back of his head, I saw the spark. I could lip-read what he said as he turned wearily and mouthed – 'Oh, shut the *fuck* up!' – and fired a rubber bullet into her belly. We just saw these stout, milk-bottle legs fly up in the air and disappear as she was knocked back into the house and on her arse.

'Chuffin' hell!' Crosier said. 'So much for not upsetting the natives!'

Even taking into account Crosier's classic British understatement, 'upsetting' didn't come close. After the last few days' events, the whole of Belfast descended into an indignant, riotous fury.

Internment turned out to be pretty much of a farce. We'd pulled in some 450 faces, most of whom had to be released either because we had nothing on them or they simply weren't involved. Our information hadn't been up-to-date. We ended up pulling some poor old buggers who hadn't been actively involved for decades. And as we were down on street level – that is, brick-in-the-face and bullet-in-the-back level – all we copped for was the increased fury of Belfast Catholics. Such a hefty load of shit was hitting so many fans we might as well have been handed a pair of wellies each and called sewage workers.

Some good news came down the line, though. The Special Branch investigation into the murder of the three off-duty squaddies had thrown up the suspected killers' names – Paddy MacAdorey, 'Dutch' Doherty and Martin Meehan. Then we further learned that the gunman who had been dragged out dead from the school after our gunbattle was not only a high-ranking IRA staff captain but MacAdorey himself. As Chris said when we heard the news – one down, two to go.

When I told him that the third man on the list, Meehan, had been pointed out to me in the Ardoyne, he questioned me continually about him. Despite the fact that, apart from his stern, hard-liner's face, Meehan looked like a pretty ordinary bloke, Chris obsessed about him to the point when Meehan became an almost mythical figure: this big, fleet-of-foot warrior who had to be tracked down.

Well, fleet of chuffing foot he certainly was. Both he and Dutch Doherty had fled south of the border now that the heat was on and their names were out.

IRA bombings increased in retaliation. Sometimes we'd be called out on back-up to the clearing-up operation. I'd seen dead bodies before but none so thoroughly dead as these. Caught in the full white-heat of the blast, they were nothing more than waste. The bits were even shovelled up and collected in bin bags, just like rubbish. And bombs are viciously democratic. They cruelly include every-one. Babies weren't spared because of their innocence; pensioners weren't forgiven because of their age. Protestants and Catholics from eight months to eighty years were blown to high heaven over the coming weeks. I sometimes thought, Well, you there, the ones that have been sprayed over the walls of that pub, or blown out the door of this bar . . . you probably prayed as hard as the next man, or woman. You probably prayed harder in the day before your death than I have for the last ten years and yet look at you now: completely given up on.

The dead only seemed to matter to two types of person: first, to the family and friends that loved them; and second, with an irony too bitter to stomach, to their enemies. To their enemies these lives mattered enough to be ended. To the IRA and the UFF, or all the other Republican and Loyalist paramilitary murderers, these people were important enough to kill but didn't mean anything alive. I started to see them as innocent sacrifices. I still differenti-ated between ordinary people (even though they were on one side or the other) and the terrorists themselves. I felt the majority of Catholics, for example, were being used by the IRA as much as anyone. The Provo leaders orchestrated riots knowing full well what the reaction, or preferably overreaction, from the army would be. This in turn gave them grounds to justify their methods: 'Look what they've done to us – we have no option but to do this in return.' It was one of their weapons in the propaganda war – response to 'injustice'.

The justifications didn't move me. I knew they were fighting for something they believed in, and even had some understanding of their grievances, but what I couldn't understand or excuse was a man calmly planting five pounds of explosive in a public place, knowing that an hour later it would be packed with men, women and children: not enemy paramilitaries or soldiers, but just ordinary people who mostly wanted to get on with their normal lives.

This was something I knew I could never do, whatever the cause. And it was something that made a nonsense of the phrase 'one man's terrorist is another man's freedom fighter'. Where was the freedom of the dead? Free to spin in their graves maybe, as they heard the killers use their deaths as an excuse for more killing.

If we had to become as ruthless as them in order to survive then we would only be ruthless with the murderers and not the innocents caught in the cross-fire.

The gloves, which had started to come off some time ago, were now more like gauntlets that had been thrown down. So now, whatever happend from here on in, the blood would be on our hands.

5

'CONTACT! WAIT OUT!'

My unit's call sign was 22 Alpha. We got a reputation. Everyone seemed to know us. The commanders back at base listened in on the radio frequencies for our call sign. They knew that when we went out, more likely than not, we'd end up in a gunbattle. They weren't the only ones listening in. So were the Provos. They also wanted to know when we were out so they could come and meet us.

After months of confrontation, now the days of walking out of the mill and into nothing more than a leisurely stroll (or even a normal riot) were over. More often than not we'd walk into an ambush as soon as we hit the street. We'd leave one at a time, covering each other as we did. An alleyway halfway up Flax Street, about five hundred yards away, was a favourite hide-out for gunmen. Invariably, shots would ring out and we'd skirmish towards them. 'Skirmishing' was the practice of moving forward gradually, one man advancing whilst the others laid down covering fire. The ambushes mostly happened at night and, as we'd already shot out nearly all the streetlights during previous attacks, in almost complete darkness.

We'd hear the familiar crack-bang-thump. The 'crack' was the noise of the bullet breaking the sound barrier (usually just as it passed you), the 'bang' was the actual gunshot and the 'thump' was the bullet hitting the wall beside or behind you. The crack and thump told you nothing, except that you must still be alive to hear them. There would be no barrel-flash, that only happens in the movies, so the 'bang' was the only thing we had to pinpoint the gunman's position. The gunshots seemed to carry through the night over the whole of Belfast. I knew the sound would cause radios to be clicked on back at Command HQ as they listened in. We'd open with our call sign, '22 Alpha', and then 'Contact! Wait out!', meaning enemy contact made, wait for futher reports. News of our contact would make its way from the company commander, Major Rocket, to the lieutenant-colonel of the regiment, Ronnie Eccles, and from him up to the top boy, Frank Kitson, 39 Brigade commander. And Command were always greedy for information. Even as we were in the middle of a firefight our radio would crackle with, '22 Alpha. What's your sit rep?' – meaning 'situation report'. So, here we were, trying not to get our heads shot off and they'd expect us to take a break and give them an update. My usual response to this madness was to tell Austin to switch off the damn radio. By the time it was all over, with the gunman usually darting off to hide, we'd switch back on to hear the chain of command in a panic. I'd say, 'Sorry, sir. We must have been in a dead-spot.' This was an area that blanked out transmission. At least it allowed us to get on with the business of not getting topped.

Other squaddies in search of action applied to join us. They weren't fearless or foolish; they didn't want to die. But they especially didn't want to die of boredom, and as the most active, front-line unit, our patrols suffered from everything but that. I came to understand the feelings of older soldiers that I'd met during my training when they'd talked about the excitement of gunbattles being 'better than sex'. It was true. It felt like a hypodermic syringe had been punched through your rib-cage straight into your heart and the stopper pushed down. And this needle's barrel was full of pure adrenalin; your blood sang with it, your ears banged with blood and your body followed the beat. You ended up either exhilarated, exhausted or dead. You knew that if you got slotted then your family back home would be devastated by thoughts of how you suffered in death, but if it hit you clean and square then the first you'd know about it was when you woke up dead, shaking hands with St Peter or Ol' Nick, depending on which way you went. Catch one in the shoulder, kneecap or stomach and that's when you'd know about it. I'd never before heard screams like those from guys that took one in the guts.

Coming out of that same old narrow alleyway at the end of Herbert Street which led from the Old Ardoyne to the New, we walked into something that, again, would lead to the rise of that familiar wave with me riding the crest of it like some demented surfer. The area was almost completely deserted; unusual for this time of day. There was none of the normal comings and goings of day-to-day living. You don't really notice these activities until they're absent and then you realize that they're not there for a damn good reason. Old horror movie clichés suddenly ring true. 'It's quiet!', 'Yeah, *too* quiet!', sprang to mind. The very old and very young of the area – the vulnerables – were glaringly absent. We just had time to exchange silent, oh-fuck looks with each other before the machine-gun blast. A swarm of bullets thunked into a nearby parked car, rocking it on its suspension. The bonnet shivered and the windscreen fell in; we were already in mid-air, flattening hedges as we each belly-flopped into a garden. The second blast ripped the guts out of a telephone pole and showered me with splinters. We all shouted each other alive, checking there was no man down. As we rose, Blakesy snapped off the first reply from the other side of the street and I followed with a volley. The next blast swerved towards Blakesy and riddled over the car. The headlights exploded. Then a shout of 'Fuck!' and the din of a dustbin ripping open. Another one bites the dust, I thought.

'They've got a Browning on a tripod!' I shouted. I'd just caught a glimpse. It was a big bastard. I didn't think there were any more than three of them with it. They were at the far end of Holmdene Gardens where it meets Etna Drive.

'Cover me! Follow me down! Keep tight! Blakesy?'

'With you, Nicky!'

We snapped into action, the mechanics of it so deeply drilled in you from training, so deeply instilled by some screaming sergeant, that it comes as naturally as breathing. We skirmished down the gardens, rising and firing as we weave closer to the target. Over the road Blakesy rose and fell over the hedges, moving with me, cracking off rounds as I leaped and rolled and then jumping himself when I got up to reply. A fist of bullets hummed past my head. I landed heavily and the hedge behind me quivered as it took the blast. I jumped up with leaves fluttering down around me, let fly with a few from my shoulder mid-jump and landed with a bump. I jumped again. I'd lost count of gardens. The next few rushed at me in a green blur, scratching my face. I was vaguely aware of something that bothered me but couldn't pinpoint the problem. Then it struck me as we neared the gun. The machine-gun was firing straight ahead, as if we were still at the top of Holmdene. As I rose, I knew that my quick glance back would confirm what I already knew to be true: the rest of the unit was still back up the street. I was down here alone. The others hadn't followed. Even Blakesy had been left behind by my charge. Another syringe of adrenalin emptied into me and shot around my body. I continued to rise, angry now but still clear-headed. I crashed over the last hedge, screaming obscenities. Suddenly I was out in the open street, running, screaming and firing. I heard the ping and pop of my bullets hitting the gun and saw the guy behind it quiver and drop. I must have looked crazier than a scalded cat. The other two panicked and fled. I leaped the body and belted after them. One swerved off and disappeared up an alley. The other pounded away until he felt me close on him. He began to turn. I couldn't exactly afford to wait and see if he was turning to put one in my face, but I assumed he wasn't going to hand me a business card. I sank a couple into him. He dropped dead-weight on to his arse and then keeled over very slowly, as if he was lying down to sunbathe.

Blakesy eventually pounded up behind me. 'The guy back there's bought it, Corporal,' he said, breathing hard.

'This one's only clipped, lucky fucker.' He moaned and rolled. 'Get Austin to call back-up and an ambulance. Then I'm gonna give those other skiving bastards the biggest bollocking they've ever had.'

I had a fair idea who was responsible. It had happened once before when Tapper led the rest of the unit away as Stan and I were left stranded. I knew Tapper would have some excuse that to him sounded plausible but I also knew, by now, that he was what some politely referred to as 'gun shy'; and some, not so politely, called shit-scared. Which is fair enough, I thought, if you know you can't take it there's no shame in that. Each man to his own talent. But you should at least have the balls to admit it to yourself, get out, and not end up compromising your unit.

As I stormed back up Holmdene, the rest of the unit was racing down, trying to con me about how far back they'd been. Tapper ran at the head. If I hadn't been able still to feel the shockwaves of those bullets passing my ear, I'd probably have felt sorry for what I was about to give him.

Back at the mill, news of my assault on the gunmen, with me at the sharp end and Blakesy covering me, spread through the ranks. We were accorded renewed respect and a certain amount of awe for this action for a long time after.

A few weeks later Tapper's fears were justified when he bought it on night patrol. A sudden crack of a sniper's rifle and that was it: dead before he hit the deck.

His replacement didn't last long. Again on night patrol, we came

69

under fire. We flattened against a wall with me at the head of the line. Being in charge, I was supposed to carry the rifle with the night-scope but as it was so heavy I got one of the lads to lug it around. This time it was Tapper's replacement. I called him forward. Still peering round the corner, I put my hand back for it. He mumbled something I didn't catch. I was still looking for any tell-tale signs of movement.

'Give me the rifle,' I said.

'Corporal . . .' He sounded nervous.

'It's alright, son. Give me the rifle.'

'Sir . . .'

'Give me the fucking scope!'

'Sir, I've shot myself in the foot.' Now I did turn to him. 'Look. I'm not in the mood for pissing about. Follow the order or I'll have you thrown in bloody jail.'

'Sir, I *have* shot myself in the foot, sir!' I looked down and saw a ragged, watery hole in his toe-cap. I hadn't even heard it go off. According to regulations, we weren't supposed to have a round ready in the chamber, but a bollocking was better than a funeral.

'Private,' I said.

'Yes, sir.'

'You've shot yourself in the foot.'

'I know, sir.'

'You daft, lug-eared, bastard.'

'Sorry, sir.' He winced as he shifted his weight off it.

'That's about sixty, Corporal,' Blake shouted from the back, measuring the new guy's brief tour of duty in fags.

The lad looked at me, puzzled. He hadn't even been around long enough to learn what Blake was on about.

Afterwards, I couldn't work out whether he'd done it on purpose just to get home. It had been known. It certainly looked painful, pumping out blood there under the streetlight, but you could suffer much worse.

Things just got better. Never ones to let a perfectly ordinary night patrol pass without incident, we entered Velsheda Park and walked slap-bang into an ambush. Street-level gunmen opened up on us with some ferocious fire. They were so close that after we'd zigzagged the street and jumped behind a wall for cover, I was surprised, when I counted up, to find us all there. Austin, who had been behind me coming across the street, tapped me on the shoulder.

'I think I caught a grenade.'

'Eh? What are you on about?' I couldn't believe what I was hearing, even from him. 'You fucking spacer.'

'I swear to God.' His voice was low, like he couldn't quite believe it himself. 'It's back there!'

He finally persuaded me. We shuffled back twenty paces on our haunches and looked around in the dark. It suddenly struck me that, if it was true, then going back to look at it probably wasn't the brightest thing I'd ever done. I was just about to point out to Austin this major flaw in his otherwise cunning plan, when he hissed through his teeth, 'There! There!' I followed his frantic pointing and saw the dull, black pineapple of a British army-issue hand-grenade lying on a grate. The pin was out. For some reason, it hadn't blown us both to high heaven. Austin just seemed pleased to have proved himself right.

'Told you, sir,' he whispered.

'I must be as big a bloody moron as you to come back here looking for it!' I hissed at him. For some reason, we'd both lapsed into whispering, as if this would keep the damn thing from going off. We shuffled back a lot quicker than we'd come and joined the rest just as they were returning quick blasts of fire down the street. I radioed through for the army technician officer (ATO) to come out and disarm it. Which was another big mistake as we were ordered to stay there and guard it. Over the next two, freezing-cold hours it took for them to get to us, we had ample opportunity to subject Austin to the biggest piss-take in history. Apparently, as he told it, he was running behind me when he saw something sail towards him out of the dark. Instinctively, like a cricket fielder, he reached up and caught it. Then dropped it like a hot potato when he realized what he'd got.

'Didn't occur to you, then, Paul,' Kev Crosier said slowly, 'that you could have lobbed the fucking thing back!'

'It coulda gone off!' He turned to us all, protesting.

'Well, thanks very much for taking me back to it!' I said to him. 'Why don't we all go back and make a campfire round it? Or go the whole hog and find a bat and whack it back to 'em? We could be here all night throwing it at each other until the fucking thing goes off.'

I chalked it up as another one of the weird, almost unbelievable things that men, fired out of their boxes on adrenalin, will do in battle.

*

Internment had been a waste of time so something new called 'lifts', or tactical arrests, was brought in. A certain area would be designated and we'd go in and lift twenty to thirty men and search their houses. By now the army High Command had realized that we had very little in the way of ground-level information about what was going on in the streets and in the minds of the IRA. We were fighting blind. We could deploy more men with more sophisticated weaponry but if we had no idea of what was planned against us then it was all useless. We'd take the arrested men north of Belfast to Castlereagh, a safe-area interrogation point. There they would be subjected to whatever methods of persuasion were employed. Most of them clammed up or only gave abuse, but enough gave out info to make the lifts worthwhile. It was our first real success in the information war.

The usual way we carried out the lifts was to go out at four in the morning. This would give us the element of surprise and also lessen the chances of a riot breaking out, because everyone was still in bed. Followed by a PIG, we'd walk down a street on patrol, almost casual (or as near as you could muster under the circumstances), and then suddenly veer off and kick in the door of whichever house we'd targeted. This was easier said than done because by now the locals had taken to removing all their house numbers in order to add further confusion to making successful IDs. So one of the lads would count the house doors as we progressed until we got to the right number. Four of the unit would be positioned at the back. Sometimes we'd actually find a guy on top of his wife doing the business as we burst into the bedroom. Depending on how much resistance they put up we'd either let them get dressed or take them out half-naked before the commotion threatened to bring out the whole street. And there was still the threat of coming out to find a sniper had got off the blocks sharpish and was lying in wait.

Occasionally, we'd be after a 'wanted' man, someone who was down as an active Provo. On one particular night we were after one of these. As usual I hit the door running, but instead of bursting in I just bounced off – the door was deadlocked: a sure sign we'd got the right house. The delay gave our target breathing space and by the time we got in, clattered up the stairs and entered the bedroom, he had leaped out of the window. I heard a sudden cry from

72

outside, popped my head out of the window and saw the bloke rolling around stark-bollock naked on top of the PIG. The unlucky bugger had landed right on the roof and broken his ankle.

'He decided to parachute down to us, Corporal,' Kev shouted up at me. 'Trouble is, he forgot his bloody 'chute!'

Sometimes things went just as badly wrong for us as we tried to arrest them. On the next action, Chris took out my unit to arrest 'Cleeky' Clarke, the bodyguard of Gerry Adams. It was an afternoon lift rather than an early morning one, but it was pretty routine so I stayed behind. Clarke's house was in Jamaica Street, a stone's throw from the mill. I watched the op from up on the roof. They went in, but by the time they came out rioters were assembling. They knew who Clarke was and didn't want to give him up without a fight. The unit got back and everything seemed fine until I asked Chris where Blakesy and Nigger were. His face froze.

'Oh shit! I stationed them at the back of the house but we came out the front. We've forgotten them!'

We ran up to the roof in time to see Nigger and Blakesy belting down the back of Jamaica Street with a mob of fifty rioters pounding after them. The boys ran for their lives, discarding their helmets, their webbing and practically everything but their rifles to try to lighten their load and keep ahead. There was a trail of army-issue equipment littered behind them. The rest of the unit joined us at the wall to shout encouragement. Nigger was sprinting so hard in blind panic that his knees were nearly hitting his chin. As they got close enough for us to be pretty sure they were going to make it, we started taking bets on who'd get in first.

The IRA devised a new method of disruption. They began hijacking buses and ordering everyone off before they torched the vehicle. Then, knowing that a patrol would be sent to clear it, they would lie in wait to pick us off. To combat this, squaddies in civvies with concealed weapons would be assigned to ride the buses, waiting for a hijack attempt. With their regulation, army no. 2 crops and looks of nervous vigilance, they stood out like sore thumbs and fooled no one, though they did provide the necessary, visible deterrent to stop the hijackings. Now the bus depot itself became the target for attack. With over a hundred buses there, the Provos had the chance to torch them all at once. So units were assigned to bus-depot guard duty. During our stint there the lads discovered they had easy access to the phone in the depot's office and took the opportunity to call friends and relatives in everywhere from England to Australia.

Months later we heard that the bus company was shocked when they received their phone bill and found it ran into thousands of pounds. The bus company complained to HQ and as leader of the unit I was called to book. I pleaded innocence, of course, saying that I didn't even know anyone in Australia.

We were now pretty adept at knowing how to bend the rules without breaking them or, when the rules were broken, at covering our arses in the event we were found out. I thought, Well, this is how it is now: they kill, we kill; they lie, we lie. And like two lawyers fighting their clients' cases in court, hopefully justice will somehow crawl out from the wreckage of death and deceit.

I soon found out, only a week later, how a well-chosen lie could go a long way to preventing your life being cut short. We'd no sooner left the mill when we walked straight into yet another ambush and came under fire. We were still in the old area off Butler Street, with no cover other than the shallow doorways. We scattered and flattened ourselves against them. The shots were coming down from high. The gunman was up on the roof of the Holy Cross school, two hundred yards away. The door behind me felt about as comforting as a coffin lid. The others in the unit were over the road on the same side as the gunman. Austin and I were the only two on the other side and we were the easier targets. A puff of brick-dust blew out right next to me and I said, 'Sod this!', pulled back from the door and kicked it. Nothing; not even a hint of give. I kicked it again and then shouldered it three times. I bounced off each time – the damn thing felt deadlocked. Austin was behind me, waiting to follow me in. As bullets chipped brick around us, Austin turned his back to the fire. As our radio man, his back was covered with the large hunch of the transmitter kit. I realized that he was hoping the bulk of the radio would shield him. So I did the same and crouched in front of him for temporary cover. When a bullet clunked into the radio, Austin rocked on his feet and I realized we were both as daft as each other for still being there. Here I am, I thought, shielding behind a man who catches bloody grenades. I threw him over to the other side of the street and followed. Stan, Blake, Crosier and the rest of the boys all took a step out and returned fire to cover us as we fell against the wall. I radioed back for help. Fortunately, the bullet hadn't taken the transmitter out. As we were still so close to the mill, it was only a minute or so before a Saracen came round the corner. Unlike the PIGs, the Saracens were armed with a heavy Browning machine-gun on a turret. We dashed out and scuttled behind it for cover as it drew nearer to the school.

I knew that the only way out of this was to use the Saracen's gun. I also knew that under the Rules of Engagement it couldn't be deployed without the say-so of a higher authority. The gun fired a huge 30 calibre shell and you couldn't just go around blasting it off like you were in the middle of the Second World War. Even though, right now, it felt like we were. I shouted to the lieutenant in charge of the Saracen to fire. He replied, as I knew he would, that he couldn't without orders to do so. Bullets pinged off the car's armour. You're safe inside, I thought, but I'm not having any of us die because of official procedure.

'I got the order when I radioed through!' I shouted. There was a brief pause from inside. Then he shouted for my name. 'Corporal Phillips, sir,' I lied. 'Now just fire that bloody thing!'

There was a God-almighty boom and the Saracen rocked with the recoil. The second floor of the school disintegrated completely. We popped our heads out from behind the Saracen, bug-eyed with shock. I knew it would do some serious damage but even I was surprised. Beside me, Crosier whispered, 'Holy Christ!' The cloud of dust began to clear. Where the corner of the school had been I could now see only sky. Like a dolls' house with the front off, we could see right inside: burning desks; a shattered blackboard; paper and exercise books singed and flapping in the aftermath of the blast. The guttering swung from the roof like a broken finger.

The next day every newspaper and TV news report from local to national was dominated by 'BRITISH ARMY USE TANKS IN IRELAND!' The poor lieutenant in charge of the Saracen was reprimanded by Brigadier Kitson and demoted. His commanders had never heard of this Corporal Phillips that he said had authorization for the gun's deployment. I later heard that he spent the next two years of his duty trying to find me.

As we were now coming under sniper fire at practically every verse end it didn't take a rocket scientist to work out that they had guns and the guns were hidden in the Ardoyne. So we went on 'block searches'. This was when a designated number of houses would be assigned to us and we'd go in, seal off the area and search the houses for weapons. We were having to take more affirmative action to stop the guns being brought into play.

We were in most danger when we tried to cross the Ardoyne on our way up to the Glenbryns in the north. This was the predominantly Protestant area where we knew we'd be safe. On the way we ran into five separate ambushes. Back at base they knew it was 22 Alpha that had gone out, but I don't think even then they could believe how many 'contacts' we reported. And for some reason we seemed to hit a lot of radio 'dead-spots'. By the time we got to the Glenbryns we felt totally knackered. Often, we'd be given a drink and a bite to eat by the Prods there. I suggested we call on a girl who lived near by whom I'd struck up a friendship with. We tramped in the house, carrying six-packs from the corner off-licence. Luckily her parents were out so Doreen and I amused ourselves in her back bedroom. If ever there was a transmission dead-spot, this was it. Unfortunately, Austin forgot to switch off the transmitter and just as Doreen and I were doing what comes naturally, I heard a call for a 'sit rep' come through downstairs. I opened the bedroom door to find a sheepish-looking Austin preparing to knock. I grabbed the receiver angrily and reported that we were pinned down by sporadic fire, when actually the only thing that had been pinned down was Doreen. Now 'sporadic' isn't the easiest word to say when you've had a few beers. It came out as 'spodadic', 'sporalic' or everything but. Another unit out on patrol that had been listening in came on the line.

'I think what 22 Alpha is trying to say, sir, is "sporadic".'

'That's what I bloody said,' I replied. I said we'd report back any changes, hung up and slammed the door in Austin's face.

As we made our way back to base, we took the scenic route around the Ardoyne. We decided we didn't really want to set an army record for running into the most ambushes in one night.

By now I was thoroughly sick of being constantly ambushed. If someone asked me, on our way out of the mill, if I thought we'd end up in another gunbattle, the usual reply was, 'Is the Pope Catholic?' There were only so many routes we could take around the Ardoyne and we'd already exhausted them all. One way we had of outfoxing the snipers was by taking a shortcut from one street to another by going directly through someone's house. So instead of walking up Brompton Park and then turning back into Highbury Gardens, for example, we'd enter a house halfway up Brompton. The whole family might be sat their in the front room having their dinner and watching *Coronation Street* and they'd turn to see us tramping through their home. I'd say 'No, don't get up, love,' to the gobsmacked mother and we'd pass on through and out the back door, straight into Highbury. They learned to get used to it after a while.

One day in particular I could sense that something was in the air. There might as well have been a neon sign in the sky saying 'Ambush Here!' A local was scurrying home in front of me so I ran up and walked behind him. I was so close that we must have looked like some music-hall comedy act going through a routine. I thought, Let's see if they're gun-happy enough to risk hitting one of their own. He started panicking at having me as his shadow and began backchatting and effing and blinding. Finally, he'd had enough and we got into a tussle. Things were getting out of hand so I whacked him off me. He shot straight through a front door with me after him and we clattered into the house, fell over the back of the front-room sofa and rolled around, fighting at the feet of the family. We brawled on the rug for a minute before I thought, Sod this, and let the poor bugger fly. It was a bit embarrassing, having to get up and dust myself off, make my apologies and leave.

Of course we would never have got the OK from our superiors for any of these techniques so we didn't enquire. Like they say, if in doubt, don't ask, as a refusal often offends. You couldn't exactly go back to the book and find under subsection B, 'Deploy your men in an orderely fashion through Mrs Kelly's front room ensuring that they leave with a cheery goodbye.' Anyway, we were already offended that some colonel or other with a few pips and bars on his chest expected us to patrol these streets like we were on some text-book training manoeuvre. So we did what we had to to avoid being slotted. I knew that, when we got back, if the shit hit the fan then the worst thing we would be hit by was a turd.

Chris Mather, being our platoon commander, sometimes came out on patrol with us. I knew when he did that I'd never end up isolated during an incident, like I had before. I knew Chris would go in as hard and deep as me. At times when we were under fire I also knew that, like me, he was hoping this might be when we'd get either of the two remaining killers of the three off-duty squaddies. Reports had come through that Meehan and Doherty had returned from the south and were active again.

During the rare lulls that we had on patrol, Chris and I would sometimes talk things over. He was the only one to whom I confessed my increasingly fragile faith. At times it did feel just like that: like a confession. It would make me think back to when I used to approach the confession box in church, the dread mounting with each step. There may be a lot of things you could accuse Catholicism of, but skimping on drama wasn't one of them. Putting the fear of God in you was obviously too big a job for God himself so he left that in the capable hands of the nuns and priests. And they always seemed to take up the challenge with great relish. I doubt whether the Devil himself would have savoured the thought of facing any of the formidable nuns that hovered over me during my childhood. They'd land on you from a great height, all flapping black wings and tight white faces, and I knew later, when I first joined the army, that no parade-ground sergeant-major could ever scare me. I'd just come out of the trenches of the most frightening religion on earth.

So there I'd be, walking down the middle of the pews like a condemned man: looming, lifesize figures of Christ flying in formation to the left of me, hundreds of prayer candles flickering to the right and, if you were really lucky, someone hunched over the organ banging out a moaning, horror-movie soundtrack to your last walk. By the time I got to the box, slipped into the quiet dark and saw the face behind the lattice grille, I was ready to confess to everything from impregnating a local widow to invading Poland and starting the Second World War.

I was never much of an angel. I seemed to have this natural aptitude for sinning. But as Catholicism deemed practically everything except breathing a 'sin', I started to feel less bad about it. A few Hail Marys and Our Fathers (or Bloody Marys and How's Yer Fathers as we called them) and you were forgiven. Easy as that. Until the next time.

Seeing people blow each other to bits here in the name of God, among other things, didn't exactly fill me with much religious fervour. I couldn't imagine there were many commandments left which hadn't been broken hundreds of times ever since we first landed. Even some of the local priests were involved and, it has been alleged, had participated in the formation of the IRA we were now fighting.

One incident in particular struck me with the sound of a death knell. We were on back-up patrol, driving around the streets in a PIG with the back doors open as usual. We came across the last stages of a riot and the scenes that normally accompanied it: bricks and bottles in the street and squaddies lining up those they'd caught against a wall. One of them was the guy I'd rolled over the sofa with a few days before. I also saw, to my astonishment, that one of the men leaning against the house with his hands held high whilst he was searched was a priest. His robes snapped in the wind as a soldier frisked him. As we passed, I had no way of knowing whether the priest was directly involved. He may have been trying to calm things down, as they sometimes did, or persuading the rioters to disperse, but the image it left me with went beyond whatever were the true circumstances of this priest's involvement.

Chris, having no religion of his own, could really do no more than listen and nod, pretty much like the old priests did. But no Bloody Marys or How's Yer Fathers were handed out. Instead he said that God wasn't saving anyone down here and He wouldn't make an exception and save me. This time it was me who nodded in agreement.

6

BELFAST EATS
THE WEAK

The worst thing that can happen is that you lose a man. When you're away from home and away from your friends and family, the men around you become first your friends and then your family. The army becomes your home. Some of the lads that had come from broken homes or from families that showed them very little care found friendship in the forces like they'd never known before. When you're living side by side, sometimes twenty-four hours a day, then an incredibly strong bond forms between you. You have to become close-knit because you may rely on these men to save your life.

There are things you dislike about each other, of course – there's bound to be – but the strongest feeling is that you're all comrades-in-arms. Even the other person's failings, like Austin's occasional bumblings, just become a funny part of their character. This close-ness is something that civilians very often don't understand. But if you think of someone whom you've worked with for years in a factory or office and have become friends with and socialized with – and then picture that person dying suddenly, then you can imag-ine the feelings that are generated. And not just dying in a car crash or some other accident, but being killed by someone who has gone out of their way to do it.

Apart from the odd aberration or occasional bad judgement, which you have to accept as part of being human, I was certain that we could rely on each other. The trouble is that, as the man said, the only things men can be certain of are taxes and death itself.

On one morning, the only thing we were being philosophical about was the boredom of being on watch-duty. We were posi-tioned on top of the flat roof of the mill as guards and look-outs. The days were over when we could casually lean on the chest-high wall and chat or whistle at passing girls as the units on street patrol came and went. In the present situation we had to be more alert, move around, stand back, and cover each other when we had to cover a unit below.

We'd been up here all morning with nothing much to do but look out over the rooftops of Belfast. You know you shouldn't relax too much but you always do. From up here things generally looked better, at times almost peaceful; we could see women hanging out washing, some kids kicking an old leather football about and the clink of empty milk bottles as a float went by.

I heard a wolf-whistle and knew before I turned that it would be Nigger. He was leaning over the wall and waving at some local girls below.

'Look at the miniskirt on that one, Corporal,' he was saying. 'It's no more than a frigging belt!' He still carried around a tatty copy of his picture in *Playboy* and I was half expecting him to start waving it.

I shouted at him: 'Wallace! Get back off the chuffing wall. How many times do you need telling?' I had told them all time and time again that those innocent looking girls that passed below might have been sent by in short skirts for some reason other than our pleasure. It was a classic 'come-on' ploy: distract, cause a weakness and then exploit it.

He gave one last wave, smiling, and then came the gunshot. We all dodged down. Something hit my back. I looked up and saw Nigger on his backside, still alive but wide-eyed and looking behind me. I turned and Kev Crosier was lying at my feet with his hat tilted over his face. He'd fallen against me. I rolled him over and could feel a wetness on my hand. He'd taken the bullet in his head and died instantly. Apparently he'd moved forward for a glimpse of the girls and the sniper had lined him up for the first shot. We didn't have any chance to return fire. No gunbattle developed. It was a one-shot hit. Down below the women were long gone and the view over Belfast looked a lot darker.

I'd always liked Kev. He'd earned the nickname 'Socks' because washing them was never a priority, but if that's the worst thing you can say about a man then he's not doing too badly. He was a good lad and a good soldier. To everyone else but us and his family, he was now just another statistic.

To the bastard that had shot him he was another successful kill to be celebrated.

Two days later we assembled in best dress uniform at Aldergrove airport. A civilian hearse glided silently on to the tarmac with Kev in the back. His coffin was draped with the Union Jack. Funerals are always times of sadness and remembrance, not all of the memories sad. Austin said, 'I hope I don't get the sock end.' We carried the coffin over to the open doors of the Hercules transporter and lifted him in for his final journey home.

Bullets can do good and bad to men. The good is when they miss and cause men to think twice, all night even, about their lives and how they can improve them. Or how they can ensure that the bullets will continue to miss.

The bad, of course, is when they hit. And when they hit it's unforgivably hard and deep. They drill right in and down, dragging a humming hot-wire of pain behind them. If, as they say, beauty is only skin deep, then a bullet's ugliness goes much deeper: straight through that skin until it makes itself a home inside you. I saw beauty raped. Faces fucked by metal. Bodies blown over a street's length. Maimed survivors turned inside out with agony.

Kev and Tapper had been two of the unlucky–lucky ones. Unlucky enough to die; lucky enough to know nothing about it. But their deaths didn't stop the world for anyone but them and their grieving families. Even we had to carry on, though the memories were still fresh. To the rest of Belfast, or Northern Ireland, or even the world, it was just another hiccup before the next one. And it was never very long before the next one came along.

We only had to wait until the following day. We heard the now familiar crack and ran towards it. A house door was open. Crying and screaming emerged from within. I hit the threshold first and saw a young man at the foot of the stairs. He'd been thoroughly pole-axed by his own death; astonished by it, in fact. It showed in his face, slack-mouthed and wide-eyed at being killed in his own home, his mother still in the kitchen. It looked like he'd been shot at the top of the stairs and then dropped the full flight. He must have been dead before he hit the bottom and remained where he'd landed: plopped on a rug; flopped over and twisted. A mess of angles, like a puppet with cut strings, his body did things in death that it could never have done in life, because it would have hurt too much for his legs to bend that way and for his elbows to cross behind his back. And he certainly couldn't have coped with that bullet without a helping hand from death. What this bullet had done to his face was the work of a real vandal.

It was a young face, too, which made its glistening splits and tufts of escaped muscle seem even worse, somehow. The gunman must have been pitilessly close, maybe on the top step as the guy came round the corner to descend. More hot-blooded, this murder, than cold. The heat not from impulse (it was, without doubt, premeditated) but from desire. Whoever killed this lad really wanted to end his life. Christ, I thought, the gunman must have been so close that he jolted, not only from the bark of the barrel but from the back-blow of blood which must have spattered him.

The guy at my feet had certainly been jolted – right out of this life and straight into whatever was waiting for him on the other side. He hadn't stood a chance. The round looked like a heavy calibre. It had kicked in the door of his nose, ransacked his head and burst out the back dragging a snot trail of brains like a thief dropping valuables in the alarm. A real breaking and entering job. Shocking how something no bigger than a baby's finger can so royally fuck up a life.

No mother should outlive her child. Or be present at its ugly, unstomachable death. She'd come out from wherever she'd been at the first sound. She was cradling his head when we'd arrived, repeating his name, and no doubt still would be when we left. I made no move to pull her from him. She made no sound now. She was beyond sound, just bucking and rocking inside whatever hell you'd have been in if you were her. I thought, How this woman will ever recover from this I'll never know. I couldn't imagine she ever would, come to think of it.

We didn't yet know why he'd been targeted. Was he a known paramilitary member, or suspected of being a member? Sometimes that was enough. It might have even been a case of mistaken identity. That also happened. Or had he been marked down as an informer? Had the gunman already seen his own father or one of his brothers die this way? Did it make more sense to him to put another family through the same thing than it did not to seek revenge? This was part of the madness. It set on course a frightening downward spiral. The more that died, the more mothers, brothers and fathers it left wanting revenge. In some sad way I thought it was an understandable, very human madness, this desire for revenge. I understood it because I felt it myself. Chris and I had made a pact to avenge the deaths of any of our men whom we lost. The difference was that we were only after the known guilty.

No doubt, though, that this woman wouldn't think that her son, whatever he'd done, was deserving of this.

Weeks of the same passed. We got into a routine of being shot at. You never get used to it, of course, but your acceptance and expectations level out accordingly. Like a cat landing on an unfamiliar wall, you learn where your balance lies pretty quickly. In the past I'd seen men adapt to all kinds of madness, from jungle warfare in the Tropics to chaos on city streets. The name of the game in the army was the same as in life in general, just a more exaggerated version – adapt or die.

We returned one night after another successful high-wire act through the Ardoyne; walking the tightrope in the dark through streets and alleys. I wasn't actually with my boys but in charge of another unit. Their sergeant was on R and R and so, as senior corporal, I had been put in charge of them. We'd been ambushed (no change there, then) but didn't lose anyone. We got back in at four in the morning and I filled in a patrol report for the Ops officer detailing the 'contact' and other relevant information about things we'd seen. The most important of these was a tractor tyre at the bottom of Brompton Park, right outside a betting shop. Wires were visible inside the tyre. It was an obvious 'come-on'. First, there would be no reason for a tractor tyre to be in the middle of an urban area and, second, if they were going to booby-trap it they'd make damn sure the wires were hidden.

Even though we'd just come off patrol, I asked for permission to go back out at eight o'clock to deal with it with my own unit. The Ops officer refused and told me to make out my report. On the rare occasion we had an uneventful patrol I even had to fill out reports for that: 'quiet on patrol', 'nothing unusual observed', basically just saying that bugger-all had happened. If we were involved in a 'contact' then the SIB boys – Special Investigation Branch – would come to see me next morning for a signed statement. The SIBs were like New York cops, in civvies and with handguns in shoulder holsters.

The temporary Ops officer, an arsehole called Captain Irving whom I'd never liked, told me to inform my 2IC on the situation so he could take out our unit to deal with it. This responsibility fell to Stan. I wasn't happy about this at all. Not because I didn't think Stan was capable but because I could practically smell the danger of this particular 'come-on'. Sometimes you get a really strong feeling that you must be there and this was one of those times. My gut instinct had never failed me in the past. I put my case to Irving again.

'Let me go out on the eight o'clock. I know this situation; I know the angles.'

'Do as I tell you, Corporal,' he replied, showing his irritation now. 'Brief your second-in-command. I won't tell you again.'

Like the rest of my unit, Stan was asleep. I shook him awake and briefed him. I told him that I'd already requested the ATO to be in Brompton Park at eight-fifteen. The ATO was the officer in charge of bomb disposal. For some reason he'd been nicknamed Felix. He'd move in with his squad and send in a robot device, which relayed information back to them. They'd probably do a controlled explosion to be on the safe side.

Stan looked at me bleary-eyed. I was worried that he wasn't taking in everything.

'Look, Stan. I can't go out with you. Felix will be there at eight-fifteen so get there at eight o'clock and secure the area. Whatever you do, when you surround it, make sure the boys are looking out, away from the device and what the ATO's doing. Don't look in. It'll be tempting to do that when Felix and the robot are farting around with the tyre, but don't do it and don't let the boys do it. This is a certain bloody "come-on" if ever I saw one. You know as well as I do that those bastards will have a couple of snipers dotted around waiting to have a go at you.'

He nodded, rubbing his eyes, saying he understood. 'Yeah, I know. I've got you. I've got you,' he said. 'I'll see you when we get back and tell you all about it.'

I looked at him. I felt like a boxing referee checking the eyes of a fighter who's just got up off the canvas, looking for signs of under-standing and recognition. I wanted to be sure that everything had sunk in and he wasn't just flannelling me. I began to go over it again.

'For Christ's sake, Nicky!' he said, laughing now, 'You sound like my bloody mother. Stop clucking. I've got it, all right?'

As I left he called ' 'Bye Mum' after me as he pulled on his pants. I still had a worrying, sick feeling about the whole thing and I was angry with the Ops officer for not letting me go back out. The most important thing was that they all remained looking away from what was going on in the middle of their circle of defence: All Round Defence it's called.

I couldn't really sleep over the next few hours, so I concentrated on writing out the report for the SIB boys.

First light came and it was a strange feeling knowing that Stan, John-Boy, Blakesy, Austin and Nigger were going out without me. Blakesy had taken over as second-in-command and the unit was made up by our two new intakes Clay and Tommo.

I checked my watch at eight o'clock – they'd be there by now – and then checked it again at eight-fifteen. Felix would be going in. The first shots came at eight-twenty-five. I could tell immediately they weren't ours. There was the low boom-boom-boom of a Thompson machine-gun and some other fire. The worst thing was the silence that followed. I didn't hear any return fire.

A report came down the line: one dead, two wounded. The two wounded were already on the way to hospital and the dead one was coming back to the mill. I went down to the medical room to ID the body with a feeling of dread. I didn't know who I was going to find there.

That frightening hospital-stench hit me as I entered. A doctor and two white-coated orderlies were stood there, along with a lance-corporal who was in charge of bringing the body back. There was no one laid out on the table. Then I saw him. It was one of our new recruits, a young lad called Mark Clay, who had been brought in to replace Tapper. I'd hardly had chance to get to know him; he'd been one of the quieter members of the squad. He was just slumped on the floor in a far corner of the room like a rag doll. His eyes were still open. I was stunned. And then, completely overwhelmed with anger, I lost it. Before I knew it I was running at the lance-corporal. He was stood chatting to one of the orderlies as if he was on a tea break. I grabbed him by the neck, breaking him off in mid-sentence, ran him the length of the room and slammed him into the wall.

'That's a soldier down there, not a fucking scarecrow! Give him some dignity! Get him off the floor now! Get him on the table and cover him before I break your fucking neck!' I sensed the others move up behind me but they didn't touch me. They'd have to drag me off. The lance-corporal stared at me, bug-eyed.

'You should be fucking ashamed of yourself. I wouldn't treat a dead dog like that!' I lowered him off his toes and back on to his heels. 'You haven't even closed his eyes,' I said finally, almost to myself. He moved away slowly and with the others began lifting Mark off the floor and onto the examination table. I now noticed that a sergeant had been stood watching through the open door. I knew he could do me for what he'd just seen, but he turned and walked away.

There's so little dignity in death anyway, however it happens, but to be left like that, to me, was the final insult, just another unnecessary degradation. They laid him out carefully, without speaking, exchanging looks with each other. The lance-corporal stepped back and whispered an apology to me. I barely heard. I just looked at Mark's face as a blanket was pulled up over it.

The full report on the incident came through. John-Boy and Stan were the two wounded. John wasn't too bad, he'd make it, but Stan was in a really bad way. Chris immediately came down to see me and filled me in on the rest. It had happened just as I said it would, just as I knew it would. I'd wanted to be wrong. When I'd left Stan, only four hours earlier, I'd walked back to my bunk wanting to be so wrong about it because I knew the only proof otherwise would be bodies in bags.

Chris laid it out. They'd secured the area, forming a ring with them all looking out. Stan had briefed them as I'd briefed him. The ATO came in prompt at 8.15 and began working on the apparently booby-trapped tyre. It was so bloody obvious that it was a fake but they couldn't chance it. Then natural curiosity had got the better of them, even Stan, and they'd looked around and away from the rooftops and doorways. Two snipers had opened up with the Thompson and another weapon. Mark got the full spray, and Stan, stood next to him, had taken the rest. John-Boy, luckily, was just winged.

I felt a sickening wave of guilt sloshing around inside me. It was like battery acid corroding me. I hated the taste. But there was no going back. It was done now. I'd just have to live with it. That was the worse thing about still being alive, you had to live with it. Small price to pay though, really, I thought, all things considered.

I knew this wouldn't have happened if I'd been there. I knew I wouldn't have let it. I'd have made the lads so afraid of disobeying me that they wouldn't have dared to look in.

'Let's go and see Stan,' Chris said. 'They don't think he'll make it.'

We found him on the emergency ward in a room of his own. He was unconscious and was wired up to machines that beeped and flashed. They seemed more alive than he was. Tubes were threaded in and out of him, running blood and God-knew-what to God-knew-where. His face was covered with tubes and tape. His face looked alien: some blood still smeared on it (the rest hastily wiped away), had dried to brown. The uniform had been cut off him. I noticed his wedding ring and wondered if I should take it off to give back to his wife. But I couldn't bring myself to touch him; I felt that if I did, all the machines would start screaming. A fatter tube ballooned his mouth open. A noise came out like he was just learning how to breathe for the first time and failing to get to grips with it.

The sound mesmerized me. I felt that if we weren't there to hear it then it would stop. As if we had to bear witness to him still being alive. And as if, and I knew this didn't make any sense, he was waiting for us to leave before he gave up. Like the silly sod didn't want to let us down again.

I backed out of the room, because it didn't feel right to turn away from him, and because I knew as sure as I knew anything that this would be the last time I'd see him.

'I shouldn't have let him embarrass me into not going over it again. You know, like when you feel stupid for repeating something. I shouldn't have.'

'I'm not going to listen to you blame yourself,' Chris said. 'When you know as well as I do who is to blame.'

We walked down the hospital steps. I felt changed by what we'd seen. I wished that I could pray for him but I knew I couldn't. What a fucking waste of time that is, I thought. Praying! To whom? To exactly which god who doesn't listen am I supposed to pray? None of them listened as far as I could see: Catholics, Protestants, Hindus, Muslims, even red Indians, all prayed to their gods and didn't get so much as a 'thank you'. The killing still continued.

If one thing more than any other was responsible for hammering down the lid on my newly dead faith, seeing Stan like that was it. Inside me I could hear the first words of the eulogy as the coffin was lowered into the ground. Catholicism still had one thing left for me, however, a parting gift, and the one thing that lapsed, collapsed or just thoroughly sickened ex-Catholics always carry with them: guilt.

I still felt guilty for Stan's death, even though I'd done all I could do. Or all I was allowed to do. And that's where the other feeling came in. This was of anger at the Ops officer, and our senior officers in general, for not listening to advice from the ones who knew best about this dirty backstreet war we were now involved in.

Stan died that night without waking. That was the only blessing, that he didn't come round to get a last look at himself and how he'd ended up.

The next night, sat in the Naafi, we were all pretty low. Things didn't improve when a unit of the Green Jackets walked past our table. The Green Jackets were a battalion drawn from London's East End and were nicknamed the Black Mafia because they were made up largely of a combination of black soldiers and cockney wide-boys who came across like failed gangsters. The one at the front wore his camouflage net tied around his neck in a knot, like a Rupert would wear it, rather than tied in the correct way as a squaddie should have it. For some reason this got right up my nose. They looked like an undisciplined bunch of tossers. Then he really put my nose out of joint when he turned and said something to his mates as he passed. We were obviously meant to hear it.

'Look, lads. It's the falling plates we've heard so much about.'

On a firing range there are metal plate targets which, when you hit them, fall down with a clang. They help in shooting practice because they give you a definite and satisfying reaction to a hit. So any squad that is known to have lost a lot of men is sometimes called 'falling plates'. It's one of the worst insults that can be thrown at you.

'Hold these a minute, would you,' I said to Blakesy calmly, even though I was boiling inside, and passed him my beer. Then I jumped up and smacked the Green Jacket right in his smug-bastard face. I heard his nose break and he hit the deck. The others stepped back. I heard a scrape of chairs behind me as the rest of my lads at the table stood up.

'Don't ever insult the Green Howards again you cockney bastard! We've seen more action in the fucking dinner queue than you ever will! Who's the falling plate now?'

He looked up at me from the floor, his hand on his nose, which was now more out of joint than mine. The rest of them picked him up and they filed past. The Naafi had fallen silent. They all knew it was true, not only what I'd said but what he'd said. Out of nearly 5,000 troops in Northern Ireland, the Green Howards numbered only 600 and we'd lost a higher percentage of men than anyone else. Can't be anything to do with the fact that we're always at the bloody brunt end of it, though, can it? I thought.

Still, I knew I'd hit him half out of anger, half out of frustration because it was true. The image of Stan was still too fresh.

The next morning I was called into the company sergeant-major's office to explain. The Green Jackets had filed a complaint. They didn't mention the insult, though, and had made it seem like

I was drunk and disorderly. I explained that I was just defending the honour of the regiment and the sergeant-major nodded and let it pass. He knew what we'd been through. Any decent soldier would have understood.

The army is no place for thin-skinned liberals. If you put up with any crap then you'd just be marked down as a soft touch and let yourself in for even more. An incident like this had happened once before when we were in Hong Kong. We were sat at a pool-side bar when some Jocks from the Black Watch walked in. They were already half cut. One of them kept coming over to us and shouting the odds, calling us the Green Cowards. A drunken Scot with a thick accent isn't the easiest guy to understand, but from what I could pick out, they'd previously been involved in a ruck with some Green Howards and they'd come off worse. We were heavily outnumbered so I told the rest of my squad to get ready to run because I was going to deck this Jock the next time he swayed over. Sure enough, he did, and before he'd even got a word out this time I smacked him. We legged it as the rest of them bolted after us. For some daft reason best known to himself, instead of running round the pool like the rest of us, Stan decided it would be quicker to leap in and swim across. The fact that he was the battalion swimming champion probably had a lot to do with it. He must have felt more at home in the water. And bugger me if he didn't beat us across to the other side. We ran off into the town, laughing as Stan squelched beside us and twenty mad Jocks tried to put one drunken foot in front of the other and follow.

My first bad dreams began the following night. The images blinked on and off as if they were caught in the flashing of an ambulance light, stuttering, first blue then red: I saw a large crucifix in a milk bottle, like a ship-in-a-bottle, puzzling you how it got in there; the streets outside, very quiet; green leaves fluttering down then bursting into flames; a baby crying in a pram full of nails; a face turning away from me, I couldn't make out whose; another crucifix, again inside a bottle, but this time someone I couldn't see was filling the bottle with petrol and the cross bobbed and clinked against the glass; an old cat I'd seen on an alley wall, looking back at me; Tapper and Kev talking and laughing, even though their faces were sheets of blood; tubes going into Stan's eyes full of petrol; the cat exploding like a nail bomb; old black robes caked in shit, snapping in the wind; my uniform with the arms and legs cut off, each piece with a limb inside; a hundred house doors all on fire slamming shut at the same time; and on and on in corpse blue and siren red until each new image only ended when it burst into flames. The cat, the cross, the leaves, the doors and Stan's eyes all on fire (I could smell the plastic tubes melting). Then I dropped back down through clouds and the feeling of falling jolted me awake.

The fluttering-leaves image stayed with me most vividly for some reason. I knew it had come back to me from the day I'd run down the gardens towards the machine-gun. I remembered the feeling and thought about the things that I remembered - how bullets hum past with a buzz, like angry bees. At times, from a distance, you can even forget how harmful they are. Until you see a face at your feet split open like a dropped melon; a human face only recognizable as such because of the odd bits and pieces that jump out at you with some familiarity – an exposed tongue sprinkled with teeth, or a single haemorrhaging eyeball blinking in something black and trembling that was a woman's head, or a man's brain coughed out of the hole where his nose used to be like so much snot. Or the small, tell-tale dot of blood on a child's forehead which indicated the first whisper of a bullet that even in the quick trip through the brain had built up to a bellow which took the back of his head off. And the disgusting depravity of a man reduced to a body-shell in his own living room in front of his wife and kids: the last image they had of him awkwardly bent, his legs soft beneath him; pissing himself his last action. And that hideous, mewling wail of people totally beyond any human ability to comfort them. Because you can't kick life back into this man they love; this son they cherished at birth, raised and adored. Only God can do that and yet doesn't. He fucking doesn't. Time and time again he refrains from easing the pain. And does what instead? Turns away with a nothing-to-do-with-me shrug? Or was he busy hacking out a deal with Death – you let this baby born of a difficult birth live and I'll trade you the one down the Ardoyne?

So I felt no guilt at turning away from this God. The last laugh is that if He was still there, He probably didn't even care.

7

A CORPORAL'S WAR

After the deaths of Tapper, Kev, Stan and Mark, Chris and I vowed to do everything in our power not to lose any more men. No more back-foot fighting, no more excuses or turning a blind eye. No more 'falling plates'. This meant, in Chris's words, 'taking the war to them'. You can't play by the rules if the rules are only being obeyed by one side.

The politicians carried on yakking; the officers above us were more at home on the parade ground or swanning around some sleepy, far-flung remnant of the empire. They weren't prepared for, or didn't know how to fight, a terrorist war. We didn't rely on them, but on ourselves, and they came to rely on us to get information back about what was really happening and how best to deal with it so they could change tactics accordingly. We were now in the middle of what I considered to be a corporals' war.

During training, the army drilled obedience into you and from this obedience came discipline. Armies run like machines and each soldier is expected to become a part. Whatever humanity you retained was down to you. What anyone else did because of their beliefs was down to them. Even in my new-found godless place I didn't mind any other soldier praising God to high-heaven as long as he continued to pass the ammunition. But we were being shot dead off-duty, blown up in bars and ambushed from every angle. We'd gone from being peacekeepers to policemen to moving targets. I decided that if I was going to die on these streets I was going to take every murderer, tin-pot terrorist and cold-blooded fanatic down with me.

Chris's forays out into danger zones became more frequent. His favoured tactic was to go into the area with two other men and, under cover of darkness, take over a house. The occupants would be locked in a back room while Chris took up position at an upstairs window. Using a Starlight night-scope he'd scan the streets below looking for gunmen.

Every time Chris went out it had the potential to be the last I saw of him, but he had the balls and savvy to pull it off.

My unit now comprised me, Blakesy (replacing Stan as 2IC), Austin and Nigger. Our dead and missing had been replaced by four new recruits – Foxy; Tommo; a guy who'd been busted back down to private called Gibson; and a hard-as-nails, switched-on bloke I'd first trained with called Billy 'Nimrod' Cooke.

It wasn't long before the new boys were christened, literally, with a baptism of fire.

Out at night we somehow got trapped in the narrow alleyway by Herbert Street in the middle of a God-almighty riot. What must have been about a hundred rioters advanced towards us. We came under a ferocious fire of stones, bricks, planks and petrol bombs. In situations like this you knew they were going to sling everything *and* the kitchen sink at you. We peddled back and loosed off a few rubber bullets and CS gas pellets, but to no effect. Nothing stopped them. Everything we threw out seemed to be absorbed by this furious mass. Petrol bombs and stones fell on us without cease. Tommo took a brick on the head and I began dragging him back. Austin was already down. I heard Nimrod shout as a bomb landed beside him and splashed burning petrol on his legs. He frantically flapped it out. More shouting bounced over from behind the houses that hemmed us in and when I glanced back and saw another mass of people behind us blocking off our retreat. I knew that we were completely surrounded.

I now felt real panic for the first time. We were in danger of being ripped to shreds. Austin, Foxy and Tommo were down and being helped back by the others. I thought of a situation similar to this from only two weeks before. Another unit had been caught in a riot and the soldier at the front had let the mob get too close. They swamped him, beat him to a pulp and then shot him dead with his own gun. I didn't want to die that way.

I flattened under the corrugated-iron roof of a coal-house as a bottle broke open in flames barely ten feet away. The noise was incredible. Then I heard a sudden boom and saw that Nimrod had stepped out and let loose a couple of rounds over their heads. The shouting clicked off immediately as the echo of the shots reverberated about us. Then the rest of them scattered and ran.

We limped back to base. By the time we got there we could hear fresh rioting starting. I knew Chris was out there somewhere in a house.

That night I went out to find him and we sat on dustbins in an alley, smoking in the dark. He bent down, laughing, and scooped up one of the cats that meowed at our feet. It gave one of those strange, human-like baby wails that cats sometimes make and then exploded with nails in his face. I jack-knifed back to life on my bunk, wet with sweat. I listened. But all I could hear above the thump of my heart was the silence of Belfast.

In the morning I rose early and searched round the mill for Chris. He wasn't in his quarters. Squaddies were milling about, coming and going, some just returning and others preparing to go out. I asked around but no one had seen him. I didn't really believe in omens or premonitions but I couldn't shake the dream from the previous night. I was convinced he must still be out there when I rounded a corner and saw him slumped in a chair with a coffee.

'You look knackered,' I said.

'Getting there. You should see the other guy.'

I didn't tell him about my night but he motioned me to sit down and told me about his.

After commandeering a house he'd sat it out upstairs, scoping the streets for gunmen. He'd heard the riot break out, not knowing that we were in the thick of it but suspecting we might be. He'd heard the gunshot and the silence. When the second wave of rioting came he radioed through to check up on the unit involved. That's when he'd learned it was us and we were all safely back. The second wave eventually broke. Silence returned. His vigilance finally paid off when the scope revealed several figures. They were probably on the run from the back-up patrols that had come out, that's when further gunshots had been heard. One of them was crouched against a motorbike holding a gun. He appeared to be commanding the others. The man turned and looked directly into the scope, his figure fuzzed in green and shadows, as if he'd sensed Chris was there. Chris shot him immediately.

Running downstairs he'd found the body already surrounded by people. It was the man's family (Chris could now see he was young) and they'd rushed out at the sound of the shot. The guy was dead. His mother and father were knelt by him, sobbing. The father kept repeating, 'He only had a spanner! He was mending his bike. He was holding a spanner!' As well as a few people approaching the scene, Chris saw the others disappearing away. He suspected one of these had spirited the gun away.

He finished his account and looked up at me. I'd already

decided not to ask but he didn't wait to see before he said, 'He had a gun, Nicky. He *did* have a gun . . .'

'You did the right thing then. You had no choice.' He nodded and looked away, his face impassive. I couldn't read anything from it and, to be honest, I didn't want to try too hard.

A few days later I saw death in one of its other forms, this one 'natural', though it looked anything but for a body to be doing what this one was doing.

It started when we were out on foot patrol, traipsing the streets with our usual mixture of nervy boredom and casual edginess. A call came through about a guy who had not been seen by his neighbours for some days. He was elderly and they were concerned for him. As he lived in a Catholic area of Jamaica Street the police had already refused to go in. So, with us apparently being full-time soldiers and part-time social workers, we got the call to go in.

'What are we,' Blakesy asked, 'meals on fucking wheels?'

We got to the house and gave it a good look over from outside: knocking on the doors, looking through the windows. I cupped my hand against the glass to kill reflections and peered inside. I saw only still, quiet dark; lived-in but untouched. I decided to use the universal doorkey that the army had given me – my size-nine combat boot. I took a few quick steps to the front door, bent back and heeled the door in at the lock. It splintered and gave slightly. The second boot flattened it back against the hall wall. While the others scanned around downstairs, I took the steps up. The smell I'd first noticed in the doorway grew more overpowering as I rose up the stairs. It became more pungent and ripe, like chronic damp mixed with spice.

At the top, on the landing, I saw three doors, one closed. As I moved towards it my nose told me I was nearing the source. I bumped it with the rifle barrel. It swung open slightly, letting out a blast of rot, and then moved slowly back on the hinges. I'd caught sight of something. I hit the door harder this time and it swung back fully and stayed. Which was more than I wanted to do. The room was black and cankerous: curtains drawn, no light but for a filtered gloom and the buzz and dart of flies.

The stench of death blew into my face. Blakesy would later describe it as 'one of the Devil's own farts'. I nearly gagged. I edged closer to check out the damp rags thrown on the bed. There was an old man in there somewhere. I saw the outline of a dry, stretched mouth, gaping. He must have lain here decomposing for the last three days. The bedsheets and his face were a blackened mess, sodden and dry at the same time, like caked mud. Bile and snot had bubbled and popped from his ears, mouth and nose. It looked like his head had exploded with old glue and then settled down tightly around the bones. I should have left then but some fascination drew me to the bed's edge. A flicker of movement around his chest made me think his heart was still there, but as my eyes widened I saw a nest of flies bedding down in the skin - tight and trembling like a fist: black bodies and white eggs. It was their bodies turning and rippling which gave the impression of a wave of breath.

I put my hand to my mouth and backed out.

Outside I swelled my lungs with what now seemed like the fresh air of Belfast as an ambulance was radioed for. Then I rang in my report and said we'd found either the best actor in Belfast or one very dead man. Well, I thought, at least he had a full innings and went off his own bat. And however neat and tidy we may be in life, when we die we're all going to fuck up someone's carpet.

We didn't have too long to dwell on things because a few days later we got the tip-off that we'd been awaiting for so long. One of the Special Branch sources revealed the whereabouts of Martin Meehan. He would be in the Clover Club on Butler Street the following day. This was now our time. This is what Chris and I had been waiting for. On behalf of all the other soldiers here and anyone else who had felt the outrage, we now had a chance to get one of the two killers still wanted for the murders of the three off-duty soldiers.

After waiting so long – hoping that every door we kicked in, every house we raided, might turn up one of them, or every gunman we shot or captured might turn out to be them – the possibility of it now happening was so real we could feel it. Meehan was not only one of the killers but an important member of the IRA's hierarchy. This would be a major coup if we managed to bag him.

It was Chris who relayed the information to me. He came down to see me as soon as he heard. He was already bristling with anticipation.

'So, we go in tomorrow, Nicky. You're the only one that's actually seen him so you'll do the ID. I want you to liaise with myself and the IO [Intelligence Officer] in the planning. According to the source, Meehan will be there from midday on so we'll probably go in about two. Brief your lads, I want this to run as tight as a camel's arse in a sandstorm. We can't afford any slip-ups.'

'Let's just hope the tip-off is good,' I said. There was always the possibility it wouldn't be. After the waiting it felt almost too good to be true. I didn't want either of us to start counting chickens yet. When I said this, some of the tension dropped out of Chris's face.

'Oh, it's good all right. I can feel it in my bones. We're gonna get this bastard stone-cold, make no mistake about that.'

The next morning couldn't come around quick enough but when it eventually did, myself, Chris, the intelligence officer and two units in PIGs all went out. We chose half-past one because this was when all the kids went back to two schools on Crumlin Road. One school on one side was Catholic and the other, on the opposite side, was Protestant. As all the kids filed back after dinner, inevitably, fighting would break out between them. Army units, nicknamed the 'lollipop patrol', would be deployed there to keep them apart. Butler Street was just off the Crumlin. So it wouldn't seem unusual to anyone that units were passing by. They'd just assume we were the lollipop patrol arriving for duty.

We rumbled down Crumlin in the back of the PIGs. The kids on either side restrained themselves just to shouting abuse at each other because of our presence. With the back doors swung open their cries floated in. It was strange to hear voices so young and so light shouting out things like 'Yer Taig bastards!' and 'Fuck off yer Proddy fuckers!' It might have been funny to hear kids mimicking their elders if it hadn't struck me how depressing it was, how deeply ingrained their hatred was and how young they were when they first felt it. If things didn't end soon, some of these kids would be the next generation of rioters or gunmen. The ones that had already lost a brother or a father were halfway down that road anyway. If I ever had a son and he joined the army he might end up fighting one of these kids in years to come. Of course that was only in the unlikely event that this all carried on that long. But that was too depressing to dwell on.

Blakesy dragged on the butt of the last cig he'd get to smoke before we went in. Our unit had been joined by Mike Nichols, one of the lads I'd originally trained with back in Brecon. He'd jumped off the back of the truck with me when we'd avoided the interrogation training. I heard the familiar signature of him cracking his knuckles come from the other end of the bench.

'Hope you're ready to crack more than knuckles, Mikey,' I said to him. 'That place is gonna be packed when we go in.'

'Don't worry about me, Corporal,' he shouted back over the engine.

Sat opposite me, Chris seemed oblivious to everything. Then he caught my eye and half smiled, as if to say, 'This is it.'

The Clover Club was a large scout hut-type building that had been made into a bar. We surrounded it with men and the two PIGs. We all jumped out and ran towards the entrance. The noise from inside grew in volume until I burst through the doors into a bawl of voices. The belchy smell of beer hit me. The place was packed to the rafters. Everything stopped and fell silent. You could hear a watch tick. We were the horror movie strangers walking into the tavern at the foot of Dracula's castle. Chris shouldered past me with the Smith & Wesson in his fist. Blakesy and Mike followed. Nigger held back at the doors. We moved around the tables, Chris at my shoulder as I scanned the faces, none of them Meehan's.

'He's not here,' I said quietly to Chris.

'Go around again.'

We circled once more, checking behind the bar. Nothing. He could be in the toilets, I thought, upstairs on the floor that housed the snooker room. I motioned to Chris and he followed me to the stairs. We shoved past a guy who was descending and got to the top step to see nothing more than a few hostile faces glaring at us over the green tables, none of them Meehan. Then I realized I'd just seen him. I whispered to Chris, 'That guy we passed on the stairs – that was him!'

'You sure?'

'Positive.'

We clattered back downstairs but he was nowhere to be seen. I scanned around again. The drinkers all glared at us as one. Chris looking increasingly on edge, and kept glancing back at me. Meehan couldn't have gone anywhere, the place was secure. I looked over the bar and there he was, knelt down with a cloth over his arm, pretending to clean glasses. I indicated to Chris with my thumb, and before I could say anything he holstered his Wesson, pulled a taped, metal bar out of his boot and vaulted the bar. Meehan rose with a bottle in his hand but Chris thwacked him and then started leathering him along the length of the bar. I could see every bottled-up, buttoned-down outrage coming out of him. There was a mass scrape of chairs as everyone in the place jumped to his feet simultaneously. They knew full well who Meehan was. Blakesy and Mike immediately snapped their guns up and everyone froze.

'No fucker move!' Blakesy barked. They all slowly sat down. The fight behind the bar ended when Chris finally decked Meehan. As we dragged him, unconscious, over the bar and outside, the whole bar rose again and pushed to the doors as we back-peddled. Meehan suddenly came round and started resisting. He was a strong bastard and he went manic. We struggled to contain him, getting in each other's way as Meehan went berserk. Blakesy finally ended it with a well-placed kick in the balls.

I turned to see Nigger holding some other guy who must have aroused his suspicion.

'This guy says he's called O'Neill, Corporal.' I looked at his ID but had a gut feeling against believing it and told Nigger to throw him in the back of the PIG too. By now the bar had emptied out onto the pavement and was raging at us. Meehan attempted to get up and do the same. I pointed into the PIG. 'And if that cunt moves, shoot him!'

The first bricks started raining down on us. Out of the corner of my eye I saw the crowd suddenly split in two, making room for something. A man ran into the gap, leaning back with the butt of a Thompson against his belly. The doors of the PIG were closing. The gunman squeezed off a few and I fired back, only just missing him. The crowd screamed and scattered. I shouted, 'Go! Go! Go!' as I ran to the doors. I turned and fired one more time. A woman crossing the street in panic ran straight into the fire. She took one in the arm. I glimpsed a cloud of blood blow out behind her as the doors were slammed shut after me.

We sped away around the corner. I ordered Blakesy and Mike to stay in the PIG and take Meehan and the other guy back to base while the rest of us piled out and carried on with the patrol.

We got back to the mill a few hours later to great news. As well as bagging Meehan, it turned out that 'O'Neill', as he'd called himself, was actually 'Dutch' Doherty. One of the Special Branch boys had recognized him as he was taken out of the PIG. We could hardly believe it. In one fell swoop we'd captured both of the gunmen we'd been after for so long. Doherty, admittedly, had been pulled in by a combination of pure chance and gut instinct, but those were the breaks, sometimes they went against you and some-times in your favour. After all that had happened I felt we were long overdue a few. The general consensus among the men, from the most humble bottle-washer right up to the top brass, was halle-fucking-lujah! Our squad were hailed as heroes and that night another barrel was put behind the bar for a right royal piss-up.

Doherty went into the hands of the military police and in the words of Ronnie Eccles, the Green Howards' lieutenant-colonel, 'he sang like a gramophone'. He had already witnessed Chris's method of persuasion with Meehan so he didn't need any coaxing. The next few days were busy ones for us as we raided houses on Doherty's info and picked up machine-guns, shotguns, grenades, ammo and many pounds of explosives.

By now I knew not to bask in any glory for too long. The adulation was always temporary. Trouble was never far away. But even I couldn't foresee what followed.

8

NIGHTMARES DRESSED AS DREAMS

On the back of the arrest of Meehan and Doherty we were now treated like heroes by the other units. We knew what it must be like to be pop stars. We were walking on air.

A features editor from the *Sunday Express* requested to be taken out on a patrol. Frank Kitson told him that if he wanted some guaranteed action he should hook up with the Green Howards. He came to us. Great, I thought, another bloody chancer who wants to dip his toe in war and then brag about it to his mates. We amused ourselves with a card game as we waited for him to join us for the eight o'clock patrol. I got on a roll and by five to eight I'd won a beautiful red Mini Cooper from Budgie O'Brian. Budgie had lost all his money and threw the car keys in the pot. Things are finally picking up, I thought, until Chris came down and told us the *Express* guy was going to be twenty minutes late and we were to wait for him. So the game continued and, of course, Budgie won the bloody car back. By the time the guy finally arrived I was already annoyed that he'd cost me a new car.

We chatted as we began the patrol and it came out that his last assignment had been on a tropical island with a beautiful model and actress called Julie Edge. The squad were all fans and already familiar with all of Julie's edges. We plied the guy for the low-down on their desert-island meeting, knowing that it would keep us in fantasies for a good few weeks, but he refused to give us the dirty details we wanted. I called a halt to the patrol and we all settled in a nearby garden for a smoke. The writer looked puzzled.

'Is this usual?'

'Nope,' I replied, 'but we're not going any further until you tell me and the lads all about Julie.' The thought of going back to

London with an empty notebook finally made him cough up with descriptions of Julie uninhibitedly stripping off on the beach, changing from one outfit to another as the photographer took pictures.

Finally satisfied we set off again, but despite all our best attempts to show him some action – going down known ambush alleys – for one of the rare times on our patrol nothing happened. We were as shocked as he was. I'm sure he thought we'd done it on purpose to get more out of him.

One day we went out on a 'block search'. This was when a certain area of about thirty houses was designated to be searched for hidden weapons and wanted IRA members. These were 'quiet' raids – no bursting in doors or shouting – we'd just enter and inform the people inside of what we needed to do.

We entered the fourth house with Chris leading us. He went through the usual routine of saying to the man of the house, 'You know who we are and you know why we're here.' This time, though, the father, who was stood in the kitchen, turned and looked very intently at Chris. For a second the silence led me to expect some fight or attempted resistance, but when I looked at the old man's face I saw an expression of such complete devastation that I knew there was no fight left in him. The sun had long since passed the back of the house, leaving only a dreary half-light filtering through, exaggerating the feeling of time standing still.

'Oh, I know who you are all right,' he said finally, his voice trembling. 'You're the one that shot my son out the back when he was fixing his motorbike. You killed my boy. Yes, son. I know who *you* are . . .'

I saw Chris visibly start. He literally stepped back in shock and stood on my foot. I looked at him and he was grey. By sheer chance we'd ended up back in the very house of the man he'd shot: facing the man's father. I looked from the old man back to Chris and it was my turn to be startled at what I saw. His face was utterly naked with pain. I expected him to say something but instead he just turned and left the house, leaving us to complete the search.

I followed him with a sick feeling rising inside me. With each step I knew that I was leaving behind one deeply wounded human being only to catch up with another. He was outside now, leaning against the wall. I felt so sorry for him, but I could already tell he was long past any clumsy words of comfort that I could offer.

That night I went to see him. As I approached he was slumped in a chair, unaware I was there, and I didn't need him to speak to know what he was thinking. But he confirmed it anyway: 'I knew when he said that, Nicky, that nothing would ever be the same again. Nothing. I just knew . . .'

We were both nearing the end of our tours of duty and I knew we wouldn't be seeing much of each other. I was left wishing I'd said more. As it was, we just shared a bottle and talked around things. Like men do. I think both of us were left, as so many people are, with one of the worst regrets: of things unsaid.

Back on my bunk I thought what a useless, senseless waste of life this whole dirty, bloody scene is. God come down, why don't you, if you're really there. Aren't you the one who's supposed to care? No, there was going to be no sudden, miraculous resurrection of my faith tonight. Not unless He made every collapsed corpse jump back to life. And there was about as much chance of that as of the Pope giving a public demonstration on the Vatican balcony of the correct way to put on a condom. What a holy joke of the highest order that is. Keep your dick uncovered to preserve life whilst killing people to stay free. Condoms and coffins – no doubt which of those were put to the most use over here.

We spent our time half in dark, half in light; split between day and night. But it was always the dark that dragged the living fear out of you: night duty, night patrol, night ambush. On a street corner, even as you tried to suppress it, out it would come, kicking and screaming into the streetlight, making too much noise in your head like a drunk you wanted to shush. What might really be waiting there for you was bad enough without also seeing ghosts on washing lines or hearing cats cry like kicked babies. And I didn't mind admitting to myself, or anyone else for that matter, that there were times when I was scared. Not admitting to that could only mean one thing: that you were plain stupid. How dumb do you have to be not to be scared when someone is trying to kill you? Especially when you have already seen men die. As thick as pig shit is the answer. There is a fine line between stupidity and bravery and I'd probably crossed it a fair few times.

Your eyes weren't the only things that had the ability to adapt to the dark: your heart did, too, to the deeds you saw committed there. We all did it as an act of self-preservation. The jokes we made got as grim as the situation. Each man's fear was his own business. It wasn't until we were alone at night that we really did our mourning. I'd felt myself close down with each death. I'd seen Chris ball his heart into a fist until those words were said to him, and then it unfurled flat and open as surely as if he'd been shot himself. Some men in history had been strong enough to remain open and accept the consequences: Gandhi, for example, or even Jesus Christ himself, if you wanted to go back that far. In his case, literally making a fist would have at least made it difficult for them to get the nails through. Christ went to his death more willingly than I ever could. Men like that are either saints or idiots, depending on your view. It's back to that line between stupidity and bravery. But we were just ordinary men, even though I'd seen some of these ordinary men have their lives cut shorter than those of many saints.

One particular fear was of capture and torture. I knew of men who had died that way. I could only imagine what they went through, though sometimes I didn't have to imagine too hard. Especially if, as with one time, we found a place used for extracting information from captives. It was located in the cellar of a house on a desolate housing estate. We raided it on a 'lift'. Whatever the time of year, the wind always seemed to be howling through the holes and spaces of this area. The locals looked as cracked and damaged as the paving stones. They always froze in what they were doing and glared as we passed. If looks could kill they wouldn't have needed guns.

We crashed in on the familiar wave of adrenalin, kicking the door off its hinges and running in shouting, only pausing for a second to shout a check with the lads planted at the back door as they, too, burst in. Usually you find reassurance in your own noise; the clatter-bang of boots and barked orders helps chase away some of the fear. This time, though, our voices just rang back off the walls, mocking us and making me feel worse. The place felt empty. Storming it didn't quell my rising apprehension at all.

I'd learned quite early on to trust my gut instinct and here it proved to be accurate again. For some reason I chose to search the cellar. As I edged down the warped, stone steps, some other sense made me stop. The stairway curved down tightly, the walls moist with a musty damp. It was dark as a tomb. I felt my way down slowly, letting my eyes adjust to the black, and moved off what must have been the bottom step and on to the uneven slope of the floor. Even with only chinks of light coming down from behind me I immediately recognized all the tell-tale signs of a torture pit, or 'romper room' as they were blackly named by those who used them.

There was nothing dramatic like chains and manacles but things more frighteningly mundane. In the middle was what looked like an old school chair. It stank of shit and piss. There were bent, crusted nails embedded in it. The seat and legs were scarred with chop-marks: some of them from misses, I would guess, and some from blows which had gone right through whichever unlucky bastard had been bound there. A bare bulb hung above it. I traced the line of the wire, fumbled for the switch and clicked it. The bulb was so dim it seemed to make the room darker, but it revealed the black patches on the walls to be what I'd thought. The glow didn't turn them red, as you'd expect blood to be, but just made them brighter-lit dark patches; and still black, as deeply spilled blood always is. Directly behind the chair three splash-lines arced up the wall. They must have severed his arteries. His heart had done the rest.

Whatever had been left of him would have been flopped into bin bags to be buried. Shallow graves were sometimes unearthed and a sellotaped parcel would be unwrapped to reveal a head, the face startled, as if surprised to be found. Where its body was would be anyone's guess.

I sagged against the wall and breathed heavily through my mouth to limit the stench. What the fuck am I doing here? I thought. How can we fight people like this?

The stinking silence was broken as the rest of the lads pounded down after me, but the hush soon returned as they formed at my shoulder. They shuffled, taking it all in. Blakesy whispered, 'Jesus fucking Christ.'

With them all there I now realized just how tiny this death cell was. No room to swing a cat, you might say, but the poor sod's torturers had obviously found just enough room to swing the axe, shovel, claw-hammer, breeze-blocks or whatever they'd used as they laid into him from all sides. In a space this confined they must have left splattered from feet to face.

None of us wanted to be down here a second longer. I didn't even want to think about the discoloured meat hook that hung from the ceiling like a dead question mark.

On the way back out I shined a torch on the steps and, sure enough, there were dried brown footprints leaving with us. I had some vague thought about getting Forensics down here to photograph them for a possible match with someone we might catch, but then admitted to myself the uselessness of it. The place would be wiped clean before we rounded the first corner.

We left in silence. At times like this a tight wire seems to form between the men in your unit, like a fuse waiting for a spark. Everyone was twitchy with outrage and shock. If there was a reception party of angry locals waiting outside for us with bottles and bricks, as there usually was, then God-only-knew what would happen. No, forget God, I knew exactly what would happen: that fuse would flare and every buttoned-down outrage would burst out. I half hoped we'd get the chance.

We filed out, blinking, and found the street silent and almost empty. An old man two gardens away looked up and then quickly away again. It was as if the street knew what had gone on in there and turned a deaf ear – or a turned up a TV – to the muffled cries.

As we drove away in the PIG, no one spoke. Like me they were probably trying desperately to stop their minds from imagining the scene in full and from filling in the blanks between the blood, the chair and the wall.

You start thinking about what you might have been doing when someone else was dying: enjoying a laugh with your mates or a drink, maybe, or even kissing a woman as another man was being ever-so-gradually butchered; care being taken not to kill him stone-dead immediately because that wasn't the same, was it? That didn't give him the space and time to know that this was it, the time when he was going to die. And not only die but die slowly and in agony. He'd been given all the time and space to realize that his screams were pathetic and wouldn't be heard, or even if they were, would fall on deaf ears; that the information he gave or pathetically and transparently invented would never be enough; that he was never going to crawl out of this hole, let alone walk out of it; was never going to see the light of day again, let alone his mother or his own children. Sweet Jesus.

And listen to me, I thought. Even in my new godlessness I was still calling Him down or looking to His son. Well, fuck them. Fuck them both. No one's saving me but me. I'd seen enough crucifixions for one day.

Still laid on my bunk after visiting Chris, I drifted off into sleep. I knew that remembering finding that torture room would drop me straight into nightmares but I could do no more than sag into the pillow and give in to them. I entered the confession box and told my sins to the face behind the grille. There was a long pause after I finished and the face slowly shook from side to side. Then he said I couldn't be forgiven. What do you mean? Why? 'No,' was the answer, 'no, I can't forgive you.' I'd never heard of a priest refusing before. 'I'm not a priest,' he said, 'not any more.' He said that listening to confessions like mine had made him renounce his vows. I tried to find the end of the curtain to pull it back but I couldn't. It was nailed down the edge. Suddenly the box began to rock violently and I heard shouts of 'Bastard!' from outside. I wedged myself against the walls as I felt the giddy sensation of it tipping over; then, weightlessness, then silence, then *crash*! Then the ripping of material as the curtain was torn back. I saw blinding sunlight. The box was on its back in the middle of waste ground with me sat up in it like a woken vampire and there were a hundred people around me. They screamed, descended and pulled me out.

Then shock pulled me out of the dream. My watch said 5 a.m. Three hours to go until patrol. I decided to lie awake till then.

Back out on patrol we walked the streets all day until it became dark. Unusually, we went down a street I didn't recognize. The streetlights were all shot out but a full moon hung above us. It dropped blue-steel on to the roofslates and picked out cobbles like goosebumps. Christ, it was cold. You could catch your death if you didn't catch a bullet first.

The lads were all behind me. I could hear them crunching quietly in formation, swapping jokes and chat; Nigger complaining as usual, Knuckles whistling through his teeth and silence from my radioman, Paul Austin, behind me.

We rounded the corner and hit the whitest sun I'd ever seen. Sunspots danced around my eyes. Can't be. Must be the flash of a bomb. But I'd heard no boom. I turned back to the lads and they were back at the other end of the street laughing at me. Pointing. I blinked and they vanished. A hundred-strong mob came screaming around the corner and tore towards me. The houses opposite each other bent forward and stretched until their gutters clanged together forming a cathedral arch. I saw the sun disappear behind it and turned to run in the new dark. I tried to kick off the rope around my ankle as I ran but it suddenly snapped taut and floored me. I felt my rifle bounce out of my hands as I was dragged back on my belly to the mob. No rifle, I've got no rifle. I've got to get my fucking rifle! I bounced and scraped down the street, my chin jarring on the ground until I was tugged out of the dark arch and back into sunlight in a cloud of dust. I flipped over and just had time to see I was on a patch of waste ground before the mob enveloped me in fists and spit, blocking out the sun. As they tore at me, grabbed and lifted me, my heart sank into my stomach and I immediately shat it out into my pants. I bobbed up and down like a cork. The sun was red now and I rose into it, fell out of it, rose into it, falling in and out of agony. I felt my arms tear off and saw them flung too far for me to follow with my legs, which were now bent the wrong way back up to my face, which was being pounded with a house-brick until I blinked silently out of this heaving sack of blood I'd become. They were all bent over me now, sweating, gasping and thrusting as if they were fucking me. And they were. I'd always said it. I'd always said it would happen this way if a crowd caught me without my gun. Then I knew I really would be well and truly *fucked*.

I shook awake wet, curled at the foot of my bunk again. I looked at my watch – six o'clock now. I must have drifted off again. Only two more hours till morning patrol. At least I'd be going out into daylight and that usually helped to blast away the blacker parts of the dreams.

We were nearing the end of our tour of duty.

A few days later as we talked about it in the Naafi, Blakesy said, 'Yeah. The end is nigh.' That sounded too double-edged to me. I preferred something less ambiguous like 'nearly home'.

'Whatever,' Blakesy said. 'Same difference. Either way we'll be out of this fucking hole.'

'Out of curiosity, Blakesy,' I said. 'What's the score on this tour, fag wise?'

'Christ. Fuck knows. Feels like we've been here for ever. It's gone beyond packets now. You're talking shit loads. Shit loads of truck loads! Even more now Tapper's not here.'

We talked about the lads not here. Tapper and Stan and John-Boy. And Kev. Paul started laughing. 'Yeah, Socks played a blinder when he pulled that old bird out of the window that time! Good job the bloody street was flooded,' he said.

I laughed and looked at Paul, thinking of how he'd got the shit end of the stick on this tour. No doubt about it. Not just because he was a radioman – that was bad enough; weighed down by a forty-pound transmitter that left you unable to use your rifle when you were reporting back – but because he'd ended up being my radioman. The radioman of the corporal who was at the head of the unit involved in more recorded gunbattles than any other. And the guy with the radio always stays at the corporal's shoulder so he can immediately report any contacts. This meant that whenever any action kicked off poor Austin would be second in line after me for an early grave.

Many a time in the middle of some gunbattle I'd jump into a garden for cover whilst still shouting into the receiver, forgetting that Paul was still connected to me by the flex. I'd hear him thump down on the ground next to me saying, 'Shit!' I must have pulled him around like a dog on a lead.

In fact, that's the image he conjured up for me: an old hound with that expression of his and the padded headphones permanently wedged over his ears making him look like Deputy Dawg or Pluto. His dopey face didn't help dispel the image, but he was a good lad.

Weeks before he'd finally caught me during a quiet moment and asked why he'd been nominated as the radio carrier. I could see that he wasn't just thoroughly pissed off at me tugging him into hot-zones but insulted that I didn't seem to think he was worth more. You don't often treat your men with any delicacy but this time it was called for. I explained that, although the other guys were hard men, most of them could barely string a coherent sentence together and certainly not without a fair sprinkling of 'fucks' and 'bastards'. I told him how, when he radioed through a contact or sit rep, it went straight through to Major Rocket and then to Brigadier Kitson.

'Think about that, Paul. The whole battalion is listening to you! You represent us, the Green Howards. That's why I chose you. We can't have Blakesy blathering on saying, "Fuck me! A fucking contact! Fucking wait out!" Or Mikey cracking his bloody knuckles over the air. We'd be a laughing stock.'

He was pleased with this and for the next few hours he had a little swagger in his step. Tommo asked me what I'd said to Paul to cause him to walk around 'like a long-knobbed bull'.

I thought I might have gone a bit over the top, but when I thought about it every word I'd said had been true. The radio procedure was fairly complex, with a vocabulary of technical terms that had to be strictly adhered to. Some of the guys in the unit, as hard as they were, just froze with nerves as soon as they were handed the receiver. But that was a blessing considering the language most of them would've come out with.

As if he could tell what I was thinking, Blakesy suddenly said, 'Remember when that padre came out with us?' Everyone started laughing at this.

At one point it had seemed like every man jack and his dog wanted to come out with us on patrol. Funny that, we thought, considering we spent most of our time wishing we were elsewhere. But by this time we'd got something of a reputation as front-line experts: 22 Alpha – the Green Howards' golden boys. Step right up for your own personal roller-coaster ride through the Ardoyne.

For one reason or another the squadron's ordained officer (who we always called 'the padre') wanted to come out with us. I remember thinking that if he wanted to get closer to his God then he was certainly going the right way about it. Chris informed me of the plan and told me to order the lads to temper their language accordingly. I said I'd try, but no promises.

So I stood before the unit, not exactly leading by example when I said, 'And when the padre's with us just mind your fucking language. You especially, Blakesy, you foul-mouthed cunt.' This didn't get the laugh I expected. I turned to follow their eyes, which were locked over my shoulder, and found the padre standing behind me.

Out on patrol in the back of the PIG, we struggled to make small talk, flattering him with the usual 'yes sir, no sir, three bags full sir'. It was all going quite well until we came under attack. A petrol bomb flew and blew open on us, carpeting the PIG's roof in flames. When we heard gunshots all merry hell broke lose and every bottled-up 'fuck', 'cunt' and 'bastard' spilled out, turning the air bluer than an eskimo's arse.

Afterwards, back at the mill, Chris came down to see me with a message from Daddy Rocket. The padre had complained to the major that he 'had been subjected to the most foul language it has ever been my misfortune to hear'. Major Rocket had apologized for his lads' 'unseemly behaviour' and made a big show of ordering Chris to reprimand us. And it *was* just for show; the major found it as funny as we did.

'Yeah, I remember Chris having difficulty keeping a straight face,' Nigger said. I reminded Blake about when we'd been in the PIG and the padre had turned on the Sunday-school chat and said, 'Tell me Private Blake – do you ever consider your relationship with God?'

'Oh yeah!' Blakesy said, picking up the story. 'And I said, "Only when I'm being shot at!" Actually, I wish I'd got the chance to apologize to the padre, Nicky,' Blakesy suddenly confessed. 'You know, something along the lines of, "I'd like to offer my sincere apologies for the foul language, Reverend – you daft fucking bastard!" '

He had a point. On a sliding scale of obscenities – with murder and mutilation at the top end – foul language came right down at the bottom. Right down at the fucking bottom. But that was typical officer class for you: more concerned with parade-ground formations and dinner-party niceties than how to avoid another poor working-class bugger being put in the ground.

They weren't all like that, of course, but there were always enough to do damage. Some of them had no more experience of combat than being slapped around by the head boy they fagged for at public school or the odd cane across the arse from their nanny. But that didn't even count because they probably enjoyed it.

We were getting into the full swing of reminiscing now and I reminded them of another incident. This time one of the officers, Captain Irving, decided it was his turn to come out to play. None of us liked this bloke. He could patronize for England. The cherry on top was that he was the Ops officer who had refused me permission to take my unit out to deal with the booby-trapped tyre. I still felt he bore some of the responsibility for Stan's death. And I knew exactly why he wanted to come out with us: every day there would be nine patrols out on the street, and every day this Captain would see them go out, see them return and then listen to their gunbattle reports. Each day he would get all fired up by tales of someone else's actions and realize how little he did himself.

When he looked at the reports, he obviously saw that if getting into gunbattles was made an Olympic sport, then 22 Alpha would be gold medallists. So he came to us. He must have been feeling particularly brave. Or stupid.

'I'd like to come out with you and your chaps, Curtis,' he said to me (some of them did actually talk like this).

'Very well, sir,' I said, and then reminded him that once we were out in the street I was in charge.

He'd agreed: 'Oh, absolutely, Curtis. It's your team, your chaps.'

The guy outranked me but I didn't hold out much hope of us returning in anything other than pine boxes if he was in charge. But then I thought that if he came out and saw the reality of what we had to deal with, it might at least make him a little more open to advice in the future, before he sent another patrol out. Some good may come of it.

I'd informed my 'chaps' of the plan. They all groaned and someone suggested bringing the padre back out with us and turning it into a suicide mission.

Funny thing is, the patrol turned out to be unusually quiet and for once we were disappointed. We'd all been looking forward to Irving crapping his pants when we were opened up on. Unfortunately, he dealt with his disappointment by pulling his Browning from his belt holster, firing two shots in the air and then running down an alley. We stood out in the street dumbfounded as he disappeared. We exchanged puzzled looks, all thinking, What is that berk doing? Eventually he re-emerged, slipping the Browning back in its shoe.

'Problem, sir?' I said.

'Thought I saw a gunman, Curtis,' he said.

'Oh, did you, sir? Did you really?'

'Yes, that's what I bloody well said, Corporal,' he snapped, taking care now to remind me of my rank in an attempt to undermine our previous agreement about who was in charge.

I turned to the boys. 'Any of you lot see a gunman?' They all shook their heads and looked expectantly at Irving. He mumbled something about better being safe than sorry and we continued the patrol without further incident.

I'd met his sort before – every one of them tin-pot, tup'ha'penny back-room boys to a man. They just wanted to get a whiff of blood from outside the slaughterhouse walls so they could tell their pals about it, and then use it to get an excited shag out of their girlfriends. And the wife as well, if she was lucky.

Around the table we all laughed at the memory of that tosser. Tommo, who hadn't been part of our unit then, said, 'Shame it wasn't a night patrol. You could have lost him out there.' Probably true, but I couldn't laugh too hard at it because it made images of the torture cellar jump back to life before me. Lost in the Ardoyne: if Irving hadn't been killed on the streets he would have wound up in bits in a basement somewhere.

I told them a story from when I was stationed in Malta a few years back. We'd just left Tripoli and had some R and R due. As usual we went out on the piss. One of the lads who had been a good friend of mine at the time was Tom McQuaid, or 'Mac'. We all had one too many beers, or, more accurately, about eight or nine too many. Mac decided then that he needed a tattoo – not *wanted* a tattoo, you notice, he said he *needed* one. I always suspected that the local bars and tattoo parlours were owned by the same guys. One generally led to the other. You'd often see squaddies weaving across the road going directly from the bar to needle shop, or as directly as they could manage in their condition.

This was before the War Department, as it was called then, became the Ministry of Defence, and everything that could possibly be stamped with the signature of 'army property' was stamped – 'WD Property': the backs of watches, shovels, belt buckles, and so on. Mac decided there was one important thing missing off the list: his arse. The next time we saw him he tugged down his pants to proudly to reveal the legend he'd had emblazoned across the top of his buttocks – 'WD PROPERTY HANDS OFF!' – and an arrow pointing down his arse crack.

The whole table was laughing now. We'd all heard daft stuff in our time but that was one of the best.

'Honest, it's true,' I said. 'We didn't believe him either until he showed us. The biggest joke of all at the time was when we told Mac no woman would need an order to keep their hands off his flabby white arse!'

I wondered where he was now and in years to come what his answer would be when his grandkids asked if he got any tattoos while in the army. Knowing Mac he would probably say, ' 'Course I have, lad. Cop a load of this!'

We finally exhausted our reservoir of stories and bedded down for the night. We weren't due back out until the eight o'clock patrol the next morning.

Things carried on as usual, with us counting down the days until we left. One morning we went out on lollipop patrol. We piled out of the back of the PIG on the Crumlin Road and positioned ourselves in preparation for the kids returning to school. Our presence there usually dissuaded them from getting into a full-scale running battle. They would just make do with calling names. But until they arrived we were sitting ducks for snipers. They knew when patrols were in position and would set themselves up to ambush.

I ordered the lads into the all-round defensive position: each one looking out and around, covering all angles of attack. It was easy to get slack, tempting to relax, but I rarely lost sight of what a lapse of vigilance could lead to. I'd seen the results of it too often.

We heard the first of the kids' voices floating down from the end of the road. Whenever I saw children playing together, laughing and arguing, no matter what part of the world I was in, I was always reminded of my own childhood. It struck me how similar kids were around the world. There was a kind of universal way of play, whether they were in the streets of Hong Kong or kicking a ball about the back alleys of Yorkshire, as I had done.

The chimes of their cries grew nearer. I scanned the road, checking on my unit. Out of the blue a clear crack rang out and we hit the deck. The shot had seemed to come from behind. We flattened and turned to it. I looked to the other side of the road and my heart sank. Someone was down. I shouted for cover and sprinted across. Already there was a stillness in the air after the crack and I knew instinctively that it had been a one-shot hit: they just fired and fled. I reached the other side and saw it was Paul. He lay on his back, bent awkwardly because of the bulk of the transmitter behind him. Blakesy was already cradling him in his arms, trying to comfort him. There was a ragged hole in the side of Paul's neck and his uniform was soaking wet. I knelt down by him and loosened the headphones still clamped to him.

'Paul? Can you hear me? Hang on, son, we're gonna get you out.' He didn't reply. He looked at me but right through me. I could see the light in his eyes dimming: headlights in fog. His face was grey with shock and blood-loss. He looked up at the sky and began to tremble. He wasn't going to make it. I was suddenly aware of the silence around us.

The rest of the lads fanned out, offering us cover. In the quiet I could hear Blakesy repeatedly cursing to himself. Paul convulsed one last time and sagged. We'd lost our radioman.

We had to turn him over to allow me to get to the receiver and call through. The ears of the headphones flopped around his neck and for some reason this one image fired the sadness of him right through me. I felt sick at what he had come to.

That night we were all really low about Paul's death. I could not help but blame myself for the situations he'd had to follow me into. I knew that didn't make sense – he was a soldier and that's what soldiers do – but, nevertheless, I was haunted by images of him lumbering after me under the weight of that bloody radio, one hand offering me the receiver, the other cupping his rifle uselessly to his side. Or his big face looking pained as he lay on the ground beside me after we'd leaped over a wall for cover; the look of his face and tone of voice when he'd asked me why he had to carry the radio. And that time when we'd been pinned down in the street and he'd just turned his back to the bullets, thinking that his radio would protect him. It had that time but not this. He'd been so close to getting out as well.

I tried to work out what it was, if anything, that separated the survivors from the victims. Paul could be pretty gormless at times but he was the last of the unit to go down and the ones before him had all been able men. Stan, especially, had been as switched-on as any of us, but even he succumbed to a lapse of concentration and paid the biggest price. It could happen as quickly as that – *snap!* – like your fingers clicking.

And then there was me. I'd been at the front of nearly every engagement, sometimes doing things which now seem plain reckless. Still here though, I thought. My old training sergeant, Johnny Jones, always said that I thought I was bullet-proof. I think most of us did until a bullet with our name on it proved us wrong. Anyway, there was a saying in the army that it wasn't the named bullet you should be afraid of but the one that says, 'To whom it may concern.'

I tried not to feel guilty for surviving but didn't have much success. There's a difference between what the head knows and what the heart feels. The guilt also made me feel uncomfortable for another reason. It made me realize something I didn't want to be true: that the claws of Catholicism were still sunk into me and the Church would have its pound of flesh one way or another.

Those priests had really done a job on me from day one; an object lesson in brainwashing if ever there was one – get the kid young, work on his mind and hopefully he'll carry this burden for the rest of his life. I suspected that lapsed Catholics like myself would be singled out for special treatment by the priests. They would mark down my name, file it away, then bide their time until they could swoop down on me over my deathbed and ask if I was ready to repent. And I probably would. Just to be on the safe side.

The time had finally come to leave. I felt I needed to but at the same time I couldn't let go. There were still too many scores to settle, too many things to do. Too much unfinished business. Yeah, I was weary of being on the streets but I thought the knowledge I'd gained about how things operated over here shouldn't go to waste. I knew I could help save lives.

The chances of me being promoted up to a particularly high level were, like the man said, slim to none – and slim had just left town. I knew I wasn't judged to be from the correct background to mingle with the Ruperts at Command HQ.

Anyway, I already knew that after my duty in Northern Ireland I was going to be promoted to sergeant and sent back to Yorkshire to train new recruits.

I had a final drink with the lads the night before my leaving. They would remain behind for another two weeks before they followed me. We made arrangements to meet up back at home and then got pissed on the barrel that had been put behind the bar for us. I was glad Blakesy was taking over from me as unit commander. As well as being as hard as crucifixion nails, I knew he was tuned-in enough to keep the boys' heads down. Still, it didn't mean I wouldn't think about them until I knew they were safely back on home turf.

I slouched in my chair at the table and watched them carrying on, taking the piss out of the lad who'd been drafted in as the new radioman to replace Paul. I could feel the beer singing through me and it made me equal parts merry and sad.

'Don't worry,' Blakesy was saying to the new lad, 'just be thankful you're gonna be my radioman and not yer Uncle Nicky's!' The lad looked at me and laughed. I wondered if we'd looked as wet behind the ears when we'd first landed. I knew it was only another one of Blakesy's tactless jokes but it swung me back from being merry. I couldn't help thinking about Paul with those earphones clamped around his hound dog expression. 'Hound dog' – good nickname. I wonder why we never gave him that.

I looked around at what was left of the original 22 Alpha. Only Blakesy, Nigger and me. We'd lost Tapper, Stan, John-boy, Kev Crosier and Paul. Falling plates? Maybe. But we wouldn't take that joke from anyone but our own. We knew well enough what had happened.

I rose early the next morning with a clanging hangover and packed my kit. From here I'd go back to Minden in Germany for a few days. We'd only brought what we'd needed, our kit and ourselves, basically. My civvies and personal belongings were in Minden. From there I'd return home for six weeks' leave.

As I packed, a lance-corporal from 5 Platoon called Chappie came over to see me. He said he thought I'd like to know that he'd overheard talk of medals being handed out and he'd heard my name mentioned. I thanked him for telling me but shrugged it off. I'd never really thought about it, to be honest. It was only over this last year after the Conservatives came to power that Ted Heath had made soldiers in Northern Ireland eligible for war decorations. The thought of it happening made me feel good but I decided not to hold my breath.

I signed over my rifle to the arms cote officer and my remaining ammo to the colour sergeant. The two were always stored safely apart at barracks.

I jumped in the back of the three-tonner that was to transport me to the airport. Two armed guards rode at the back as those inside were now unarmed. With me were another fifteen men from three other units which had been in the Shankill, Lynhill and Ardbow. Of these, only Ardbow was an area that really saw any action and still nowhere near like the Ardoyne.

As we left the mill and jolted down Flax Street, the regimental police sergeant in charge said, 'We're going through the Ardoyne now, lads. So keep your wits about you.'

I realized he was taking the chance to play the big man, as if he'd seen action here. But the position he held meant he would have barely seen the outside of the mill. I looked at him hard and I could see that he knew I knew. It was then that he seemed to recognize me: 22 Alpha had become well known amongst the other squads. He looked as embarrassed as he rightly should have.

When we got to Aldergrove airport the Hercules transporter was waiting for us on the runway with its huge engines running, roaring like some great animal with its belly open. Last time I'd seen one of these we'd been pushing Kev's coffin into the back of it.

I'd vowed not to look back down at what I was leaving when we were airborne. But as we reared into the climb and I felt myself press against the seat, I knew I had to. That familiar green was soon flecked with grey as the clouds closed in and we cut up into them. Then it was gone. And so was I.

9

FROM GREEN TO BLUE

Back in Germany two pleasing things happened. One was my reacquaintence with Helga which, though I knew it would only be temporary as I was due to go home soon, was a much-needed boost. I'd never before had a girlfriend with legs as long and hair as blond as hers. Girls like that were pretty thin on the ground where I came from. To be honest, I never really knew what she saw in me. Maybe I seemed as exotic to her as she did to me. The uniform helped as well. I think when we'd first met I'd made out that Yorkshire was a really wild, exciting place. Even then I hadn't been so Catholic that I wouldn't lie if it helped me get my leg over.

The other surprise was finding out that my reputation, and that of 22 Alpha, preceded me. Six hundred of the battalion had gone to Ireland, leaving fifty behind to look after the barracks and administration. All the time we'd been there, the lads in Minden had received regularly updated sit reps from Belfast. It was one thing being known in the Ardoyne (everyone seemed to know what everyone else was doing there) but to land in another country and find you didn't have to explain what you'd done because they already knew was really strange. I was aware of eyes following me when I walked around. They seemed to look with a mixture of respect and envy (because of what we'd done) and a certain amount of awe (because I'd managed to get out). These reactions always surprised you, initially anyway, because at the time when it was all happening, you just got on with it. Then I realized that if this was one of the rewards of surviving, I might as well make the most of it because it might not come again. From the time when I'd been here on the parade ground with my clipboard, I had always taken the few chances I got to lighten my duty. Most squaddies came from backgrounds where things weren't given lightly; they had to be fought for. The ones who were ex-Barnardo's boys, for example, were always first in the dinner queue.

118

So I had a few easy, pleasant days for a change. I was bought beers and given a bed blanket without a hole in it, and so on. Not much, really, but it meant a lot.

I sailed back to Britain and my seasickness made me remember why I'd joined the army and not the navy.

With my mum and dad I was pretty much the same as I'd been on my last visit, only worse. They didn't get much more than 'yes', 'no' and 'don't know' out of me. I realize now that my dad in particular probably knew more than he let on, but at the time I didn't even think about whether he did or not. Nothing was mentioned about my duty; or my faith (or lack of it). That would have been too big a bombshell, for my mother especially.

The streets of my home town were far too similar to those of Belfast for the memories to erode; row upon row of tight, workhouse brick and flat, coloured doors. The same grey sky too. As I walked the streets, simple things like the entrance to an alley (or ginnel, as we called them), a line of hedges, a front door slamming or the far-off cries of schoolkids would jolt a memory out of me. As if I was an old shop till, the images would *ker-ching* up in succession as I progressed down the street.

I still had the Star pistol I'd bought in Belfast. Sometimes I went down to the local woods by the canal and shot at trees. The deadwood exploded particularly well. God only knows what the local coppers would have made of this if they'd caught me. I'd have probably been thrown inside.

I didn't have to wonder what my mum would make of it, though, because one day she found the pistol in my room whilst she was hoovering. I always slept with it under my bed. She went absolutely bananas.

'What in God's name is this doing here? I thought I'd brought you up to have more sense, Nicholas Curtis!' she said, slipping into that universal mum-speak of using your full name when you are in trouble. I thought, Bloody hell, I've gone from ordering men around in a war zone to being told off by my mum!

It was a blessed relief when the rest of the lads finally came over and I could join them. We got together for a much-missed pint of Tetley's or two. Well, six or seven to be more accurate. Things had carried on pretty much as before in the two weeks after I'd left. They'd been through nothing more dramatic than being stoned, bombed and shot at. Business as usual. No one lost, though.

A great shock was in wait for me, however. Sitting down one day to have lunch at home, I switched on the TV to watch the news. The lead story was the escape of Martin Meehan and Dutch Doherty. I nearly dropped the plate off my knee. They'd been sprung from the Crumlin Road prison by other IRA members. I couldn't believe we hadn't been able to hold them. I knew that by now they would have been spirited away to safety down to the south of Ireland. A newspaper lay folded beside me that my dad had brought in. I hadn't even looked at it but now I flipped it over, and who should be on the cover but Doherty himself. The whole of the front page was dominated by a photograph of him cowering against a wall. It was incorrectly described as having been taken at the moment of his arrest in the Clover Club; like we'd had time to stand around taking pictures in the middle of the raid! It had actually been taken back at the mill after Doherty had got out of the PIG. The squaddie that had taken it (nicknamed 'Click-click' because of his habit of carrying a camera) was a friend of mine.

The headline read 'PATRIOT SAYS THE IRA – TRAITOR SAYS THE BRITISH ARMY'. After his escape he'd gone to the papers with his version of the events. Over the page was another photo of him, clean-shaven this time, showing off his wounds to the world's press and stating that he'd held out under severe interrogation by the army. Another version was given by a security officer who said that Doherty had given the information willingly and his wounds had been inflicted later by other IRA members when they tortured him to find out if he'd sung. During his time in Crumlin Road prison, Doherty himself had admitted to the officer that he'd been present when the IRA had broken the arm of a suspected informer during questioning. Everyone knew these things happened. In fact if the IRA suspected you of grassing you were lucky to end up with only a broken arm and not a bullet in the mouth. One of the tell-tale signs as to the reason why someone had been shot was the presence of an ugly mess in the head where the mouth should have been.

It was obvious that when he'd found himself back in the fold of the IRA, after they'd sprung him, he realized he'd gone straight from the frying pan into the fire. In order to save his own life he'd had to play the hero and convince them that he hadn't said as much as he had. There was the very real possibility that the cigarette burns on his legs were self-inflicted in order to bolster his story about his treatment. Obviously, part of his deal with his now suspicious colleagues was to go to the press with his version. It was just another shot fired in the propaganda war.

Where his story fell apart was in the fact that we'd made success-ful raids as a result of his information. They weren't just carried out on a whim. There were too many houses in the Ardoyne for us just to have got lucky finding as many weapons and explosives as we had during that one operation.

I was thoroughly gutted by the news. It felt like all our hard work had been for nothing.

Upon the Green Howards' leaving of Northern Ireland they were given the freedom of the city of Middlesbrough (the Green Howards' main recruiting centre in the north-east) and the regi-ment paraded through the centre. Chris came up from down south for the parade but as we were still officially on leave we couldn't take part. We watched the lads march by in no. 2 dress, their boots buffed up to a mirror shine.

It was the first chance I'd had to talk to Chris since we'd ended our tour. We both had a good rant about the Doherty/Meehan escape and the press coverage. He confirmed that Doherty had blabbed without needing any coercion. He said he'd been shocked at this. I knew that in the months preceding their arrest, Chris had built Meehan and Doherty up in his mind to such an extent that he wasn't prepared for the reality of what they actually were: just ordi-nary men. Hence the shock when one of these 'hardmen' blurted out information on the IRA. Maybe watching Meehan get a leather-ing at the hands of Chris in the club had fed Doherty's fantasies about what might happen to him. Or maybe, like a lot of men, he was only full of bravado behind the barricades or while plotting to plant a bomb. Either way, I knew I'd witnessed men at both the heights and depths of human behaviour so nothing really surprised me any more.

Chris and I arrived at the post-parade night function being held at the city hall with all the local dignitaries, only to find our way barred by a squaddie on the door. If we hadn't been on the parade, he said, we couldn't come in. Saying we were Green Howards who had served in Belfast didn't cut any ice with this idiot in front of us who I could tell hadn't even been out of barracks. Trouble was just brewing when an officer inside caught sight of us. He knew who we were and told the guard to step aside. It's not that we wanted any special treatment but we certainly didn't expect to be barred from our own regiment's piss-up.

The final straw came on New Year's Day.

I was suffering from the usual post-Christmas boredom (eaten and drunk too much, watched too much crap TV) when I opened the paper at the New Year's Honours List. Among the usual gongs handed out were medals awarded for services in the Troubles. I was elated to see that Chris had been awarded a Military Cross. This was just reward for his bravery and involvement: great news for him and all the Green Howards. I knew the lads would be as pleased for him as I was. The downside was that I didn't get a mention. This wouldn't have been so bad if it wasn't for the fact that the regimental sergeant-major had been awarded an MBE for gallantry. For bloody *gallantry*! It would have been far more gallant of him to admit to the fact that he – and the rest of the brass that were down for awards – had done bugger all to deserve it.

I returned to Catterick to take up my post as training sergeant. God, it was boring, drilling seventeen-year-olds around the parade ground. The most exciting thing to happen was during the first two weeks when we were still waiting for enough of the new intakes to arrive to justify beginning their training. We had nothing better to do than wait, until the adjutant came through with a request from the director of a film that was being made near by; he needed soldiers to act as extras. We needed something to lessen the boredom. And we would be paid: nine quid a day.

Three days later on the film set, the director, a guy called Ken Loach, was probably amazed to find us the first 'actors' there. First, because we were used to dragging our arses out of bed at unearthly hours and, second, because we couldn't wait to see what was going on.

The film was to be called *Days of Hope*. It was set during the First World War. I'd taken up about twenty-five trogs (as we called new recruits) from the barracks with me. Appropriately enough, they were to play young men in a bar being recruited into the army. Typecasting I think they call it. I was supposed to play the officer in charge until Mr Loach approached me and rather delicately pointed out that he thought I looked too young to play the part. Which was pretty ironic considering that's what I did in real life. So I was demoted!

Mr Loach approached me again towards the end of our stint with another suggestion. I'd already noted that he talked to us with a lot more diplomacy than he did to the actors. Realizing we were the real thing, he probably feared getting a smack in the mouth if he ordered us around too strongly. This time he pointed out that I had managed to get my face in virtually every shot since we'd arrived a week before, which was true. I think I'd got a little stage-struck and whenever the opportunity arose I'd order my lads back and make sure I was in shot. He tactfully suggested we give the cinema-going public a break from my mug. I thought, Fair enough, but secretly I was a little miffed that my best chance yet to be Errol Flynn had come and gone.

But it was a good laugh and the food was brilliant, much better than what we got back at base. So we milked it for all we could. I realized that an actor's life is similar to a soldier's in that it's a good deal of boredom spiced up with occasional 'action'.

Back on parade, now that all the trogs had arrived and we were well into the routine of initiation, I thought that all I'd learned on the streets of Belfast was going to waste. There was a training ground for Military Recon Forces and I felt I would have been better there than here, shouting at stamping rookies. In the time since I'd left Northern Ireland I'd seen how things had changed; I saw how the war now needed to be fought and I wanted to be a part of it. I knew I could contribute in a much more constructive way than I was at present.

I knew I couldn't stand it any more. I decided to get myself busted back down to corporal and returned to unit (RTU). One night, four corporals and I went to the local working men's club. The place was packed with drinkers from eighteen to eighty, the men knocking down pints, the women nursing their halves and sherries while they played bingo. I fished four CS gas pellets out of my pocket and dropped them in the ashtray. One of the corporals asked me what I was doing.

'I'm just about to demote myself,' I said. 'And if they don't find out that you were here with me, you might be in line for a sudden promotion.'

I placed my cig in the ashtray and we moved to leave. Just as we got to the doors the pellets flared up. Then all hell broke loose. We stood outside and watched the show. Within minutes the club was engulfed in choking smoke and people were literally flinging themselves out of windows to escape. One of the corporals made a joke about me being a bad loser at bingo and we left.

I'd had to sign in at the club because I wasn't a member so I knew the army would find out it was me. But that was the idea.

The next day I went straight to the noticeboard and saw, as I expected, that I was on orders to report to the adjutant officer. Great, I thought, that's me RTU. Job well done.

I entered his office and stamped to attention like a good soldier. Finally, he looked up from his reports and began reading out my citation for a Military Medal. I carried on staring dumbly at the wall behind him until he finished with, 'Well done, Curtis. It's well deserved.' At this it sank in and I looked at him and thanked him. I was unsure whether to mention the gassing. Maybe they hadn't found out after all. But curiosity got the better of me.

'Oh, don't worry about that,' he said dismissively. 'It's already been sorted out. We've been in touch with the Chief Constable and smoothed it.' Then he led me to the officers' room and I was handed a drink and greeted by all the big boys there. I was still in a state of semi-shock. In the space of a minute I'd gone from thinking I was going to be busted to a back-slapping session with the colonel. I walked out on air and floated down to my pigeonhole. I hadn't even bothered to check if I'd got any mail earlier. There were fifteen letters waiting for me, all of them congratulations from all the GOCs, right up to Frank Kitson himself. The one that pleased me most, though, was from Chris. I spent the rest of that night getting drunk and grinning like a hen-house fox. I woke up next morning with a 24-carat hangover, fully clothed in bed but missing one shoe. God knows where it had got to.

Over the following days I gradually found out what had happened when an officer I knew tipped me off. It started when he congratulated me on the award and said, 'It should have been higher.' I asked what he meant and he explained. Apparently, my citation had been sent by the 2IC for approval with everyone else's but I hadn't been told about it because the board took one look at the actions I was commended for and realized they had a problem. Because of the number of gunbattles I had been involved in, I should have been upgraded to a Victoria Cross, but for various reasons this couldn't be allowed so they returned my citation and the number of incidents listed was halved. The officer explained that the giving of a VC was such a rare occurrence (and often only given posthumously) that awarding it would have brought world notoriety to myself and the regiment: the kind of publicity they didn't really want when the ongoing Troubles were still such a politically sensitive subject. It made some kind of sense so I didn't torture myself by dwelling on what might have been. Anyway, I was happy with what I'd got.

A letter from Buckingham Palace arrived inviting me down for my investiture. When I phoned my mum with the good news she congratulated me and said she thought that it was the same thing my dad had got.

'Don't think so, Mother. I think he'd have told us if he'd got a Military Medal. I think he was put in for it and then mentioned in dispatches.'

'Oh, that was it,' she said. 'I knew it was something like that.'

I had to laugh – 'something like that'. Trust my mum to bring me back down to earth with a bump.

On 30 January 1972 fourteen people were shot dead by paratroopers in Derry during a civil rights march. News of what became known as 'Bloody Sunday' spread around the world. Speculation as to the events of the day began to rage and carried on without any sign of abating. According to the IRA, the dead were all innocent, unarmed civilians who had been wilfully murdered by the British army after the march had degenerated into a riot. The soldiers told a different story.

The march had indeed culminated in a large-scale riot. The paratroopers, who had been brought in for this eventuality, were ordered in. Gunshots from the crowd were heard (both sides agreed on this one thing alone) and then panic ensued. The paras, believing themselves under attack, opened fire. The paratroopers' commanding officer, Lieutenant-Colonel Wilford, may not have been in the literal firing line on the streets but he certainly was after he got back to Command HQ when the enormity of the event was beginning to sink in.

Something he was later to say struck a chord in me as it reminded me of the problems our units had faced in Belfast. He said that during a briefing before the march he had mentioned the probability that the march would end in rioting and asked what he should order his men to do in this case. His superiors didn't really give a satisfactory answer. The question was glossed over with, 'We'll face that when it happens,' answers. He later admitted his regret at not pursuing it.

From what I could see, the officer and his men were left with little other course of action if they truly believed they were in danger. The two biggest mistakes were, first, letting a march of such huge scale take place (everyone knew it would culminate in massive rioting) and, second, bringing in the paratroopers to deal with it. Their reputation preceded them and was well earned. They were not feared for nothing. They were the hardest, most tightly drilled unit; only one step down from the SAS. Wilford himself admitted that his men would not stand and be knocked down 'like Aunt Sallies' as so many other units in Derry had already. Parts of the city were complete free-for-all areas for the locals and complete no-go areas for the army. And the belief among the officers was that it was an outrage that any area of Ireland that was designated as being British (that is, all of Northen Ireland, including Derry, which is on the border) should be off-limits to the armed forces of Britain. The marchers, on the other hand, were as equally firm in their nationalist beliefs that they should be able to march wherever they pleased and reclaim their country from the 'invaders'. All in all, it was a recipe for chaos and I believed it should have been foreseen how disastrous a confrontation it would be.

I knew that you could not reasonably expect favour or pause for reassessment during battle from men who had been highly trained to act quickly and authoritatively when they believed themselves to be under attack. Lives had already been lost because of lapses and this would have been in the minds of the paras. As a consequence, if unarmed rioters had indeed been shot, then this seemed one of the horrible, tragic inevitabilities of the chaos of that day. As for the rioters being 'innocent', this was a questionable point. As they were involved in a large-scale riot and attack on soldiers, the most they could be called being innocent of were the consequences. If they weren't aware of these, then they were pawns of an IRA leadership, who played their own part in exploiting that day. Those men would have known full well the likely outcome.

They may have lost that particular battle but it helped them win the propaganda war and also win over Catholics who, until then, had had no involvement in terrorist activity. It wasn't long before reports came through on how their ranks had swelled with new volunteers in the immediate aftermath of Bloody Sunday. You should never underestimate the ability of the higher echelons of an organization, whoever they may be, to write off the lives of those much lower down the order if they think it will help move their cause one step nearer to success. I think the dead on that day were victims of hidden agendas.

The arguing, accusations and counter-accusations raged on. Still drill-training new recruits, I watched from afar with the sinking feeling that, far from nearing a conclusion, things were now moving further down the wrong path.

During this time I kept getting called back to Northern Ireland to attend the trials of Provos my unit had arrested. By the time the cases came to court the commanding officer involved in the arrest may have been restationed elsewhere so he had to return to the scene, even if he was now in another country. I returned some twenty to thirty times. Some of the trials would go our way and we'd secure a conviction; just as many times, it seemed, we wouldn't. Seeing someone walk that I knew full well to be guilty was a constant frustration and one I never got used to. A guilty verdict would make all the travelling and hanging around outside court well worth it. Any other result made it all a boring chore, a real drag. The journey back was even worse.

One of the trips back, however, turned out to be anything but boring. I got the call to return to Belfast for the trial of a guy we had picked up last year. Chris was on the job with us that time and I knew he'd be called up too. We travelled over together, and caught up on the time we'd missed. He still had that contained strength about him but was quieter than usual, as if he was braced for this return. Almost as if he'd been forewarned.

Back in Belfast we found ourselves with hours to kill before the afternoon trial. We waited at the HQ in Lisburn, prepared for an uneventful day. Which it was until, while wandering around the Ops room, Chris overheard a report come in. It said that a foot patrol had seen a man who they suspected was Martin Meehan entering a Belfast bar, but they needed verification – a spot-on ID from someone who knew him.

Chris rushed out of the Ops room and pulled his jacket off the chair beside me as he repeated the report and made for the door. Without any prompting I was out of my chair following him, taking the stairs three at a time.

By the time we got to the bar the enormity of what we were about to do was sinking in. The elation we'd both felt at the capture of Meehan and Doherty had been short-lived because of their later escape. Chris had taken it badly. Capturing Meehan had always been something of a personal crusade for him. This was the chance to redress the balance.

We'd driven down from Lisburn with me at the wheel. After we parked we sat for a moment in the car with the engine off. Just as I was about to get out, Chris took a quick look around for witnesses and then unsheathed the Smith & Wesson from his shoulder holster and clacked back the slide hammer, putting a round up the spout. I also had my Star pistol with me. It was illegal for us to be armed at all but we could think of worse sins. Better to be jailed than nailed.

He turned to me: 'That bastard's not getting away this time,' and then got out before I could answer. He didn't expect an answer anyway; he was just voicing his thoughts. He didn't even need to do that. I knew already. He looked wired.

'Let's just be certain it's him, Chris, before we blow the whole place to fuck.'

He nodded absently and walked ahead.

The foot patrol had made themselves scarce, perhaps waiting around the corner so as not to alert suspicion. They would be expecting any operatives going in to contact them beforehand, but in the rush to get in there before Meehan left, this procedure went right out the window.

It was a hot day and the bar sounded full. Beer-noise came out into the street through the tilted windows. It blared in volume whenever someone banged in or out of the doors. Chris was ahead of me when we reached them. I stopped him.

'Let's go over how we're going to play this.'

He paused as someone came out, and let him pass before he replied. 'We approach the bar and order. When you're waiting for the drinks you scan the place. I'll walk around looking for him.'

'OK. If you see him, though, Chris, come back to me first before you make a move.' He nodded as he was already turning to enter.

Inside the bar was heavy with that curious daytime pub-gloom, despite the sun outside. We walked into the full weight of it: the smoke spirals; the clang of voices; the drinkers clotted around tables and bar, too involved in it all to notice another two fellas coming in off the street. Good. My heart was kicking like a mule. We didn't have any back-up. First golden rule already broken.

I turned to say something to Chris but he was moving away from me, deeper into the throng, as if he'd immediately spotted someone. I followed him. He reached the bar ahead of me, turned, rested his gaze on someone as if to double-check, and then came back towards me. The guy he'd clocked was sitting at the bar, oblivious in conversation. It was Meehan.

Chris reached me, face ablaze. He spoke through his teeth. 'It's him, Nicky.' Even as I was opening my mouth to ask if he was sure, Chris was turning back to the bar repeating, 'It's him!' and diving into his jacket. I saw the blackness of the Smith & Wesson appear in Chris's hand, his fist so tight and white I thought it would explode with the gun.

'Meehan! Meehan!' Chris shouted, arrowing in on him. The air seemed to flatten out, stretch tight and then sag when pierced by screams and shouts and chairs scraping back. I fanned my Star over the clump of men at the bar. Instantly, it struck me that Meehan hadn't turned at the sound of his name; something you would do instinctively, overriding even your determination not to. Chris was homing in, unaware. As the guy turned, I had a quick slow-motion vision of his head splattering open like a melon, seeding the bar and thickening his pint. Then I saw it wasn't Meehan at all, just an astonishingly scared man looking down the black of a barrel. I took a sidestep and shouldered Chris off balance. The barrel dropped in shock, I grabbed his arm and propelled him back to the doors. 'It wasn't him, Chris!' We hurried out and darted over the road. 'It wasn't him.'

He was already protesting, disputing the call.

I had to talk over him. 'Believe me, I know. It wasn't him!' I glanced back over the road and saw the bar spilling out on to the pavement, some hurrying away, some shielding their eyes in the sun and pointing after us.

I was already in the car with the engine on and preparing to reverse out when Chris caught up and leaped in. We shot off.

Chris sagged next to me, deflated. Defeated. I knew how much he'd wanted it to be true. He ran his hands back through his hair and exhaled at the sky. Without taking his eyes off the roof he asked again.

'Yeah, I'm sure,' I said. I checked the rear-view mirror again for any follow up.

'I wanted him just as much as you did. You know that.' He nodded in agreement. I tried to fill the silence. 'It did look like him, though. Bloody hell, he was a real dead ringer that one.' Pretty fucking close to being just dead, I thought.

'Maybe we should have stopped and bought him a drink,' I added. Bad joke, and it didn't get any response. Chris continued to look out of the window as I sped us back to HQ with the bad news. So much for this being another boring, by-the-book trial visit.

The next day the papers were full of the incident. The reporters had got hold of the guy mistaken for Meehan and reproduced his picture alongside one of the real thing. It proved that he looked almost identical to Meehan, but a lot more scared.

The only other return visit that broke from the uneventful norm was when I was again accompanied by Chris, and we found ourselves slap-bang in the middle of the wholesale destruction of Belfast.

Killing time again before our appointment in court, we went for a drink in a city-centre bar called the Abercorn. It was early on a Friday afternoon. Chris showed off by producing a fifty-pound note at the bar. I doubt if he could have caused more drama if he'd pulled out a pistol. Fifty-quid notes were of a fairly recent issue and as he handed it over the barman looked at it like we'd just produced a positive pregnancy test in his mother's name. There was much holding up to the light, passing along the bar and then double and triple checking watermarks, trying to remember if the Queen had a beard or not. Every self-appointed 'expert' in the joint sauntered over for a good gander and threw in his two-penneth-worth of opinion (which is more than I would have paid them for it). You know the type, those alcoholic Einsteins who know so much about everything that they don't waste their valuable time doing anything. It's reward enough, apparently, for them to screw themselves to a bar stool and right every wrong in the book until closing time.

Finally, the barman emerged from the scrum of the impromptu conference at the end of the bar and walked back towards us like a doctor about to give the good news of a negative cancer test.

'OK boys.' He smiled. 'Whadd'ya like?'

'Service within the next fucking hour would be nice,' I said, smiling back, 'and two pints as well.' He started to pull them, still looking at me but sour-faced now.

Halfway through our pints, and only a few minutes since we'd dropped the bombshell of producing the fifty, the IRA decided to start dropping a few of their own. We heard the first familiar dull *boof* of a distant explosion. A ripple of concern rolled along the bar but not enough to sway anyone from his drink. Then came another. And, minutes later, another. They were getting closer. The last one was near enough to carry with it the tinkle of glass and visions of billowing bomb-dust. I watched the beer in my glass tremble slightly and was surprised to find that I didn't follow suit. Still, from the reaction of the drinkers, there was some way to go before the drama of producing the fifty-quid note was equalled. And Chris and I carried on as normal. I started to get an inkling that maybe we'd been over here too long on our previous duty, and already seen too much of what life can throw at you. The fact that we weren't particularly fazed by what seemed like Holy Hell on a pushbike riding through the city and lobbing around explosives like Sunday papers was disturbing in itself.

Over the next hour we walked from bar to bar, hands in pockets, to the sound of the city being torn to pieces around us. We could have fled in panic, of course, but that would have brought the risk of running right into the wrong spot at the wrong time and waking up dead on a rooftop looking down on our own burning bodies. So we remained as unconcerned as only two jaded, war-weary idiots can be and continued to walk in and out of bars to the smell of powdered brick-dust and the sound of some other poor bastards being splashed over the pavement. It was a major redecoration job by the IRA. You've got to give it to them, I thought, the heartless bastards certainly knew how to paint a town red. Albeit with the blood of their own countrymen. But that was OK: a small price to pay for 'freedom fighters'.

Hours later the TV news was full of pictures that shocked the whole country, and the rest of the world that had the displeasure of seeing them: soldiers and police on clear-up duty literally shovelling the remains of bodies into bin bags. This was the IRA's answer to Bloody Sunday. In the space of seventy-five minutes they had detonated twenty-two bombs throughout Belfast: nine dead (a miracle it was so few) and over a hundred maimed. I watched the reports with horror, both at the result and the fact that we had been in the middle of it. Oh, and one more thing to add, according to the IRA, *we* were to blame for the deaths; that is, the security forces. They said they had given adequate advance warnings for each bomb and the army and police had neglected to act quickly enough; that is, not acted quickly enough in the chaos of twenty-two bombs going off in a crowded major city on a Friday afternoon. Which meant, in other words, that the IRA had fucked up big-time, and they couldn't admit it. The planning had been wrong and they didn't give the security forces enough time. And that's giving them the benefit of the doubt that they didn't actually intend to kill anyone.

If any reminder was needed that I was being wasted back on the mainland teaching spotty recruits how to stamp properly, then this was it. The sooner I got the chance to return here the better.

Another point for me to ponder was the fact that, without aiming to, or even wanting to, I'd once again been at the heart of one of the defining moments of the conflict. You could feel it immediately. I didn't need weeks or even months to look back on this with the benefit of hindsight. The fact that the day was quickly

131

christened with its own grim title spoke volumes. It became known as Bloody Friday.

A few months later, in June 1972, Mum and Dad accompanied me down to London to receive my medal. It was starting to sound like a joke whenever someone asked me what I had planned for next week and I'd reply that I was going to London.

'Oh, why's that?' they'd say.

'To meet the Queen,' I'd say, as you do.

The night before, I'd gone with some of the lads for another celebration so I was sat there in the Daimler that picked us up from the hotel with a banging headache. My mum gave me one of her little yellow pills to 'help steady my nerves', as she put it. I don't know what it was but within half an hour I felt I was floating. It certainly cured the headache.

We glided through the gates of the palace and assembled in the grounds. There were a few hundred others there, all dressed in their finery. I was in my best no. 2 dress with a red sash across my chest from shoulder to hip. Who would have thought it would come to this? From the little smart-arse kid I was in a northern pit town to a decorated soldier at Buckingham Palace. If only the nuns could see me now, I thought, there would be more than a few 'Jayzus, Joseph, Mary Mother of Gods' flying around.

We entered the palace and walked down a long corridor lined with guardsmen wearing chest plates and plumed helmets. Inside it was everything you'd fantasize about it being: a riot of the plushest carpets and rugs, incredible paintings and the grandest, most ornately decorated rooms you're ever likely to see. Yeah, they've definitely had the painters in, I thought. The gold, braided bell-ropes alone probably cost more than all my personal belongings.

In a side room the Queen's equerry ran through the offical procedure: address the Queen as 'Your Majesty' for the first time, and then as 'ma'am' thereafter and only bow from the shoulders down, not the waist.

The OBEs and MBEs for industry, charitable works and so on were handed out first. Nearly an hour later the time finally came for myself and the other soldiers present to go through. As we walked down the corridor the swell of music grew louder until we were ushered through into a huge hall. At the head of the hall stood the Queen; before her were seated hundreds of the relatives and spouses of the invested and behind and above them was an orchestra playing Elgar's *Nimrod*, making the occasion even more stirring.

I gradually moved towards her, awaiting my turn. I was struck by how small she was and also by how beautiful she looked, with the most flawless skin. Things moved along pretty quickly, until she got to me. We shook hands and she placed the MM on the hook already pinned to my tunic. I'd expected nothing more than a few standard questions but I was astonished by her knowledge on what I'd done. She had obviously read the citation. We talked about me being stationed in the Ardoyne. She made mention of what a dangerous area it was and then actually asked me about particular gunbattles I had been involved in, 'especially that one in the gardens,' she said. Again I was surprised by how well acquainted she was with my time there. Finally, she asked something of me which was completely unexpected. 'Tell me,' she said, 'what actually drove you to do the things you did?'

I could sense her genuine interest in this. Like many people, who when they are on the outside looking in with no experience of that strange exhilaration of battle, she probably wondered if I was driven by bravery or madness. A scene immediately popped into my head from an old Errol Flynn film I'd seen when younger. In it he was asked the same question by a previous Queen of England from centuries ago, an ancestor of the one now stood before me. It seemed to me that he'd given the perfect reply so, without pause, I said, 'I did it for you, ma'am.' She smiled and thanked me.

As soon as the words came out I'd nearly bitten my tongue. It sounded so cheesy and sentimental, but it seemed to go down well enough. As a kid I'd always made first claims on being Errol Flynn when we chose heroes to be but it was obviously more difficult to carry off in reality than when we were just playing. I must have lacked his style. I just hoped that Her Majesty had never seen the same film.

Back outside the palace with all the other guests, we posed for photographs. I'd never seen my dad look smarter but as he dipped into his pocket I knew he was going for the tin of tobacco to roll a cig. It had probably killed him to go for so long inside without one. I asked him if he'd at least wait until we'd got the photos done and he tutted and put the tin away.

Mum and Dad, having sat through the whole ceremony from beginning to end, told me that in comparison to most of the other investitures the soldiers' had taken longer. I was quite touched by this. The Queen had spent more time with us, and me in particular for some reason. I was surprised myself by how long she had talked to me. Mother nudged me and said to Dad, 'D'you think the Queen fancied our Nicky?'

'Give over, Mother!' I said, and they started laughing. I could see that Dad was as proud as Punch and that pleased me as much as anything. I unhooked the medal with its red, white and blue ribbon and laid it across his palm. I told him that I wanted him to keep it for me. He said he'd take it back to the colliery and show all the lads at the pit. He may never have said much, but that said it all.

Over the next few months I kept hearing tales about Chris from soldiers newly stationed or passing through the barracks. They told me he'd spent hours talking to the padre and then 'gone religious' and left the army. I heard he was now part of a born-again Christian group. When I got some leave I tried to track him down. The only information I had was that a friend of his ran a local gun shop. This fitted in with Chris. He always had a great knowledge of firearms.

The shop's door chimes caused a head to pop up from behind the counter. The guy stood up to greet me with a box of bullets still in one hand. I explained who I was looking for and he gave me an address only half a mile away.

Chris's wife didn't recognize me but when he appeared in the hallway behind her he moved towards me with a warm welcome and embraced me. It was great to see him. We sat in the front room, sharing a couple of beers. It was odd to see him in civvies, relaxing in a home environment. He asked after all the lads and we caught up on old news. I was struck by how calm he seemed, in marked contrast to the anxiety he had felt during our last days in Belfast. I'd really felt for him then and thought how sad it had been for such a great man, and fine soldier, to be brought down by what had happened. I'd thought that it always seemed to be the good men, the moral men, who ended up most damaged by war.

I suggested that he seemed a changed man now. He said that he was and explained what had happened. After being confronted by the father of the man he had shot, he'd spent the rest of his tour of duty racked with guilt and doubt. He knew he had done the right thing, in fact the only thing that he could have done in the circum-stances, but nevertheless the words of the father remained with him.

It was while he was walking across some waste ground that it happened. In a quiet moment he found himself – as he had been for sometime – thinking about God.

'Then it suddenly hit me, Nicky,' he said. 'It felt just like a light-ning bolt striking me on the neck and travelling down through my body. It's funny, you read about it happening to other people.'

He said it felt like a real, physical jolt, almost enough to knock him to the ground. That was the moment when he'd felt 'God come into me', as he put it, and all his worries and troubles lift from him. I could see it was true. He looked more contented than I'd ever seen him. He talked further about his conversion and eventually it became what we used to call the 'Sunday-school chat' that the padre would give us.

I said, 'Look, Chris, I'm not ready for this yet.' I knew the newly converted were always eager to try to bring you over to the fold, or, in my case, back to it. Lost sheep were always the most coveted. I was envious of him for what he'd experienced and pleased too that he'd found some peace, but it still didn't mean anything to me personally. It didn't change how I felt.

As I listened to him, it occured to me that he had shown his usual bravery in facing up to things. A different kind of bravery in a different kind of battle – this one spiritual – but bravery none the less. I could see a lot of his hurt had vanished. Maybe it would happen to me in time, but not now. Not yet.

As I left we wished each other luck. I was unsure of whether we would meet again, not because we didn't want to but because I knew I was due to return to Belfast and I also knew that once I was there, anything could happen.

So I left him to his own personal journey and walked away to continue mine.

PART TWO

UNDERCOVER

*'Let he who desires peace
prepare for war.'*

10

BACK TO THE FRONT (LONDON CALLING)

Dying of boredom is a terrible thing. It's a long, slow, lingering death. You don't even realize how bad a state you're in until you wake one morning and find your bunk has become your deathbed and someone is pulling the sheet over your face.

The familiar descent down through Irish cloud had sent the usual shiver of nervous adrenalin through me. Though it bled out of me pretty quickly when I found myself stationed in Craigavon, near Lurgan, a short distance from Belfast.

This is a rural area – beautiful but boring. If you found those qualities in a woman you'd put up with the dullness because of the beauty until even that waned and you eventually moved on to someone else more interesting. It was like that for me. Despite the ugliness of inner-city Belfast, and the Ardoyne in particular, it still had a strange attraction that outweighed the danger. In fact, for a soldier accustomed to that peculiar high-wire act of survival in combat, the danger *was* the attraction.

In Craigavon, because of the distances involved, there were no foot patrols. We travelled everywhere in the back of a Land-Rover. We couldn't go out when we had time off so we remained confined to barracks, overdosing on crap TV and each other's company. The only interesting thing that happened was when I met a warrant officer from the Intelligence Corps. He told me that they needed more recruits for the corps because the war had now got dirty. I'd noticed the change myself.

There was now much less overt action on the streets. The outbursts of major rioting and gunbattles had died down and been replaced by more covert and dangerous methods by the IRA. It was like a pub fight which, full of obvious displays of aggression and bravado, has ended but the two men involved still harbour hatred for each other. And they know where each other lives and start plotting less public but more damaging revenge. It was like that for us and the IRA now. We each knew where the other lived and that it was only a matter of time before someone decided to pay a visit. This knowledge of where we were and how and when we patrolled was less obviously damaging than an actual attack, but just as dangerous. And as any fireman will tell you, it's not the flames of a fire that are most likely to kill you, but the smoke.

The year 1972 saw more deaths than any other up to that point. The ill-wind after Bloody Sunday had definitely blown no good. The British Embassy in Dublin was burned as a result. IRA membership increased. Bloody Friday was a display of just how much power the Provos now possessed.

More violence erupted. Sectarian murders continued to increase, as did car bombings. The IRA took their bombing campaign to mainland Britain and a truce only lasted two days before collapsing back into the usual mayhem.

The same year had also seen the army's Military Reconnaissance Force's activities brought to wider public knowledge when two undercover operations were attacked by IRA gunmen. In one, a laundry cleaning service called Four Square was set up to allow the MRF to analyse clothing taken from Catholic areas for forensic evidence. The ruse was discovered and the driver, an MRF officer, was shot and killed. In the other operation, a massage parlour business that had been set up by the army in order to glean information from visiting Provos was raided in a bungled IRA machine-gun attack. This massage parlour was where an SDLP councillor revealed the names of the three IRA gunmen responsible for killing the three off-duty squaddies. His revelations were recorded by bugging devices on the premises.

The Provos' HQ in Derry was also raided in this year and the no-go areas there and in Belfast were closed down by an army operation called Motorman.

By 1974, while I'd been in mainland Britain for two years training new recruits, things in Northern Ireland had changed. Out of their original thrown-together formation, the IRA had now reassembled into a far more efficient organization. They had their own hierarchy of officers, staff captains and foot-soldiers, put together in a kind of dark mirror of our own structure. Their active service units (ASUs) operated in cell systems drawn from a communist model. These cells comprised only four members (including one leader) who had very selective information pertaining only to their own activities. It was like taking out every fifth domino from a long row so only one cell would fall at a time without taking the others down with them. The IRA was now a far more difficult organization to crack, making successful information gathering vital.

The previous year had seen the IRA weakened, almost to the point of collapse, by an MRF operation. They recruited a former Provo intelligence officer and sent him to meet two journalists with a fabricated story of IRA officers syphoning off £150,000 from IRA funds. The MRF supplied the tout with enough details of MRF procedure to make his cover believable. The journalists fell for it and ran the story. The ensuing paranoia and suspicion among the ranks of the IRA led to a bout of in-fighting that brought them to the brink of self-destruction. This led to a protracted 'inside' war between the older, more traditional elements of the organization and the younger, more militant factions. The power struggle was finally won by the newer hard-liners led by Gerry Adams.

Adams was a man I had good cause to remember. As he had come to greater power and his face appeared more regularly in news reports, I recognized him as one of the gunmen in a street battle I had been involved in. He had just missed shooting me by about as narrow a margin as I'd missed him. When I'd got back to the barracks I'd immediately recognized his face on his 'P card' as I looked at the array of suspects' photos pinned up in the Ops room. Providing you get a decent look at them, you tend to have good reason to remember and recognize the face of someone who's just tried to shoot you. It also turned out that he was one of the planners of Bloody Friday. At the time Adams was the commander of the IRA's Belfast Brigade battalions, making my narrow miss of him during our earlier gunbattle even more regrettable.

MRF success had taken out many top IRA members through a combination of heavy troop presence and the rapidly improving surveillance techniques. But as we got better at undercover warfare, so did they; not only to combat us, but to fight the threat of emerging Loyalist paramilitary groups. These groups, such as the Ulster Volunteer Force (UVF) and Ulster Defence Association (UDA), had formed as reactions to the current political deal-making. They feared an agreement was nearing between the Republicans and the British government to form a united Ireland.

The truth of something I had realized when on the streets now came fully into focus: 'knowledge was power'; knowledge of who was who; what they were going to do; when they were going to do it; how it would be organized and so on. All these things were needed to piece together the full picture. They helped pinpoint exactly when the next 'punch' was going to be thrown, so we could get in during the draw-back and strike first.

On returning to England I was sent for by Command HQ of the UK land forces. I was to be interviewed as a potential recruit for the Intelligence Corps. First I was supposed to be 'positively vetted' by the int officers, but because I was already known to them after what I had done in uniform, I was PVed immediately. I was given one week to hand in all military equipment and report to Company Int HQ in the wooded depths of Middle England.

Brigadier Frank Kitson had originally formed the MRF to operate in Northern Ireland. This is where the idea of placing guys on the buses to prevent the hijackings had come from, among other things. They were getting men out there and disrupting terrorist operations, but their success was limited because the soldiers weren't particularly well trained. So the intelligence training camp had been opened on the mainland for the cream of the forces to be recruited to undergo intensive, specialist training. I was to became part of this force.

We were trained in all manner of undercover techniques: electronic surveillance (house-bugging, phone-tapping, installing area-listening devices and wearing body-wires, lock-picking); accent coaching (so we could at least attempt to pass ourselves off as locals should the need arise); and following suspects on foot and in cars whilst avoiding detection. We practised vehicle-tailing on the motorway. Three cars in radio contact would follow the target, alternating with each other so one car was never in sight long enough to arouse suspicion.

For the foot surveillance we'd move into the nearest big city and practise tailing another recruit through the streets and shops (Woolworths was always a favourite, for some reason).

We also grew our hair out from the regulation army crop in preparation for what was to come.

Eventually I was sent to Warminster to be briefed. I was told I was to be sent back to Northern Ireland and stationed at a border crossing. My brief was to recruit and pick up 'sources', identify suspected members of the Republican movement and gather information that could be used by combat forces in the field. Without this, they were running blind, or walking dead, depending on how bleak a picture you wanted to paint.

As the real power now lay in information, and that information had to come from somewhere, this is where the sources came in. They had to be carefully cultivated and then rated according to the strength of their information. The rating system ran from A to F (for the source himself) and from 1 to 6 (for the information given). A new source would first be rated F6, until he proved his reliability and the importance of his information. Then he might move up to, say, a C or B as he became more trusted. An A source was the best. So an A source giving particularly good info would be an A1.

Cutting through the crap of all the terminology – 'deep-cover', 'low-intensity op', and so on – in cruder terms intelligence meant finding out exactly what the fuck was happening. The war had now gone underground. The water was further muddied by lies, bluffs, propaganda and the IRA's own form of intelligence gathering on what *we* were doing.

In light of all this I arrived at the village aware of the responsibility I carried: the good I could do if I was successful and the damage that could be inflicted if I screwed up.

Earlier in the year no-warning car bombs had already killed nearly thirty people and recently the IRA's bombing campaign on mainland Britain had escalated. In two major atrocities five were killed in the Guildford pub bombing and nineteen were left dead after the bombing of two pubs in Birmingham.

The border post was a stop/checkpoint at the edge of the village. It consisted of nothing more dramatic or imposing than a small station building, two search areas and a watchtower containing two armed guards. Although the actual geographical north/south border was several hundred yards behind us, our post was considered to be the demarcation point from one to the other. In the area between the last checkpoint building and the stream that marked the border on the map, we had a Caltrap.

I lived in a large caravan in a stockade on the edge of the village. This was a compound used by the Ulster Defence Regiment (UDR) for weekend training but as I couldn't live in the main building they put my caravan in the car park. Initially, I was supposed to camp down with the guard-duty squaddies in the tiny Portakabins they lived in but as I was due to be here for longer than anyone else, I thought, sod that. I'd had enough of the stink of other men's feet and insisted they bring a caravan down for me. It was a big, state-of-the-art thing with all home comforts, like a TV, a lounge and even a bar. The lights and fire were run from bottled gas but I got them to run wires from the main electricity supply in the UDR building through the caravan window so I could use an electric blanket. One of the main problems was condensation and the damp it left on my bed. So every night when I bedded down with this electric blanket on I was actually risking electrocution! But rather that, I thought, than freeze to death.

The Alsatian I'd bought recently moved into the compound with me. His kennel was next to the caravan and the helicopter landing zone. Whenever the chopper dropped on to the LZ (carrying supplies, mail or visiting officers) the caravan would rock violently in the downforce of the blades. Every few days I'd wake up a few feet closer to the village. Eventually they brought in a fork-lift truck to keep moving me back before I slid right down to the coast. And the dog in its the kennel with me. Eventually the noise drove the dog spare (he'd hear the chopper well before me and begin howling) and I had to give him away.

All was fine apart from the fact that every night I had to leave the checkpoint and walk up through the village to get to the caravan. Hardly an ideal state of affairs as it left me open to attack if anyone was so inclined.

This particular border crossing was important because it was where the Provos from Derry and East Tyrone would cross to travel south to County Monaghan, to a place used as an IRA HQ for battle-plan meetings.

Cars would come and go between the north and south. We noted, recorded and reported all relevant information which may help identify both suspected and known terrorists.

One ploy of theirs was to hijack a truck in the south, plant a bomb on it, threaten the driver with retribution against his family if he didn't comply and then tell him to drive to the checkpoint. We never had to search the trucks for the explosives because as soon as it pulled in the driver would leap from the cab screaming blue murder – 'There's a fuckin' bomb on board!' – and we'd all leg it up into the village after him as the truck was blown off its wheels behind us, ripping the buildings apart in the process. Sometimes a brand-spanking-new checkpoint would be up on Monday only to be in bits again by Friday.

So, in order not only to lessen the chances of this but to save us from a half-marathon every week, we began stopping the trucks as

THE WAY IT WAS. (BELOW) A
LITTLE GIRL OFFERS HER
SANDWICH TO A SOLDIER AND
(RIGHT) A SHOPKEEPER OFFERS
TEA TO BELEAGUERED SOLDIERS
IN THE 'HONEYMOON' DAYS OF
1969. (CAMERA PRESS)

THE WAY IT BECAME. BY 1970 THINGS HAD GONE FROM BAD TO WORSE ON THE STREETS OF BELFAST.
(CAMERA PRESS)

ME AND SOME OF THE LADS IN A FLOODED STREET. THIS WAS THE SCENE OF KEV CROSIER'S ATTEMPT TO RESCUE AN OLD LADY STRANDED IN THE FLOODS.

A SNAP, TAKEN BY US, OF THE FRIENDLY NATIVES. ALSO THE SCENE WHERE PAUL AUSTIN CAUGHT A GRENADE — LITERALLY!

(ABOVE) FLAX STREET MILL, 'HOME SWEET HOME' ON MY SECOND TOUR.

THE REWARD FOR REGULAR PATROLLING AND ENDLESS PATIENCE. ME IN THE ARDOYNE HOLDING WEAPONS DISCOVERED DURING A HOUSE SEARCH.

THE ARDOYNE STEEL BAND. LOCAL WOMEN WARNING THEIR MENFOLK OF OUR PRESENCE. (CAMERA PRESS)

PROVO GUNMEN IN A SHOW OF STRENGTH AT AN ILLEGAL CHECKPOINT. (CAMERA PRESS)

THE VIEW OF THE ARDOYNE FROM THE ROOF OF FLAX STREET MILL. THIS WAS WHERE KEV WAS SHOT AND KILLED WHILST STANDING NEXT TO ME ON LOOKOUT DUTY.

THE LAST JOURNEY. STAN, ME AND JOHN-BOY CARRYING KEV'S COFFIN TO A HERCULES TRANSPORTER TO BE FLOWN HOME.

WATER CANNONS, ONE OF THE MANY WAYS WE TRIED TO BREAK UP A RIOT. IT WORKED FOR A WHILE — UNTIL THE IRA GUNMEN CAME OUT TO PLAY. (CAMERA PRESS)

THE GUTTED REMAINS OF FARRINGDON GARDENS. PROTESTANT HOUSEHOLDERS, FLEEING BECAUSE OF INTIMIDATION, DESTROYED THEIR OWN HOMES RATHER THAN SEE THEM FALL INTO CATHOLIC HANDS. (CAMERA PRESS)

Two of the decorated soldiers I was proud to serve alongside. (Top) My platoon commander, Chris Mather, who was awarded a Military Cross. Here he is talking to an American newsman from CBS. (Right) The legendary Captain Robert Nairac, who I worked with on undercover operations. He was posthumously awarded a George Cross. (PA News)

BERNADETTE MACALISKEY (NEE DEVLIN). A FEW YEARS AFTER WE MET, SHE WAS SHOT BY THE UVF, BUT SURVIVED. (CAMERA PRESS)

ME AND THE REIGNING MISS WORLD OF 1976 IN MY OFFICE AT DUNGANNON. I AM POINTING OUT PHOTOGRAPHS OF WHAT WE CALL THE IRA BUT WHAT SHE CALLED *BANDIDOS*.

soon as they crossed the stream. This way they were far enough away from the actual checkpoint to make the planting of bombs pretty futile. I don't think that killing a few sheep and covering half of us in cow dung would really have been considered much of a coup by the IRA.

Despite all this it was still considered safe to go for an occasional pint in the village pub. One day I got chatting to a bloke there and realized he was in a position to give me some information. Unfortunately, I didn't yet know who all the main players were in the IRA network. I needed to get in touch with someone who did to verify the info and find out if we could use it. I contacted our field controller, Jack Marshall. Jack liaised between all the int cells and so knew just about everyone who needed knowing. We arranged for the guy to meet me and Jack in my caravan.

Making yourself known to a Catholic who may have potential as a source always carries risks. Using a Protestant was of little use because, to them, all Catholics were 'bad bastards'. They might just tell you the names of people they had a particular grudge against. The really dynamite revelations came from Catholics themselves and, preferably, ones who were either fully involved or on the fringes of the IRA. An ordinary Catholic would only be valuable if he happened to live near to someone we wanted, then we could pump him for info on the target's appearance, what car he drove, when he left the house and so on.

Initially, I wondered why someone involved in a cause to which they were committed would give us anything, but the reasons soon became apparent. The simplest one was the age-old bribe. Down the years the 'thirty pieces of silver' hadn't really devalued much in effectiveness since Judas and Jesus. The Provos drew their ranks from the disaffected working classes, most of whom were on the dole and scraping to make ends meet. The source might be paid up to £300 if it was really good info. Usually they would be paid in cash but, occasionally, longstanding sources would have it paid straight into their bank accounts. This happened rarely, though, because the bank worker doing the transaction might have Republican sympathies and become suspicious of large amounts of money regularly going into an account.

Obviously, you wouldn't tempt any of the hard-liners with this method; mostly just the ones dithering on the fringes. The more committed ones were handled in other ways. One was the promise of immunity from prosecution. We'd search someone at the roadblock and, though they weren't carrying anything incriminating, we'd produce some rounds of ammo that had been 'found' on them. They would protest their innocence of course, and we'd say, 'OK, if you want to take your chances in court that's up to you.' They knew as well as we did that they'd get completely stuffed by the judge. Looking down the barrel of five years in prison was usually enough incentive to get them to give us a few names. Sometimes, the real do-or-die members would just say, 'Go ter fuck yer Brit bastard!' and we'd have to let them go. But often it worked.

The best scenario was when we actually found weapons or explosives in their car. Then we could lay into them with threats of being banged up till doomsday. Then you really would find out the extent of their resolve and if they were willing to risk spending, say, at the most, the guts of ten years inside. For some that was too long and too dark a tunnel for them to see any light at the end of it.

The day came when the guy from the bar was to visit me. Usually, when meeting a source, I'd wear a body-mike with the wire leading from the recorder in my pocket, down my arm to the microphone hidden in my wristwatch. Real James Bond stuff. As this meet was due to take place in the caravan, we decided to use a larger tape-recorder for better sound quality. We hid the main bulk of the machine in an overhead cupboard, ran the wire down the wall and up the leg of a folding table and taped the mike underneath it. The wires were all carefully positioned so as not to be visible.

When the guy arrived he already looked skittish. I'd forewarned him of Jack's presence so as not to scare the Jesus out of him. Eventually he settled down. He sat on the bench on one side of the table with Jack and me on the other. We cracked the seal on a quart of Bushmills and the whiskey started to oil his wheels. In common with most Irishmen, the guy could certainly talk. I began to wonder if we'd run out of tape. I didn't know exactly how much of it was pukka, though. No doubt Jack would fill me in on this afterwards.

It got to the point where all that whiskey was obviously making his bladder jangle so he got up to go to the lav. Unfortunately, when he rose he kicked the folding leg of the table, which collapsed, the microphone pulled the wire tight, the wire pulled the tape-recorder and the whole damn machine shot out of the cupboard above him and cracked him on the head. He staggered and fell back on the bench. Jack and I jumped up and looked at each other, gobsmacked. Funnily enough, earlier, when he'd been trying to impress on us the truth of what he was saying, he'd said, 'And may God strike me down if there's one word of a lie in what I'm telling you boys.' As he lay there in a heap, he slowly came round to realize he hadn't actually been struck down by the hand of God but by a Philips High-Fidelity tape-recorder.

'Holy Christ! You fuckers are taping me! Why the fuck are you taping me?'

I could see that Jack was trying as hard as me not to burst out laughing. In fact, I was sure if he opened his mouth that he would do, so I spoke first. 'You don't expect us to memorize all this, do you? You've been here over an hour. Don't worry, it's only for our use, you know that. We're not gonna broadcast it on speakers around the bloody province.'

This was meant to reassure him but it didn't. He seemed to think it was a veiled threat to do just that if he didn't give us what we wanted. He started to shout again. 'Fuckin' hell! Do you boys know my life will be worth shit if word of this gets back to the wrong people?'

We tried to reassure him again but he shot out of the door like a dog from a trap. The last image we had of him was him bounding across the compound holding his head. I turned to Jack, who was in stitches by now, and said, 'Another successful day at the office, then?'

One day I got a call to report to Brigade HQ for a briefing. Whilst sat in the outer office someone else entered the room. I hadn't heard him come in but just felt his presence. He was a tall, dark-haired, handsome bloke with an unusual air of confidence about him. He stuck in my mind because there was something about him that reminded me very much of my later impression of Chris Mather: the same natural, officer-bred authority at odds with a squaddie's toughness in his eyes; the same kink in the nose that looked like a relic of boxing days; and the same swagger of a soldier totally at ease with his own abilities. He strode past and disappeared into the office.

I asked quietly of the officer beside me, 'Who is that?'

'Oh, that's Robert,' he said with a noticeable respect in his voice, as if the one name should be enough. 'He's part of the hush-hush operational guys that have been brought over.' This didn't really tell me a great deal more but added to the intrigue.

Back at the border checkpoint I got a call through one day telling me of the imminent arrival of a man crossing from north to south. I was given a description of him and the car and told to expect him at about eleven that night. The voice said, 'Let the car through. Search him but not the car. He's "friendly forces".' Nothing more dramatic than this was said but I noticed the voice was weighted with the importance of this person. We were to pretend to search him in order not to arouse suspicion in anyone watching and then let him through without any hassle.

When the car eventually arrived and pulled alongside me I bent down to the driver, and despite his newly grown beard I recognized him as the man I'd previously seen in the HQ office. He handed me a driver's licence which, although perfectly authentic-looking, was obviously fake as it gave him an Irish name and address.

We searched him and his companion but left the car untouched. I knew it would contain weapons.

He drove away into the dark. The other guy stayed behind and joined us in my office. I now recognized him as one of the blokes I'd trained with on the int course back in England. As we sat down for a coffee he took his pistol from its shoulder holster and laid it on the table. It was a Browning 9mm and I noticed that the right-side butt grip was missing. Even if I hadn't recognized him he wouldn't have needed to explain who he was. This told me everything. A doctored Browning was the tell-tale sign of 14 Int undercover agents.

As we talked I learned that the man in the car was an officer called Robert Nairac. I'd already heard whispers about him. He was extremely highly rated as an intelligence agent. His speciality was deep-cover infiltration as he had a great ability to mix among the locals, adopting different guises and perfect Irish dialects in order to pass himself off as one of them whilst gathering information. This was a very dangerous game to play, something akin to tip-toeing through a minefield. One wrong step could blow your cover and the fall-out from the blast would be your certain capture, torture and assassination.

He told me they were down here on a reconnaissance mission, or 'reccie'. Nairac had gone down to case the house of a Provo member whilst the other officer remained here with a radio in case Nairac wanted to get in touch.

We sat out the next few hours destroying the best part of what remained of my coffee and cig supplies. Outside it was as black as pitch – the land enveloped with that truly scary darkness that only the countryside has at night. No hint of the reassuring glow of city life here. It made my mind wander to where Nairac must be right now. He was out on a very lonely limb, that much I knew. I felt the familiar kick of adrenalin go through me at just the thought of attempting to pull off such a manoeuvre. Nairac and Chris obviously shared more than just a certain demeanour: their balls must have been forged in the same steel mill as well.

As the minutes turned to hours and the hours piled up, and Nairac still didn't return, I wondered if this was a bad sign. He could have been rumbled, killed and dumped in a ditch. The guy with me showed no alarm. He seemed accustomed to this scary uncertainty.

Nairac eventually returned several hours later, picked up his partner and left to drive back north. Nothing of the mission's success or failure was told to me.

Far from putting me off, the night's events made me want to become more involved. This is what I'd wanted after all – to be able to make a difference. This was obviously the way to do it.

One of the major difficulties we faced was the constantly changing appearance of 'wanted' men. For example, a beard could easily be cut down to a moustache and then removed completely to leave a clean-shaven face. Hair was also cut, restyled and dyed. It didn't take much to alter an appearance dramatically. On top of this was the blizzard of false IDs, documents and driver's licences that threatened to snow us under.

I'd get a call from another int cell saying that such-and-such a person was going to be driving down through the checkpoint and could I supply info on their current guise. However, there was no accurate information accessible to all units at one time.

I came up with the idea of installing a hidden camera at the checkpoint, enabling us to update our information data-base rapidly with fresh evidence. This was considered by everyone to be a real breakthrough. I would now be contacted regularly by other branches of intelligence for updates. The army was eager to justify the large numbers of troops on the streets who, by now, were mostly just kicking their heels.

A1 information was like gold dust, as rare and as frantically sought. In this context the checkpoint was like a mine which I ran: tapping for seams, sifting and assessing the value of our finds. Appropriate then that I was beginning to be regarded as one of intelligence's golden boys because it wasn't so much nuggets of information I was giving them as solid gold bars. All the int cells were now much more genned-up and efficient due to the new photographic evidence. The first of many congratulatory cases of whiskey from the other officers came winging my way.

Although I wasn't promoted by rank I became much more important because of what I knew. This was the position I'd always wanted for myself – a front-liner with the chance to feed information to those still in the immediate firing line and helping to limit the lives lost; maybe even contribute to the resolution of this conflict.

The fact that troops and officers moved in and out of Northern Ireland on four-month tours meant that there was no continuity of knowledge between them and the incomings. I, on the other hand, remained in almost continual service and became increasingly valuable in my position as a LINCO (liaison intelligence non-commissioned officer: the army would never call you by five words when one would do).

When the MoD called in their top brass for a report on intelligence progress they were given the good news about my up-to-date photos operation and even more congratulations came my way.

I now had power way beyond my rank, even more than some of the officers above me. It got to the point where they even hated me going on temporary leave because they had no one to replace me.

Much to everyone's suprise, the IRA announced a temporary ceasefire to last from the end of December to January of the new year after meeting a group of Protestant clergy for peace talks.

I hoped it was more than just empty promises riding on the back of the usual swell of Christmas sentiment. But anyway, it came as a welcome relief. I hadn't relished facing the sickly combination of blood and tinsel over the festive season.

I took the opportunity for a week's leave and flew to Canada with a mate of mine who served in the SAS. We had talked about opening an 'outward bound' trekking business together when we left the army. He had already been out to Canada and seen a possible location.

Staying in a cabin in the shade of Canadian mountains made the troubles of Northern Ireland seem a thousand times more than the 3,000 miles away that they actually were. I had my first real stretch of nightmare-free sleep in a long time, drifting off to the howl of the wind rather than sirens and gunfire. It brought home to me how, when you're as deeply embroiled in a situation as I was, you can so easily forget the rest of the world even exists. And that you could be part of it. I even saw a grizzly bear and experienced that simple shock at the reality of something I'd only seen in wildlife programmes. Even in the distance it looked hugely impressive, rearing up on its hind legs, swaying and sniffing the air like some great hairy wardrobe.

I also took a trip out to Halifax in Nova Scotia on the east coast. This was the closest mainland territory to where the *Titanic* had struck the iceberg. A plot of land on a hillside had been turned into a memorial for the dead. All their names were carved into row upon row of black slate headstones. Each one bore the same date of 15 April 1912. It was eerie looking up from them and then out over the moving mountains of the Atlantic.

One headstone in particular, to a young officer called Everett Elliott, had an inscription that affected me more than the others. It seemed to be an ominous reminder of my own situation. It read, 'Each man stood his post as the weaker ones went by, and showed once more to all the world how Englishmen should die.' I thought that, however noble this sounded, I didn't want it to become my epitaph. I'd already seen Englishmen stand their posts and die; and not just out of self-sacrificing duty like the *Titanic*'s officers, but needlessly because they were ill-prepared. Like Stan Overend and Paul Austin.

It showed how even here on this wind-whipped, God-forsaken bump of land thousands of miles away, there was still no escape from the Troubles.

Too soon I had to return to Aughnacloy. I arrived to find that the ceasefire had been extended on 2 January. It broke down on the seventeenth but between those two dates there was an act committed of such significance that it became partly responsible for the truce ending. It was also significant for one of the men rumoured to be involved, a man I was already familiar with: Robert Nairac. And it brought the first whispers on the wind of the involvement of the SAS. In fact, this incident alone seemed to encompass every single element of the dirty war: murder and recrimination, accusations of responsibility, terrorist and army intelligence intrigue, conspiracy theories, and a spiral of rumours, suspicions and lies all circling each other in a confusing dance around the 'truth' and yet another corpse.

The body of John Francis Green, or 'Benny' as he was known, was found in a remote farmhouse in County Monaghan on 10 January. Green was a prominent IRA staff captain. His escape from internment in Long Kesh prison made him as famous among the ranks of the IRA as he was infamous to the security forces. He had been on the run ever since. He finally holed up in the farmhouse of a Republican sympathizer. This 'safe' house turned out to be more dangerous than expected. For Green it proved fatal as he was ambushed and shot dead.

The killing was immediately attributed to the most obvious suspects, a Loyalist hit-squad from the UVF. But I began to hear differently. Through my contacts in intelligence and through the more informal exchanges of information after int meetings had ended, I heard of the rumoured involvement of Robert Nairac.

There had already been open talk (and resulting controversy) about a 'shoot to kill' policy by the security forces against known terrorists. My first thought when hearing the phrase 'shoot to kill' was that there was no other way to shoot. Soldiers are never trained to aim to wound. This was, admittedly, just an initial glib reaction to the wording. In reality it referred to the supposed policy of targeting the most important and active paramilitary members (who for one reason or another could not be charged) and having them taken out by the security forces.

The first mention of shoot to kill, to me personally, had been by a sergeant-major. He was the same guy who had kicked Martin Meehan in the balls during his arrest. This guy had told me of his plan to lay men in wait outside the home of two brothers who were members of the Irish National Liberation Army (INLA). They were to be shot as they arrived. His source's info was duff, however, and the two never showed up.

I had no evidence myself that this was policy passed down from on high rather than just men acting on their own intitiative out of frustration.

Everyone had become accustomed to the difficulties of success-fully securing a conviction against men known to us as active terrorists. I knew of a detective sergeant in the RUC CID who had hundreds of unsolved murders on his books alone. Our case against the suspects would go before the Director of Public Prosecutions for review. Too often the DPP would decide not to risk public expense and the court's time on a case he couldn't be certain we would win. This was all well and fine, and to a certain extent understandable, but the overall feeling was that far too many of these cases were allowed to slide. Even when they did get to trial and even when these 'bad bastards', as they were commonly and accurately known, were up to their elbows in corpses, they often walked free because of legal technicalities, the reluctance of witnesses to testify or these same witnesses being threatened with retribution against themselves or their families if they didn't withdraw their evidence. Jury nobbling got to be such a problem that they were eventually done away with altogether in favour of a bench of judges. Then the judges were targeted for assassination. It was not only a major problem but a source of incredible frustration to see these men walk free to carry on killing. It was insane. It seemed like the plug had been pulled and democracy was disappearing down the hole in a swirl of bloodied water.

Recently an old adversary of ours from my time in uniform had appeared in court: Chris's nemesis, Martin Meehan. After the time when we had arrested him and Chris had knocked seven bells out of him, Meehan had sued the army for wrongful arrest. I thought this was the biggest and unfunniest joke I'd ever heard in my life. Many months later (by which time I was out of uniform) the legal process had finally ground around in its usual ponderous way to Meehan's hearing. Despite all manner of high-ranking officers being present at his arrest, as I was the unit commander I was the one put down as the arresting officer. I duly appeared in the witness box to give evidence.

My identity was protected insofar as I was only referred to as 'soldier A', but still, I was stood there for all to see. Over the last three years I'd had to appear in court many times, only to find myself facing the friends and family of the accused, all sat in the public gallery glaring at me.

During Meehan's trial I got that familiar sick feeling of things not going our way. In the middle of the complex, tangled web of what was termed 'legal due process' (or what we called 'barristers' bullshit') the real reason why we were all assembled here slowly slid away and became lost between the pages of textbooks and cited precedence. Eventually, our brief cut his losses and approached the bench to surrender the case. Meehan walked free, richer for £800 compensation. (It wasn't until a few years later that he got his come-uppance when he was convicted of the kidnapping of an informer and jailed for twelve years.)

Among certain members of the security forces it was already known that intelligence info on Provisionals was finding its way into the hands of Loyalist groups who then acted upon it. Nairac had a none-too-secret history (told to me, personally, by a field controller) of information-trafficking to Loyalists who shared his desire to weaken the Republicans by hitting them hardest where it hurt the most – in the loss of their most important members. The word on the grapevine was that Benny Green had been whacked not by the UVF but by a hit-squad comprising Nairac and two of the SAS.

Although the SAS were not officially deployed in Northern Ireland, their name was cropping up with increasing regularity. I didn't yet have any evidence other than these rumours that they were operational but, then again, that was in keeping with the nature of this select and very secretive force.

And yet it may have been just a very deliberate act of 'black' propaganda by Box 5 (as we called MI5) to begin these rumours of the SAS on active service. Their formidable mystique was enough to spread fear and paranoia through the ranks of the IRA. In that case it wouldn't have really mattered whether they were operating or not, as the simple belief that they were would have done the job. This was all part of the intelligence and counter-intelligence game: to muddy the waters enough to destabilize clear-thinking in the enemy camp. It was like a more sophisticated version of my old trick of shooting out streetlights. If you were going to be fired on you'd rather it be a shot in the dark.

Anyway, no matter who slotted Green, the whole of intelligence was on a high at him being taken out. The next thing that concerned us was the transportation of his body from the south back over the border to the north and his home in Lurgan. We would take this opportunity to observe the funeral cortège accompanying the body. Funerals and their processions were always a good time to scout for the dead man's associates. More often than not there would be some in attendance, particularly for someone of Green's stature. Nothing was sacred, not even your last, lifeless journey to a hole in the ground.

It was a trick used by them as well as us. On the occasions when Provos infiltrated the security forces they worked side-by-side with men they were gathering enough information on to kill. After the hit, if they had befriended their victim well enough, they would attend his funeral. As they were consoling the guy's widow and family, they would be scanning the other mourners for security personnel who could also be killed. So even the paying of respects to a dead colleague could sow the first seeds for you joining him not long after.

The southern Irish police force, the Garda, informed us of the imminent transportation of Green's body; but only the time, they didn't know what route would be taken. Their information had to be given to us as part of procedure, they didn't like doing it.

With the Garda being drawn from the Republic of Ireland, of course they were always loath to collaborate with us on anything. The Garda Special Branch in particular always seemed to make a profession of getting right up my nose. Whenever they came north – sporting shoulder holsters, coming on strong like a cut-price Sweeney and spouting matching dialogue to boot – they would flash their ID cards and say they were Special Branch. My usual response was that that may have been true down south but up here they weren't so special so they should sit down and shut the fuck up. We'd keep them in a holding bay for a few hours until they cooled their jets.

We knew the most likely south-to-north crossing point would be the official checkpoint near Keady in County Armagh. Keady was so staunchly Republican that it contained something you had to see with your own eyes to believe: 'sniper signs'. These were warnings to troops put up by Provos in the form of a red triangular sign (just like a conventional road sign) with the black silhouette of a gunman painted inside and the words 'DANGER SNIPER AT WORK' underneath. The troops were the last ones who needed reminding but the signs served their purpose as an act of bravado and a very public display of the lawlessness of these no-go areas.

The alternative to the Keady checkpoint crossing was the possibility of an illegal crossing somewhere else along the border. This seemed unlikely to me in light of the heavy publicity following Green's death, but it was something we still had to cover.

I took the border-patrol duty and found that one of my companions was to be the big man himself, Robert Nairac. I already had the impression that he had official sanction to do pretty much as he pleased so his presence on the patrol would have come at his own request. I also knew that if rumours of his involvement in Green's death were true, he would want to be up close to the action. This dovetailed perfectly with my view of him as probably being more deeply immersed in the intrigue than anyone else I had encountered, or could even think of.

On the day, myself, Nairac and two supporting intelligence officers from Armagh got into our vehicle. I'd pulled a big-engined two-litre, bottle-green Datsun out of the car pool. I wanted to be sure we had enough power to out-accelerate any Provo ASUs we might run into. They would be patrolling the border too. This wasn't exactly a walk in the park we were going on. Despite prior knowledge of the cortège and a watchful security presence, we could be traversing the border along some very dangerous no-go zones in the most southerly corner of the Murder Triangle (the area between Omagh; Keady and Lurgan); right through the yards and muddy backwaters of the most hostile bandit country. And not so much on a wing and a prayer as in a green Datsun with ammo.

We were all tooled up. The two intelligence officers in the back with Uzis at their feet and Robert and myself up front with our Brownings. It was my mission, so I drove. As I fired the engine, Robert leaned over with deliberate exaggeration and checked the fuel gauge.

'Already done that,' I said. He smiled, tapped the dashboard as if for good luck and then, suddenly serious, said, 'Let's go'.

As we drove, Aughnacloy began to seem like a large, life-filled city compared to the windy desolation of the land we were knifing into. The long, thin ribbon of road ahead often appeared completely empty until a vehicle suddenly careered out of a corner blind-spot or zipped out of the trough of a road-dip and flew past us. Each time this happened I checked the rear-view mirror, expecting to see the tell-tale sign of brakelights burning on as the car stopped to turn and chase.

On first leaving I had switched on the car radio but this attempt at mimicking the events of a normal journey backfired: it only seemed to exaggerate the hard reality of what we were doing; and where we were going and why. This was no bugger's idea of a family outing. Except maybe the Addams Family.

The tinny stereo threw out ridiculously happy-sounding tunes, putting us even more on edge. The last thing I wanted to hear was some Yank disco group.

Eventually we reached the border. I kept as best as I could to the north side. It wasn't the crossing of the border that worried me, even though it was illegal to be on an operation in what was classed as another country, but the fact that if we got involved in a contact there we really would be in trouble.

After about half an hour I saw something move in the distance. It quickly grew in speed and size and formed into a dark saloon car racing towards us. The instances of being passed by other vehicles hadn't happened with enough regularity for us to get used to it. We simultaneously tensed with each and every one. Something about this one seemed yet more ominous: the dark size of the car perhaps, or its speed, or the way the light flashed in blocks over the windscreen, making it impossible to see inside. We were closer than we'd ever been to the expected crossing point.

The combined speed of our cars whipped away the distance between us. Now I heard their engine for the first time. It sounded as big and healthy a bastard as ours. It bore down on us at speed. The sun moved behind clouds and the windscreen darkened. The car was full of men. I relaxed then when I saw broom and tool handles sticking up beside them – they were just farmers! – then as the vehicle grew in my windscreen I saw these 'handles' were machine-gun barrels. We hadn't produced our guns yet, but instinctively I still knew they had sussed us. On a day like this, four guys in a car could only be one thing: security forces or a Provo ASU. And they knew we weren't one of theirs.

Then the oddest thing happened; probably the oddest thing I've ever been part of at the beginning of an imminent gunbattle ... absolutely nothing! We roared past each other without making a move. We barely dared to look at them and they hardly looked sideways at us. As I watched for the glow of brakelights I knew they were doing the same, but they just faded in the rear-view mirror. I held my breath for the reappearance of the car with the windows down and all guns blazing. Nothing.

I glanced around the car but no one said anything and I thought I'll be damned if I'm the first to do it. It was as if we all immediately came to some mutual understanding: that we realized it was somehow a negligence of duty not to engage the gunmen, so it was best not to mention it at all. A similar feeling must have passed between them as well. Like an instinctive, common consent to let this one pass; as if we were all saying, 'Look, we both know why we're here – no point turning an ordinary reccie mission into a double slaughter.'

Which, in a way, was true. We considered this a fact-finding mission rather than a proactive sortie. The other mob were obviously a tooled-up Provo ASU scouting the area as some kind of advance protection unit for the cortège. No telling now who would have come off worse if we had got into a Bonnie-and-Clyde style firefight. I think our arms training would have given us the edge but if both sides had been wiped out I think the damage to army intelligence would have been greater than that to the IRA. As well as the two int officers, if Robert and I had been taken out the loss of our combined intelligence knowledge would have meant more than the deaths of a few foot-soldiers to the IRA.

I looked over at Robert and he gave me that knowing half-smile I'd become familiar with. We knew we had just sailed perilously close to the wind. Some mysterious collusion had occurred between us and them back there. It was significant to me because it was one of the rare occasions when I was forced to acknowledge some kind of shared humanity between myself and the enemy. It was so easy to dehumanize them, in fact it was absolutely essential for a soldier to do that to enable him to do his job. But we had just had an insight into the equally fearful hearts that beat inside them, too. We had all been linked by the same fear.

It reminded me of the stories I'd heard of the unofficial Christmas truce that occurred in the trenches during the First World War when British and German troops refused to shoot at each other. I guess by that time they were all equally exhausted by the scale of death they had witnessed.

What had just happened was a one-off, though; I knew that. If we happened to pass again, things would be different the second time around. Then we would be just a bunch of murdering bastards to them, and they would be the same to us.

Still, I'd never experienced anything quite like this before. I think there was also an element of male pride involved for all concerned. No one liked to think that he was the one who should have said something. And that's all it would have taken: for just one man out of the whole shebang to make a move. That would have been the whistle to a big and bloody kick-off. No doubt about it, it could only be described in one phrase: un-fucking-believable.

We carried on until we reached the Keady checkpoint and caught first sight of the procession. It was bigger than I'd expected, four or five cars behind the hearse. It confirmed my earlier opinion that it would have been difficult and foolish for them to attempt an illegal crossing elsewhere.

I wound down my window to get a clearer view. The sun had broken through now but it was still bitterly cold and my breath smoked out before me. My lungs filled with the scent of grass. We looked down from the rise of the hill we had stopped upon. The roof of the hearse shined like water as it crawled into the checkpoint. A heat haze wobbled off the engine. I looked up at a noise and saw the fat bulb of the brigadier's helicopter holding itself above the scene below. Its surveillance cameras would be zooming in to record faces and vehicle registrations. After my success at the Aughnacloy border with the hidden camera, the idea had been taken up at the Keady checkpoint. I knew those cameras would be operating, too.

In many ways it was just another standard operation but there was an air of solemnity about the whole proceedings. They were bringing home one of their dead. It was still a rare occurrence for such a high-ranking IRA man to be taken out so we were out in force to bear witness, partly out of further intelligence gathering duty and partly, if the truth be told, in celebration.

We got back to Aughnacloy without any more incident. I even snapped the radio back on in relief and then quickly turned it off again when I heard the same blare of God-awful music.

In my office, Robert settled down for a coffee before he was due to leave. 'That was a close call,' he said to me. 'But I knew it was too good to be true. I get the feeling there's always some element of unexpected danger about your missions, Nicky.' It was a sign of the man that he meant it as a compliment.

'Isn't there always that risk?' I said. He just nodded. The risk was an important part to him, that much I knew by now.

I decided to test the waters with him about the killing of Benny Green. I didn't know if the whispers of his involvement were just of the Chinese variety, twisted in their travels beyond anything recognizably true.

I said something like how it had been a good day's work by whoever had done the job and he just nodded and agreed. Then he looked at me with more than simple expectation of the next question, but with what looked like encouragement, too. It was the sign for me to jump in with both feet.

'I'd heard that you were involved in it, along with the SAS.'

He pressed his fingertips together in a cathedral arch, on which he rested his chin. 'I don't doubt, Nicky, that you've heard such a thing, but you and I have both heard a lot of things in our time here. And no doubt we will hear a lot more.'

It was neither a denial nor an admission but I realized it was all I was going to get. He continued to look at me over his fingers but his eyes betrayed nothing either way. His face was as impenetrable as his answer.

Was he cautiously admitting his involvement but in a way as not to compromise himself completely? Or was he just knowingly planting that thought in me as a way of further bolstering his own reputation – an act of bravado? Maybe this is how the whispers had started in the first place, through Nairac's own carefully worded hints. I didn't mention the fact that I'd already been told outright of his liaising with the SAS by Jack Marshall's 2IC at Brigade HQ on that first occasion I'd seen Nairac. Or that there was also a widely held belief that he supplied information to the UVF and UDA, enabling them to take out Provos. Perhaps this was the route that had led to the killing of Benny Green.

I thought of that time a few months earlier when I'd let Nairac through the Aughnacloy checkpoint. I still hadn't learned of the nature of that trip south of the border. Had this been a reconnaissance mission as the prelude to Green's death? I was only sure of one thing: every answer threw up another half-dozen questions.

It seemed to me there was a side of him that secretly yearned for recognition for the undoubtedly brave and clever way in which he operated; wider recognition than that already given to him by the very select few who were privy to the whole truth of what he actually did here. During a previous briefing, when Nairac's name was mentioned, I'd already overheard another int officer say, 'He thinks he's Lawrence of bloody Arabia!' I now knew enough to know he would take that as a compliment.

He rose and we shook hands, and wished each other further luck of the kind we had experienced today.

The truce was now well and truly over. All manner of things had brought it down: the increasingly unworkable demands of the IRA; the growing wave of hunger-strike protests by IRA prisoners; and the accusations of 'dirty tricks' and 'shoot to kill', all resulting in the inevitable slide back into shootings and bombings. The truce had also been weakened by the fact that its very existence sparked off fear amongst Loyalist groups of some political power-sharing deal which could lead to a British withdrawal and leave them out in the cold. They responded by dispatching their own bomb- and bullet-happy death squads.

You could also throw into this mix the vicious in-fighting between the two main Loyalist terrorist groups, the UDA and UVF, and the feuding between Republican factions. There was only one conclusion that could be drawn: murder was in no danger of going out of fashion. In the Troubles, peace and understanding were the only commodities in short supply.

My own greatest personal and operational success came some

weeks later, one Sunday, when a coach approached the checkpoint on its way south. While in the north drinking traditionally came to a halt on Sunday, the southern bars observed no day of rest. The coach was more than likely on its way down to the Four Seasons in Monaghan.

Scanning the faces of the forty or so people on board, I recognized one woman as a prominent Sinn Fein councillor. Trying not to arouse suspicion, I got her taken off with the first half-dozen due to be searched in the holding area. Their luggage was searched separately. In the councillor's bag a WRAC found a diary and was smart enough to realize its importance. She immediately brought it to me and as I flicked through it I couldn't believe our luck. It was like a *Who's Who* of Sinn Fein: addresses and phone numbers of everyone from high-ranking officials to well-known Republican sympathizers.

This was a vitally important document of the people behind the political activism, and these politics were what drove the ground forces of the IRA: the organ grinders behind the monkeys.

I knew I had to get it copied, but the nearest copier was back in Aughnacloy. I left instructions for the searches to be conducted as slowly as possible and sprinted up to the village.

I had to go through the laborious process of opening the diary at every page and flattening it to the copier's screen. I worked quickly, knowing I was racing against the ongoing searches. I got back down to the checkpoint breathless but ecstatic to find the final searches were just being completed. The WRAC slipped the diary back in the bag.

The boys had done a really good job of conducting the searches at a snail's pace while also stripping down the bus under the pretence of searching for weapons. Trouble is, they'd done too good a job and now couldn't put some of the bloody bus back together. The bits lay on the ground as they stood around scratching their heads like puzzled scientists wondering where they'd gone wrong. We called in some local mechanics to throw it all back together and the coach finally chugged away. We weren't too fussed if it broke down and left them stranded as long as they got away from here.

Still on a high, I immediately typed up a military intelligence source report (or MISER) in my usual manner: slowly and badly. In all my time of typing-up reports I had only improved in one area: how to make more mistakes per minute. Eventually I telexed off the

MISER to Int HQ. I knew it was dynamite stuff so I just sat back and waited to hear the bang.

It wasn't long coming. HQ were overjoyed with what they received. All the top intelligence officers came down to the border to see me for a back-slapping session. They arrived with all the fanfare and attendant security of a royal visit. They asked if there was anything I needed.

This was the opportunity I'd been waiting for. I reeled off a list as long as both arms: brand-new high-tech cameras, my own photo-copier (running into the village was a farce) and a landline telephone, which unbelievably I didn't have. All we had was an old 'ringer'-type phone like those they used in the trenches. I had to turn a bloody handle on it to charge the damn thing up.

'In fact,' I said to them, 'why don't we just rebuild the whole checkpoint?'

I felt I was pushing it, to say the least, with this last request. The visiting colonel was standing before me, surrounded by his minions. Without hesitation he turned to them and said, 'Give Sergeant Curtis anything he wants.'

I tried to remain composed even though inside I was thinking it was like scoring at Wembley.

Within a short time the checkpoint was totally transformed. The most significant change was the construction of a 'Dutch barn'. This was a sideless structure with a large, high roof supported on pillars, something like a modern petrol station. Now, at night, the place was ablaze with light.

The secretary of state for Northern Ireland, Merlyn Rees, came down for the official grand opening and to put his face about and blah-blah-blah to the press. He came over to me and we got on great. He even invited me to dinner. Never one to pass up on a free lunch I went to it and when I returned all the other officers started calling me D'Arcy because I'd been hob-nobbing with the top brass.

After all this HQ really did think I was the dog's danglers. I was promoted by appointment (rather than rank) to take over the battalion intelligence in Dungannon. Rank promotion didn't really bother me too much. It wouldn't have enabled me to do much more than I was doing already. Anyway, all the higher-ranking officers now relied on me. This felt so good. I knew if my old gang back in the Green Howards had known of this they would have cheered me on.

Essentially, I still felt like a front-liner at heart who had managed to claw his way up the pecking order. Although I was a sergeant now I still felt I was fighting what I'd previously thought of as 'a corporals' war'. The essence of that still rang true. But now I couldn't be ordered about by some wanker like that Ops officer back at the mill. At least my position had been earned and not given. It reminded me of one of my dad's favourite phrases when he thought some of his coal pit's management had screwed up: 'Some a them an't got t'sense they were born wit'.'

I thought my old man would be proud of me now. I felt quite proud of myself, too. I only had to think of the men I'd lost in the Ardoyne, which I did often, for it to strengthen my resolve not to waste this position of power I had.

Just prior to leaving, as I lay in my caravan at night being buffeted by another helicopter take-off, I marvelled at how a bit of balls and a little common sense could take you far.

11

DEEPER AND DOWN

I moved to take over the LINCO's post at Dungannon. This was in East Tyrone, thirty miles north-east of Aughnacloy and in the middle of the Murder Triangle. Sectarian and paramilitary killings here had reached atrocious levels. This was where the blood and snot really flew wild. The area spanned East Tyrone and also Armagh, including the south of Armagh which crossed the border.

This was real bandit country. The IRA's interrogation and execution squads were based here. The open countryside was far more difficult to police than streets of heavily populated urban areas covered by the security forces. Down here there were few, if any, witnesses to the IRA's actions. In a remote farmhouse, for example, they had all the time in the world to torture someone at their leisure with little fear of discovery. Sometimes these sessions went on for days before the victim was finally executed, his body found in a ditch and his wife finally informed that she was now a widow and her children fatherless.

The IRA's hypocrisy over these matters was as stark as the blood on a butcher's apron, and stank as much. At the same time as they were demanding fair trials and conventional war status for their members, and the civil rights and Geneva Convention protection that went with this, they were also stripping men down to their underwear to be tortured before shooting them in fields like dogs. One of the most astonishing things (which would have been laughable if it wasn't so disgusting) was that after an execution committed on a Saturday the killers would often attend mass the next morning. Did God still take their prayers, knowing they were bathed in blood? Did the priests ever take confessions to these acts? It would take a man of stronger faith than I ever had to listen to such a confession and then not act on it because of the belief in some higher retribution. I had no intention of waiting around to see if any of these men ended up on Hell's guest list – a life sentence in prison would do just fine, for the time being.

My job here was to take over existing sources, run them and find more whilst also linking all the separate intelligence units.

This time I was given a room of my own rather than a caravan. At least I knew when I bedded down at night I wouldn't wake up the next morning twenty feet from where I'd fallen asleep.

My promotion had been for two reasons: one, because of my successes at Aughnacloy; and, two, because of the cock-up made by a previous int officer, Sergeant Tony Poole, in Dungannon. Poole, a field int NCO like myself, was intelligent enough but, in common with some of the int officers, wasn't exactly blessed with 'street' savvy. He had dropped a bollock of such magnitude that when I heard about it I couldn't quite believe it. He had recruited and developed a seventeen-year-old lad called McVeigh as a source. His task was to infiltrate the IRA meetings at a well-known pub down in Monaghan and discover the Republicans' north/south escape routes. These were the routes that terrorists who had been wounded in the north would take down south to enable them to receive medical treatment before returning to active duty. Taking them to a doctor or hospital in the north was too high a security risk. The escape route was only used for members of great importance to the IRA; their ordinary foot-soldiers would be left in the north to their own devices. The location of the routes had been sought by everyone in intelligence since we first learned of it. We knew if we found them we had the chance to get some of the big-time boys after they'd been winged in a gunbattle. The escape routes were intelligence's Holy Grail.

The source was graded A1 because of his importance and given the codename 'Hot Dog'. The plan was for McVeigh to plant ammo in his own house that would be found the next day by troops and the RUC. This gave him a justifiable reason to flee south and seek sanctuary at the Four Seasons, saying he was 'on the run'. From there he would develop a role within the IRA and supply information.

Initially it all went to plan. His house was searched, the ammo was found in the appointed place, a warrant was issued for his arrest and he fled south. Where it all fell apart, as I could have told them it would if I'd been in on it, was that the Provos immediately suspected his story. The IRA were vicious, not stupid. I never underestimated their savvy. They knew that if he had been involved enough to have weapons and ammo in his house then they would have already known about him. And they didn't. So they beat the crap out of him and got the truth. Hot Dog had now flipped from the frying pan right into the frigging fire.

We always knew when we found someone's body if they had been killed for being a source. The IRA murdered them with a ceremonial deliberation to let us know that they knew. The guy would be shot in the mouth and a pound note stuffed in the hole, plugging his silence for ever. It was an extremely crass and very literal interpretation of 'blood money' but you didn't get any brownie points for subtle hints. Sometimes, if they were feeling particularly creative, they'd nail the poor bastard to the floor as well.

McVeigh was obviously far too young to attempt to carry off such a cover. Most seventeen-year-olds still stutter when having to lie to their fathers let alone when faced with a group of terrorist hardmen staring them down. But he got lucky. His captors decided he would be worth more to them as a propaganda tool than as fertilizer in a local field. He was dispatched back north to confess his sins to a priest, Father Faul. This was a very clever move.

He immediately went public. His denunciation of what he called, 'the British army's use of innocent civilians in the dirty war' was widely reported in the press. Sergeant Poole had foolishly told McVeigh not only his rank but his real name. This was the most elementary mistake you could make when dealing with a source. He was named by Father Faul in his pronouncements, and you can hardly work undercover if every man-jack and his mother's dog knows who you are. So Poole had to go.

This is where I came in. I was to control the regimental int boys. My first job was to contact and re-establish the sources in the area, most of whom had been neglected over the months: some of them had been contacted so little they thought their job was over. I decided it was time to pay them a call, let them know they had a new handler and remind them how pleasant it must be for them to wake up every morning not staring at a prison cell wall.

One method was to lift twenty or so men from their homes and bring them in for 'screening'. Out of these twenty there would be perhaps only one (or, at the most, two) who were old sources. We lifted them among a group so as not to arouse suspicion of them in particular. I told them that Poole was gone, I was their new handler now and I expected results. They each knew me by a different name so that when they called the barracks, and their call bypassed the main switchboard to come directly to my office, I knew exactly which source it was by what they called me – 'Tom', 'Dick', 'Harry', or whatever.

Another way was to put a vehicle checkpoint near a guy's house on the day he was due to sign on at the dole office, as a good portion of Northern Ireland's menfolk regularly had to do. We'd check everyone coming through (again so as not to compromise the source by singling him out) and I would wait in the back of a Land-Rover. When our target came through the checkpoint he'd be thrown in the back of the truck with me. Sometimes they refused to carry on with the task. I'd point out how a leaflet-drop from a helicopter with details of their previous activities could easily be arranged. The threat of being revealed as a 'grass' usually turned them back to us. They must have felt like they'd joined the bloody Mafia – once you're in, you're in.

You have to be as hard as the people you're fighting. I'd already run into guys who took pleasure in cruelty. I didn't want myself or any of the ground forces I felt responsible for protecting to end up looking down the business end of a burial service just because I hadn't done my job properly. So the hard line with the sources was 'Cough-up or we'll cough you back out into the community you've betrayed.' The truth was that a source got precious little respect even from the people he was giving information to.

The method of getting them as they were going to sign on was a difficult one to swing. Obviously, we couldn't put checkpoints everywhere in the hope of getting the right guy at the right time, so we needed an 'in'. Mine was Heather.

My and the other int officers' social lives revolved around either the barrack's mess (which was boring) or local Protestant bars and discos (which weren't and, being Prod-run, were safe). Dungannon was broadly split into two areas by Irish Street, which was, logically enough, Provo land, and Scotch Street, which was Protestant.

It was at one of these discos that I became friends with Heather. In situations like this soldiers often ended up copping-off with local girls. There were even such things as squaddie groupies, believe it or not. But there was never any romance between me and her. Like the rest of the lads I had brutally simple tastes: a pretty face and fine pair of pins just about covered it. And Heather, lovely woman though she was, wasn't exactly pretty. She struggled to make the grade as plain, in fact. One of the lads cruelly described her as having 'a face like a slapped arse and an arse like a butcher's fridge'.

Anyway, we got on with her and her female friends and, after we felt we could trust them, ended up going to parties at their homes. One of her friends was Catholic so we had to be sure we didn't get into anything we couldn't get out of. We were aware of the Provos' history of using 'honeytraps'. This was when their female members tempted squaddies to their deaths with promises of sex. It was an age-old counter-intelligence ploy, probably as old as war itself. This is how the three off-duty Scots soldiers had been led to their deaths. And more after them. Even after it became known that this was happening, some of the lads would still fall prey. I guess one thing that was still difficult for men to fight was the light-headedness resulting from blood fleeing their brains in order to support a stonking hard-on.

In order to justify us going to these parties I'd put Heather and her friends down as sources, but only 'numbered' sources, not 'named'. I didn't want to endanger them. I'd make up some crap when I got back to the int office like, 'Source 12 says Prod feelings running high after last Provo bombings.' In fact, their label as sources eventually became true. It was from Heather, a junior ranking civil servant, that we gleaned the info on sources' and suspects' signing-on times. She didn't have to do any of this but she did, but only to a certain extent. Being what we in Yorkshire would call 'on the bonny side' or big, in other words, she wasn't exactly overwhelmed with male attention. I thought a little pillow talk might yield some more results. I informed one of my int sergeants, Dave Shaw, of the plan. Now Dave wasn't known for being particularly choosy. It was said he'd shag an infirm Alsatian if it paused too long. In fact, he cast his net so wide we started calling him 'Trawler'. But even Dave blanched at my idea.

'Oh, no. Not me. Why me?'

'She's always had an eye for you,' I explained. 'Think of it as your duty. Anyway, you're not called Trawler for nothing. You've got a reputation to uphold!'

'Yeah, but this is the kind of thing that can ruin a man's reputation, Nicky. Anyway, trawlers don't catch fucking whales! So fuck off!'

I gently pointed out how easily I could transfer him from this job, which I knew he liked, into something far nastier or, even worse, boring. He reluctantly agreed. He couldn't do anything else.

And so the Great Heather and Dave Love Saga began. Because of his comment about whales, he soon had a new nickname – Captain Ahab. He'd return the next morning after another info-gathering/love session to our cries of 'Thar she blows!' and 'Been roaming in the Heather again, Dave?' But, like they say, war is hell.

Around this time I also became reacquainted with Robert Nairac. From time to time he would visit me in Dungannon with other 14 Int boys and ask me about a particular person's movements or for my help in tracking them. Or he'd be on a reccie in the area and call to let me know so we didn't compromise his position. A G2 Int boy would always contact me beforehand and forewarn me: 'Give Robert anything he asks for.' It felt like I was expecting royalty. I had picked up more about him since the last time we met when he'd come through the Aughnacloy checkpoint and the more I learned the less the 'royalty' tag seemed like a joke. He really seemed to be considered the 'kingpin' of undercover ops: intelligence's golden boy.

He was an ex-Grenadier Guardsman and regimental boxing champ; ex-public school, too, but hard with it. After joining the army he must have been an obvious natural for intelligence. He was part of the SAS-trained 14th Intelligence who spread their men out into other regular regiments which acted as a cover for their real role. Nairac's guise was as commander of 4 Field Survey Troop, which provided maps and aerial photos.

On his first visit we sat in my office talking. He was clean-shaven now. The beard he'd grown earlier for the cross-border reccie had obviously been part of a disguise. We talked about things but he'd never really revealed to me exactly what he was doing or why. He still reminded me of Chris, though Nairac's confidence, unlike Chris's, was tinged with arrogance. I didn't mind this, though; I'd found that arrogant, difficult men were usually the most interesting.

He knew I'd been decorated and eagerly asked me about the gunbattles in the Ardoyne. I knew he'd served a tour over here but in common with most of the thousands of other soldiers he hadn't really seen any action. It was odd, here I was trying to find out about him and all he was interested in was talking about me. I suppose we were both equally bored with repeating tales of our own experiences and wanted to thrill to someone else's. It was also a good way of him avoiding revealing too much about himself. But there was another reason behind his questions. I think when he knew I'd been through the mill, and seen some hard times and survived them, he knew he was safe with me. And that told me that he was a switched-on operator because I knew that just one of the many fears of undercover work was of someone else's incompetence blowing you out of the water. No king's reign would last long surrounded by court jesters.

I mentioned the time I'd passed him through the Aughnacloy checkpoint but knew better than to press for details of the mission. He just nodded and then gave me a demonstration of his ability to adopt different Irish dialects: from a hard Belfast accent to the softer Derry brogue. This was a bloody difficult thing to do. The Irish could usually spot a stranger or a 'faker' within seconds, particularly in the more isolated provinces where unknown faces were treated with intense suspicion. I think his Irish background stood him in good stead on this score. His mother was Protestant and his father Catholic. Like me, he had been raised as a devout Catholic and, again like me, he had gone through the same feelings upon landing in Northern Ireland for the first time, his knowledge of the conflict's history giving him the belief he might be able to do some good.

I found that despite the obvious differences between us of class and rank we had far more in common. He had that kind of savvy and natural, in-built bullshit-detector that was universal to all good soldiers. I was pleased by this. It was gratifying to meet someone who deserved the respect they were given.

One day I got the usual call informing me of his imminent arrival. We were to go out on a daylight reconnaissance mission. Myself, Nairac and two others in support drove out to case the farmhouse of a suspected Provo. Robert was going to return later to break into the house and search for evidence. I took a Cortina out of the pool of cars we had to choose from and we drove out of Tyrone and into County Armagh. We were all in civvies, of course, and in a civilian car, but there was still the risk of us being suspected and challenged. There was a lawlessness in these areas that was far more difficult to control and police than on the city streets. We were tooled up to the eye-teeth, each of us with a handgun in a waist-band or shoulder holster. The boys in the back had Uzi machine-guns on the floor.

We passed the farmhouse and pulled over. Robert made some notes and pretty soon we left. We couldn't afford to hang around too long and risk arousing suspicion.

Not far from the farmhouse, as we drove back, I noticed that the petrol gauge was red-lining. I cursed whichever daft sod had taken the car out before me and had forgotten to fill it up when he got back. We could be in real trouble now – deep in the middle of hostile territory and possibly about to run out of juice. By now the light of the sky was already beginning to dim and glimmer with evening dark. Storm clouds were moving in. The empty road and wide surrounding fields looked desolate and lonely. But this didn't reassure me that we couldn't be rumbled. It would only take one passing car or a suspicious local to make a quick call for a nearby hit-squad to descend on us. Through the rear-view mirror I could see the lads in the back getting twitchy. I knew that, like me, everyone else had now suddenly become much more aware of the comforting weight of the weapons they were carrying, but none of us relished the idea of becoming engaged in a running gunbattle.

From my knowledge of the area, I knew there was a small petrol station not too far from here if we could manage to reach it. I also knew it was run by a notorious local family, the Gurneys. They were a large clan of real bad-to-the-bone boys, most of whom we had down as suspected Provos. Their farmhouse was a few miles from the station and I'd already come down here on a reccie and entered the building looking for evidence. Breaking-and-entering missions in rural areas differed from those in urban ones because it usually involved no 'breaking', just 'entering'. Down here it was like England in the 1940s and 1950s when people felt safe enough to leave their doors open.

On the previous occasion, I hadn't found anything more incriminating than the usual Republican paraphernalia, including a picture of Michael Collins taking pride of place in the living room. Their family-run petrol station wasn't exactly the ideal place for us to stop, but we had little choice.

I drove on, eye-balling the gauge as much as I did the road – as if this would miraculously change the reading. We reached the crest of a hill, rounded the next big, slow bend and breathed easier when the petrol station finally came into view. It was a ramshackle affair of rusty, swinging signs and old Shell Oil stickers, but right now it looked like a little bit of heaven dropped down on Irish earth.

I bumped the car over the pot-holes of what passed for the forecourt and Old Man Gurney himself came out of the cabin in his overalls. He was frowning slightly. I could almost see a question mark pop out and bob above his head in a cartoon balloon. I let

Robert do the honours. He stepped out smiling and addressed Gurney in a faultless Armagh accent: 'Fill her up.' Through the open passenger door I heard the old man say they had run out of petrol. That's obvious bollocks, I thought, he's fucking sussed us. Nairac tried to make the best of it.

'Aw, com'on! You must have. We're nearly out. My ole lady'll fuckin' kill me if we get stuck down here!'

Sat in the car, we tried to look nonchalant but it was pretty near impossible. While Nairac was trying to talk the guy around I saw Old Man Gurney turn to the cabin and nod slightly. I looked to the cabin. The young woman inside disappeared into the back. I saw the telephone wires leading to the cabin. That's it – enough of this crap. I said, 'Get ready!' to the guys in the back and slid across the passenger seat, pulling the Browning out of my waistband. I jumped out, spun Gurney around, cutting him off in mid-ramble, shoved him against the car and jammed the 9mm into his neck. I spoke quietly into his ear, 'Fill her up you lying, old bastard before I blow your fucking head off.'

He stared at me hard but for only a second before his resolve crumbled. He moved to the pump. Robert moved to the open passenger door but remained standing, looking around at both ends of the road. I noticed the boys in the back had pulled the Uzis up off the floor into their laps and heard the *chuk-chuk* noise as they armed them. The old pump clicked round slowly. I kept the gun on the old fart and darted a glance at the cabin: no one there. She was still in the back on the phone, or maybe laid out on the floor for safety. Robert got in and started the car even as it was still being filled. It seemed to take for ever, but I knew hardly any time had passed before we heard the first sound of another engine. It was going fast, revving hard. I turned and saw a black car rounding the bend, keeling on its suspension with the speed. I turned back to see Gurney fleeing, already halfway to the cabin. The other car veered off the road and skidded on to the forecourt, its passenger doors already opening. Robert was gunning the engine now. I jumped in through the passenger door and he screeched us away. The acceleration slammed the door for me. The pump was still in the car. The tube drew taut and as we reached its length I heard it wrench and snap. I turned and saw it whip around the forecourt, spraying petrol everywhere. We pulled out just ahead of the black car and swerved wildly back on to the road, clipped the farside hedge and sped away, trailing leaves and smoke. The car flew out after us and loomed up in my wing-mirror. They gained on us with the gathered momentum of their run-in. We tried to build up speed. I turned and could clearly see their faces. They were such a fierce-looking bunch of bastards that there was no doubt who they were – a nearby Provo ASU tipped off by the girl in the cabin. Luckily their car was no faster than ours and we gradually began to pull ahead, but only because Robert was taking more risks on the corners than the driver behind, throwing the car through the curve with an abandon that would either save us or turn us over. He screwed the arse off the Cortina until the car behind started to fade away. The chase had been given up.

We didn't let up the pace for a few miles until we were sure we had lost them. We pulled over when I saw that the petrol pump nozzle was still lodged in the car's side, stuck out like a dagger. I jumped out and flung it into a field. On the way back Robert turned to me, smiling, and in reference to my treatment of Gurney said, 'So which charm school for advanced etiquette did you attend?'

As by now I was aware of his own reputation, I replied, 'Probably the same one as you.'

I eased back into the seat. I noticed Nairac's eyes in the rear-view mirror, narrowed slightly by a half-smile. I understood. You never planned near-misses or narrow escapes but when they did happen and you got away, you couldn't help but get off on the excitement. We didn't fully relax until we crossed into County Tyrone and neared Dungannon. I made a mental note that the first thing I'd do was check the log book to find out who had used the Cortina before us.

I carried on establishing and milking sources. By now, after the work I'd done at Aughnacloy border, I had a reputation with the int boys above me for producing the goods. They expected more. HQ were even greedier for information than when I'd been on the streets.

It was less hand-to-hand combat now than out-and-out covert counter-insurgency. And the agencies begging for usable information (sometimes even fighting amongst themselves for it) were many and varied – army intelligence, army undercover units, IRD (Information Research Department), MI6 – SIS (Secret Intelligence Service), MI5, and the RUC and RUC Special Branch. They all spun an interconnected web in which, it was hoped, they would catch their prey. We'd long since learned our lesson from the disastrous internment operation which had failed because the intelligence information was either too old or just plain inaccurate. That was the first of what I considered to be the two major bollocks that we'd dropped; the other one being Bloody Sunday. The natural human reaction to being pushed too hard was to push back harder.

One of the problems, though, was the lack of trust and cooperation between our own agencies. The armed Northern Irish police force, the RUC, resented the army moving in and taking over despite the fact that we'd originally had to go in because the RUC were badly trained, understrength and overwhelmed by the emerging conflict. And the RUC Special Branch boys thought the war was theirs and also resented our involvement. Then there was the Ulster Defence Regiment (UDR) – a local Protestant volunteer force, although they were under the overall control of a regular British army officer. Finally, there was little love lost between MI5 and MI6. MI5 were responsible for 'internal' security and as Northern Ireland was British they claimed it was their area. MI6, on the other hand, were the 'external' security service who had their fingers in all foreign pies (from Russia to Cuba) and, as the IRA had their HQs in the south of Ireland, MI6 counted this as 'abroad' and under their jurisdiction.

In fact, the nickname that we all used for MI5, 'Box 5', had come about through a much earlier split in the intelligence services. During the Second World War MI5 was formed to handle internal security. After the war ended they were housed in London in the same government building as MI6. In order to differentiate between the mail for MI6 and MI5 two mailboxes were created for sorting purposes; hence, 'Box 5', 'Box 6'. You could always tell pukka security forces personnel by their use of these references.

Anyway, whatever name the organizations went by, everyone seemed pretty loath to do anyone else any favours. So all the threads of the security web would quiver their information back to central HQ but not necessarily communicate with each other. Each squad would jealously guard its own sources and information.

The UDR, in particular, could not be trusted by the rest. It was comprised entirely of Protestants with Loyalist sympathies, some of whom were either members of the UVF or had family members who were. So if I had sent a MISER with information naming suspected Provo members to the UDR, I could lay good odds on them passing it straight on to the UVF boys who would then use it to plan a hit or plant a bomb. Often the MISERs would only contain as-yet-unconfirmed suspicions that still needed to be verified, but to the UDR and UVF 'suspicion' of being a Provo was enough. These suspicions were sparks to tinder and were already responsible for the explosion of assassinations within the Murder Triangle.

Often a whispering campaign against someone in the area (sometimes without foundation) would escalate into a succession of violent acts. On the strength of these suspicions a guy would be shot or, if he couldn't be tracked down, his brother or father would be done in his place. Retribution for this act would then follow, and on and on. For every man, woman and child killed there would be family and friends crying out in the wings for justice. And revenge was considered 'justice in action'.

In truth the area wasn't as overrun with Provos as the number of acts that were committed led many to believe. The IRA didn't take just anyone into the fold. They were far more select in their recruitment of members because of the risks to their security by taking someone untrustworthy or not fully committed to their cause. It only needed a handful of ASUs operating in an area to do a lot of damage.

In light of all this, the fortnightly, Monday-night int meetings we had at the UDR centre in Dungannon were pretty farcical. In attendance would be Big Sid (all six foot four of him) from Special Branch; Raymond, a detective constable with the RUC CID; Jack Marshall, my field controller; George Jackson, chief inspector of the RUC in Dungannon; various odd-ball RUC Special Branch officers; the major of the UDR, Ken Maginnes; and myself, the one who linked them all. All in all, with these representatives of the security forces present and correct, you would think it a recipe for successful information exchange. Wrong.

For a start, we could take full advantage of the free bar in the officers' mess. Second, conflicting interests, jealousy and sheer bloody-mindedness between the different branches led to no bugger giving away anything he didn't have to. Big Sid and I were in both the best and worst positions. We were the only two around the table who really knew what was going on and were determined to hang on to our own info. Jack and I felt that on occasion we couldn't give too much information away for fear of it inadvertently landing in the wrong hands.

Maginnes always chaired the meeting, sat at the head of the large mahogany table like an unelected king. After the rest had thrown in their two-penneth-worth of low-grade info Ken would finally come into the fray. He would give me a report on Paddy

What's-'is-face supposedly being involved in this, that or the other.

This was when one of two things could happen; I could say I had nothing and end up looking like an uninformed idiot (which didn't exactly sit well with me being in intelligence to begin with) or give them the full chapter and verse on what I knew. This option would be more flattering to me personally – no one likes to look like they don't know what's going on – but potentially far more damaging to the area. So I'd strike a balance between the two, always erring on the side of caution, and give them info which I knew they already had or that wasn't of any real importance.

At one meeting things went as per usual. Maginnes looked at me expectantly and said, 'So, LINCO, what have you got for us?'

Here we go, I thought, another test of my ability to talk a lot while saying bugger all. 'Well,' I began, 'the latest source report says that the guy we suspect of being the second in command of the Coalisland boys has stopped drinking in his usual bar and moved to another nearer the border. Significant this, I think,' I lied, 'because it throws up the possibility of the ASU widening their area. Maybe thinking of some kind of border crossing.'

Maginnes nodded seriously. 'Yeah, that guy's a bad bastard all right. Keep an eye on it.'

At this point Jack and I avoided making any eye contact for fear of bursting out laughing because the standing joke between us was that, to Maginnes, every Catholic from the Pope down was a 'bad bastard'.

One time I actually brought up the subject. I turned to Maginnes and said that I'd been keeping count of all his mentions of so-called 'bad bastards' and so far it was around the four hundred mark. In their dreams the IRA wished they had that many members in the area.

But Maginnes wasn't an idiot. He knew what I was doing but couldn't do any more than complain about it behind my back. To be honest, I didn't give a flying tu'penny fuck.

I'd send my MISERs to HQ in Lurgan from where they would be sent to HQ, Lisburn. If it was crack-on info from an A1 source, Lisburn would then send their own report headed 'FOR UK EYES ONLY', meaning it was only accessible to our own security forces: MI5, MI6 or army intelligence. This was especially important if the info was on Loyalist terrorists. We didn't want them to be fore-warned by bodies sympathetic to their actions.

Intelligence had their own branch called G3 who specialized in information gathering on the Loyalist terrorists. To begin with, this info didn't really bother me because the Prods weren't shooting us; they were only targeting the Provos who *were* shooting us. As sectarian killings increased, however, and threatened to destabilize the whole area, we began to take more interest. Army intelligence's Special Branch had operatives from 4 Troop (Robert Nairac's boys) keeping the Protestant paramilitaries under surveillance. At times I felt like I needed to be permanently in a helicopter just to keep above the rising tide of bluff, blame and bullshit.

One day I got a call through to attend a big intelligence briefing at Command HQ in Lisburn. Anyone who was anyone in int was going to be there. I prepared myself for the announcement of some big, new battle plan or revelations of such importance they could only be relayed in person.

I travelled up with other officers from Dungannon. Figures from all brigade areas were there – LINCOs and FINCOs (Field Intelligence Non-Commissioned Officer) from Armagh, Bessbrook, Belfast and so on; British army intelligence boys; and any other operatives who needed to be in the know. We assembled, fifty or sixty of us, in the Lisburn barracks' cinema, which doubled as a conference/lecture centre, sat down and waited with an air of anticipation.

Presently, a G2 int officer entered and introduced the man with him as a fellow intelligence operative. This guy was in his forties and wearing a three-piece pinstripe suit with matching Paisley tie and top-pocket handkerchief, which flopped as he moved to sit down. His waistcoat carried a fob-watch with dangling silver chain. I thought, This guy looks like one of the biggest Hooray Henrys ever to draw breath but, then again, he may be more switched-on than his appearance suggests.

He crossed one pinstriped leg over the other and began: 'OK, chaps. I'm here today to address you on the subject of source recruitment and intelligence information gathering. As you are probably already aware, the unearthing of accurate and usable information . . .' at which point he paused for effect and scanned us with his eyes '. . . is of paramount importance. To this end you should go about it thus . . .'

He then proceeded to spew out more crap than a backed-up shit-house drain. My heart slowly sank and the benefit of the doubt we'd all given him flew straight out of the window. His idea on how we should 'go about it thus' was particularly priceless. We were to inform troops on the streets to sidle up to the local folk in their area and 'start chatting to them' (you know, just like you do when you're viewed as an oppressive invading force) and then 'try to win them over' with gems such as, 'Wouldn't you like to help bring an end to this terrible conflict?' Little matter that a lot of them were already trying to bring an end to it in their own fashion by shooting and bombing anything that didn't wag a tail.

He carried on in this manner, seemingly unaware of the waves of disbelief that I could feel coming from everyone else. Around me there were so many shoulders sagging I thought the room was being pumped with sleeping gas.

I couldn't quite believe it. I thought, The distance between this guy and reality is big enough to sail the *Titanic* through towing the fucking iceberg behind it. It also occurred to me how appropriate this seafaring image was – time for a little mutiny. When, finally, I'd had enough, I raised my hand. 'I'd like to ask a question?' I said.

'Certainly,' he said, looking eager to respond. 'But first may I ask who you are?'

'Sergeant Nicholas Curtis MM, liaison intelligence non-commissioned officer for Dungannon,' I replied, deliberately giving him my full title with the gong added on for effect. I didn't want this arsehole to think he could carry on talking down to me.

'And your question, Sergeant Curtis?'

'Quite simple really. I was just wondering exactly who the fuck *you* are?'

He paused, startled, and then began waffling in vague terms. 'Let's just say I'm in the security forces.'

'Yes, but what are you?' I continued. 'Box 5? Box 6?'

The G2 officer, who had been bristling with embarrassment all the way through this guy's speech, intervened and tried to smooth things over.

'But he hasn't told us anything of use,' I protested. 'Or that we don't know already.' The meeting was all downhill from there. It gradually dissolved and old Henry was ushered out to very few 'hoorays', presumably to be put on the first rocket back to whichever planet he lived on.

The int officer who had originally brought the guy in returned sheepishly to apologize. He obviously hadn't been briefed beforehand on what the guy was going to say, otherwise he wouldn't have dragged us all in for it.

But to me, as soon as I'd clocked the guy, it had been no great surprise. He was just another ex-public-school Box 5 or Box 6 book-learned bastard with his head so far up his own arse he was on speaking terms with yesterday's dinner. The laughable thing was that, in the relationships between all the different security groups, I knew that army intelligence were not thought of highly by MI5 and MI6, and yet this was presumably one of their most highly regarded operatives; and the guy was a joke with no punchline.

Jesus, I thought, I can't wait for the next time I run into the guys from my old unit. This was one to go down on our Jokers Roll-Call of Honour with the padre, the gun-happy ops officer and every other dozy bastard it had been our misfortune to run into.

So, back to Dungannon and back to business. At least I'd got a brief holiday out of it.

Back in the real world, information sourced by different agencies would be collated, compared for verification and then sent to me. If I received info about the shooting of a policeman, for example, I would send a MISER to G2 who would in turn pass it to Int HQ Northern Ireland. From there it would go to MI5, who would compare it with information they had already received on the incident from other sources.

I would then be asked to set up another meeting with my source to get further details to be cross-checked before any action was taken against the suspects. This involved me arranging a second meeting with my source in, say, a pub. I'd turn up wearing a body-wire and ever-conscious of the weight of the 9mm tucked in my waistband. I'd try to get further details of the suspect – what was he wearing? With whom might he have planned and carried out the hit? This would adequately confirm the validity of what I had been told.

Meetings were always high risk in terms of leaving yourself open to assassination; a tout might have been rumbled by the Provos and forced to become a double-agent in order for his life to be spared. Though this would only be temporary. They were always killed by their own eventually. No one trusted someone who had turned once, let alone twice.

So when I went to a meet I never knew exactly what I was walking into, or my chances of walking out of it. Back-up was a way of minimizing the risk. I'd place other undercover operatives in civvies inside the pub.

I always tried to attend with an empty bladder to avoid having to visit the lav. The toilets were, naturally, an impossible area to make safe and were notorious 'hit' spots. It was simple enough for you to be followed in and topped with one in the back of the head. The gunman would be caught on the way out but that was scant consolation for the poor bugger he'd topped. And all the other undercovers in the pub couldn't rise at the same time and go for a slash with you without it looking like a secret agents' day outing.

I would also station an armed patrol near by, but not too close in case it gave someone the jitters. If I thought I was on particularly dodgy ground I'd have a helicopter hover above. This was high enough to avoid detection from the ground but close enough for its high-tech surveillance cameras to relay ground movements to the back-up forces.

Recently another int officer called George Store, whom I knew from my MRF training, had stepped too far out of procedure. We had shared similar duties as he worked on the border checkpoint at Keady before being promoted to Enniskillen in County Fermanagh, thirty-five miles east of Dungannon. One day he took it upon himself to meet a source, but without back-up. He was almost immediately clocked as a stranger, captured, interrogated, tortured and shot. His half-naked, swollen body was found in a shallow stream. His recklessness not only cost him his own life, but his wife her husband and his children their father. And we lost a man who, up to then, had been a good operator.

I don't know in what moment of insanity the idea had seemed to him to be a good one but I hoped it was a madness that I never suffered from. In this arena nothing was clear, clean-cut or obvious. The executions may have been 'clean' (a clear shot at the head of a bound man couldn't be anything else) but the overall feeling caused by corpse on corpse was a seeping, dirty one. These deaths seemed much more sordid, degrading beyond belief. They were lonely, frightening little ends to lives that at the time when you heard of them felt like they had the power to haunt you to your own grave. Bodies tied, bound, hooded and naked; burned, beaten, drilled-through and ditched; caked in their own blood and their last petrified shit. One poor bastard had had his head completely wrapped in parcel tape with just a hole left for his nostrils because they didn't want him to suffocate before they pumped half a dozen bullets into his face.

Without doubt we were wading thigh-deep through the filth of the lowest possible human behaviour. And it was human, or more accurately 'inhuman', in a way that only man could be. It would have been degrading to other creatures to bring them into this by referring to the killers as 'animals'. I'd never seen a wildlife programme that showed animals kill with this amount of premeditated pleasure in another's suffering. At this level, at this depth, I knew right from the off that the street fighting in Belfast was a world away. It seemed almost honest by comparison. There I'd at least had the chance to fight my way out of any situation I found myself in. I thought if I could now watch film of myself running down through those gardens to attack a machine-gun post without back-up I'd probably think, You mad bastard. Fortunately, I'd lived to learn. The Last Post had been blown over many that hadn't.

Rather than laughing all the way to the bank, this country's undertakers just slowly and solemnly marched there in a never-ending procession, carrying another fee or large chunk of some parents' life savings.

This was the real underworld. Minute details would sometimes escape into the newspapers or TV news and give some hint of what lay below, but they were only the tiny, visible parts of a pretty fucking big iceberg.

'Nothing clean, clear-cut or obvious': too frigging right. I was now operating in a theatre of lies and counter-lies, bluff and double-bluff, information and misinformation supplied by agents and sometimes double-agents; we'd counter their lies with lies of our own which they might decide were true until they began to have doubts about the motives of the supplier. Was he really one of them? Had we planted him? Should they kill him or send him back to us to work for them again? Would we find out and do the same? And could we ever really trust and rely on our own sources. If they were suspected by their own side they would be sent to us not realizing they were carrying false information and we might send some of our own to their deaths because of it. In the absence of hard intelligence we'd have to play a waiting game or try to second-guess whatever the next move might be.

Sometimes they would go to the lengths of setting up a legitimate business. Offices would be rented and decorated, clients sought and provided with whatever was being supplied while all the time it was a front for a bomb factory or weapons store. When it was eventually discovered (as they always were when an A1 source came good) the place would be raided and the stash found. News of the arms discovery, however, would not be given to the press. The IRA would then wonder if it had been found and whether to send in more men later to recover the stuff. But then there was the risk of the place still being under surveillance. Here there were enough 'white men speaking with forked tongues' to make an American Indian's head spin. It was a case of having to fight fire with fire or risk getting burned to oblivion.

The information we gathered had to be used carefully, sparingly or sometimes not at all. Occasionally a piece of good info couldn't be used, especially if it came from a valuable tout, because it would compromise his position and leave him open to discovery. This decision was never mine, it would be made by the big boys at Intelligence HQ and I was glad of that. It wouldn't have been easy knowingly to sit on something realizing what the probable consequences would be. Once I passed on my knowledge about the location of a culvert bomb and found out that it hadn't been acted upon for fear of exposing the source. We could only hope that no one died as a result of it.

This was one of the unavoidable and most difficult aspects of playing the 'long game'. It sometimes cost lives, but all eyes were on the ultimate prize of winning the war rather than every single battle. The hard fact was that there were those considered to be 'expendables' on both sides. The higher up the ladder you rose the more danger you were in, because the 'result' was greater from knocking you off, but you were also afforded more security cover as a consequence of this. Ironically, the ones who rose to greatest prominence were the safest of all. The most visible spokespeople of the terrorist organizations, both Loyalist and Republican – Gerry Adams, for example – were actually safer than their high profiles suggested. I often heard outside observers of the Troubles wonder why these figures were not assassinated. The little-known fact was that the leaders on both sides secretly negotiated a mutual 'hands-off' policy on each other's most prominent men. They knew that the retributions from their murders would be wholesale slaughter when even harder, less 'reasonable'men took over. In this, as in all wars, the higher-ups wanted to protect their backs.

In fact, occasional collusion between Loyalist and Republican paramilitaries was an 'open secret' to those of us in the know. For example, a member of a Loyalist group was known and feared even by his own people for being a bit of a 'loose cannon'. It got to the point where his profitable sideline in racketeering and other criminal acts made him something of a liability. Both sides wanted him taken out. The IRA had difficulty in arranging for him to be whacked because of his knowledge of safe houses and routes; he rarely strayed from safe Protestant areas. So other officers from his own organization relayed information of his movements to the IRA and assured them of the safe escape of their gunmen from the Prod area where the hit would take place. They arrived one day, found him where they had been told he would be, did him, and fled safely back their own area of Belfast.

And if you peeled another layer off this diseased onion you'd find that this hit was not sanctioned purely to prevent damage to a 'noble' terrorist cause. It was partly done because the other Loyalist paramilitary officers also had profitable rackets that were being undermined by this man's business.

The gloves very rarely came off completely. If that had happened – if every active Republican tried to kill every active or suspected Loyalist and vice versa; if every single opportunity had been taken to bomb and kill every 'legitimate target'; if sectarian killings had reached their full potential – then the streets would have been piled up to the gutterings with corpses. Everyone concerned seemed to like to fool themselves that they acted within codes of honour or modes of acceptable 'war' behaviour when the reality was that they had already given up on doing the honourable thing – that is, trying to talk out, accept and work through their differences – and retreated to the bomb factory and bullet box. I dreaded to think what unholy shite the IRA came out with to justify bombing the English pubs in Guildford and Birmingham. Twenty-eight innocent people blown to high heaven for simply being English, which, I suppose, to the IRA was reason enough. Guilty by birthright. All we could do was try to limit how much they killed each other and ourselves.

My nightmares, unsurprisingly, returned with a vengeance. The fears of being discovered and left out on a limb were now even greater. I was no longer surrounded by all the reassuring army paraphernalia of being in uniform when you took comfort from simple things like the power invested in you by pulling on combat dress and the more obvious strength drawn from publicly wielding a fully loaded rifle.

The nightmares were of the usual sweat-inducing variety as before – my isolation, capture and murder; Christ laughing at it all from the cross, and so on. In one dream I found myself again unarmed and being pursued at night through a darkened church by a mob of gunmen. In a screaming rage, one of them tipped over the back pew, sending it crashing into the next one, which crashed into the next. I ran wildly up the middle of the church as the domino effect of falling benches chased me and caught me. I was running on the spot now, watching them clatter ahead and beating me to the altar. The continuous boom was like gunfire. Or was it actually gunfire? I couldn't tell. I woke up before I found out. Another time the same dream ended with the figure of Christ wrenching his outstretched hands off the timber of the cross and bursting into applause. The nails were still embedded through his palms, the points clearly and visibly sticking out the back of each hand. From the dark recesses of the church I heard the gunmen join in the clapping. I took this to be a sarcastic comment on the futility of my attempt to escape but again I jolted awake before finding out.

I lay in bed and remembered something I'd once read that said: 'We will be very lucky, any of us, to get out of this world alive.'

12

LOADED

The only things worse than my dreams were the real events I woke up to almost every following day.

One morning I awoke feeling like death warmed up. It was the last day of July 1975. I'd had one of those fitful night's sleep where the bed sheets turn into a straitjacket. If the dreams were particularly bad, they left a frost over my skin that seemed to sensitize every hair. I dragged my carcass out of bed and tried to thaw myself out with black coffee and a wake-up fag.

The TV in the corner was on with the sound turned down. When a news report came on it flickered madly with quick-cut images of the kind I had become familiar with: shots of blanket-covered bodies and some blackened wreck of a vehicle with its guts blown out. An RUC face talked to camera. They were giving it big coverage so I turned up the volume.

A pop group called the Miami Showband had been ambushed in Banbridge, south County Down. Their bus was blown up and five people were dead. This was indeed big news. The Miami Showband were famous in Ireland because in spite of all the musicians being Catholic, they continued to play gigs in Protestant towns such as Banbridge. Some viewed this as courageous and others as foolish. I sided with the latter view. Just because the Showband presented themselves as an example of how Catholics and Protestants could set aside their differences and peacefully coexist, it didn't mean they would be protected from attack. The tolerance the band showed in playing for Protestants, in spite of the deep religious divisions, had obviously not been reciprocated by whichever Loyalist group had wiped them out. In this war there was always some blood-hungry bastard waiting to exploit someone else's good intentions.

I switched off the TV after getting the broad details. This was all that you did get from them. I would find the truth behind the headlines elsewhere.

Within hours the UVF made a statement admitting responsibility. They maintained border patrols because of Provisional IRA crossings from the Republic to the north. They said one of their patrols had become suspicious of the vehicle and stopped it to be searched. A bomb went off and they came under fire. They returned fire, killing three of the band. The other two dead were UVF men killed by the blast. Again, this was only half the truth.

I learned the full facts through a combination of what was revealed through the RUC Special Branch inquiry (three of the hit-squad were identified and arrested) and what I found out from my own contacts in the intelligence network.

That night the UVF were actually masquerading as a UDR patrol. One of the captured members admitted that they had been planting the bomb on the bus when it accidentally went off, killing two of their own men. The rest of the patrol had then opened fire on the unarmed band members in order to eliminate them as witnesses. The UVF's idea had been for the Showband to get back in their bus unaware that a bomb had been hidden there. A timing device would ensure that it exploded as they crossed the border. Loyalists would then say this was an example of Republicans transporting explosives and use it to demand tighter border-crossing controls. And blowing up some Catholics along the way would have just been a happy bonus on top of the political gain.

Two pieces of evidence that emerged jumped out at me from all the rest. The first was that one of the surviving Miami musicians said he had heard a man with an English accent in the patrol; second, a Star pistol used in the attack was proven to be the same one that had killed Benny Green. This was startling news because it added weight to the rumours of the involvement of one man in both events – Robert Nairac.

Among those in a position to know, it was already an open secret that Nairac was colluding with Loyalist paramilitary groups, feeding them the whereabouts and movements of known Provos so they could be hit. But these Loyalists had been proving increasingly erratic and unreliable. This led to Nairac's request for the shipping over of a unit renowned for its professionalism and secrecy – the SAS.

The covert actions of Nairac's own regiment, 4 Troop, had already led many mistakenly to believe them to be the SAS. The main task of 4 Troop was to observe suspected terrorists. Sometimes their ops required them to dig themselves into an observation hole in a field near the suspect's farmhouse. The preparation of this hole may take a week, each step done under the cover of night, before it was ready to be occupied. Two of the troop would then cover and camouflage themselves and lay in wait. Strict radio silence was maintained, only to be broken if their position was compromised and they needed to call back-up, or if they saw something important enough to report, such as the movement of arms. It was a really tough gig, demanding great discipline and stamina. They had to shit in plastic bags, for example, in order not to leave any evidence of occupancy. They may not have been the SAS, but they were only one step down.

Personally, I thought that Nairac was indeed passing on information to the Loyalists, but I didn't believe he was literally 'in at the death' of either the Benny Green or Miami Showband ambushes.

The Miami Showband murders proved, once again, that links existed between the UDR and Loyalist death-squads from the UVF and UDA. It seemed to me that a decision had been made at the highest level that this job would be the preserve of only an undercover agent of Nairac's stature.

I began to realize that in my past missions with Nairac I had been working with one of the major operatives in the whole of counter-insurgency operations: 'Lawrence of bloody Arabia', indeed.

Despite my involvement with him, Nairac still remained something of an enigma to me. I had him down as one of those figures who revealed different aspects of his character to different people depending on whom he was with at the time. This was part of the chameleon nature that made him so valuable as an undercover agent and so skilled at adopting various disguises. He was known to frequent rabidly Republican bars in the guise of a Belfast 'stickie'. It was even reported that he went so far as to jump on stage and join in drunken renditions of 'Danny Boy'. This kind of character submersion not only required balls of iron but a great self-confidence in your own abilities.

I suspected that each person he worked with probably had his own personal and slightly differing view of Nairac.

I thought back to when he had first contacted me to go out on reconnaissance missions. During one we had cased the farmhouse of a known Provo outside Coalisland. This was on the most southerly edge of Lough Neagh and approximately seven miles east of Dungannon. Coalisland was a deeply Republican area. So much so that it was near impossible for me to get any sourced information out of there. I relied instead on the local RUC police sergeant of the area to supply me from his own sources. I was told of the RUC sergeant by Tony Poole when I had taken over from him at Dungannon. On my return from Canada I'd brought him a pukka lumberjack shirt to keep him sweet. When I had asked him about my own chances of recruiting sources his exact words had been, 'Probably about the same as you finding rocking-horse shit.'

I had already contacted him to let him know we would be in his area and what we would be up to.

After the reccie Robert had said that before we returned to Dungannon we should go for a drink to wind down. I'd suggested a bar in a safe Protestant area a few miles away. He suggested McCrory's Bar in Coalisland. I'd thought, Never mind the 'winding down', this must be his idea of winding me up. McCrory's was an infamous Provo hang-out: a safe bolt-hole for every bad bastard life-taker and widow-maker in a five-mile radius. As well as all the off-the-peg thugs who frequented it, McCrory himself was a nasty, tailor-made bastard of the highest order.

'You're joking, aren't you?' I'd said. 'Have you gone totally fucking insane?'

He'd replied that it would be OK if I stuck with him and let him do the talking. Thinking back to it now, I realized it could only have been the respect I had for him as an operative combined with his cracking job of careful persuasion that got me to go with him that day. Any other time, any other person and I'd have driven straight back to Dungannon, probably laughing all the way there.

We entered McCrory's bold as brass and walked straight into that belchy beer-smell common to bars the world over. It usually smells good and means things warm and welcoming await you but to me, there and then, it smelled stale and dead.

Fortunately, the place was only quarter-full that afternoon rather than heaving, as it would be later on. But the air still felt oppressively heavy to me. We settled on bar stools away from the men at tables. As I watched Robert ordering at the bar, all the time I was thinking how we didn't need to be here. There was no reason I could think of why we should drink here rather than in a safe Prod bar. No reason, that is, other than Nairac's desire to show off to me his famous abilities. To me, that wasn't reason enough. I decided that I'd probably underestimated how highly he had regarded my service history. I hadn't thought of it at all, in fact, until then. This seemed to me his way of flexing his own particular muscle for my benefit.

We were both armed. That was one thing. Looking at Robert's back as he sat at the bar chatting away, I was unable to detect any sign of the Browning beneath his long, black leather trench coat (which is exactly how it should be – well hidden) but I knew, nevertheless, it was there. I remember wondering that if things went to pot and we were sussed and attacked if I'd be able to resist putting one into Nairac as well for getting us into this. I grimly amused myself then with some quick mental arithmetic, adding together our combined number of bullets and then dividing them between the men in here. We might have just made it, providing we could miraculously clang each one down with a single shot like ducks on a fairground game.

Robert chatted away to McCrory who was behind the bar, taking care to keep me out of it because I was no way as good at faking the accent as him. Then he rose and disappeared, I presumed, to visit the lav.

Minutes ticked by and he didn't return. I waited. And waited. Fuck. Alarm bells started clanging. McCrory disappeared from behind the bar seconds after Nairac. I began to have visions of him already laid out on the bog floor with his balls in a sling and blood pumping from his head into the trough drain, mingling with fag ends. Fucking hell. Had the idiot blown it? Maybe he'd tried to be too clever for his own good. And for mine.

Perched there on the bar stool I felt as naked as a newborn baby. I just prayed that none of the other drinkers decided to get friendly and come over for a chat. Then I really would have been in deep shit.

This planted the idea that maybe he'd gone for more than a piss. I got up to follow him in. Even thinking about it now made me go cold at the thought of what I might have been walking into. I didn't know if they'd already sussed us, attacked Robert and were waiting for me to follow. It was time to do the right thing. And that was to find out if he needed me.

As I got off the bar stool I unbuttoned my jacket to let it flap freely, giving me easier access to my 9mm.

A dividing wall partitioned one part of the bar from the other. As I went through the doorway I caught sight of Robert talking with

McCrory, hunched together over a table like old pals. They were in such deep conversation that neither of them noticed me. I moved away and into the toilet, just washing my hands and taking enough time to make the visit believable.

As I returned I saw that they were still immersed in whatever they were discussing. I found it all bloody puzzling. Had Robert managed to recruit McCrory as a source? If he had, then he'd really pulled one out of the hat. But knowing McCrory's Republican credentials, this seemed too implausible to be possible.

He'd obviously established some relationship with McCrory. It made sense then why we were there. It hadn't been as risky as I'd first thought. But what the fuck was he up to?

Robert returned after a few minutes and we left and drove back to Dungannon. In the car I mentioned seeing him and McCrory talking but he just passed it off as 'passing the time of day' or some such bollocks. Whatever had been passed between them it was more than the time of day.

Later I telephoned the RUC sergeant in Coalisland and told him what I'd seen. He was, to say the least, surprised, as I thought he would be. Even when I explained more about Robert's position and function he still found it almost impossible to believe that he could have recruited McCrory as a source, particularly because the sergeant himself ran all the available sources and he was sure he would have known about it.

Then he suggested something which hadn't even crossed my mind. He asked how well I knew Nairac. 'I mean, do you trust him one hundred per cent?' he said.

I said I thought I could trust him as much, if not more, than anyone else.

He said, 'You don't think he could be doing the double, then?' That hit me like one on the chin. He was suggesting that Nairac could have been working as a double-agent. I dismissed it immediately, but then, because the doubt had been planted, I began to consider the possibility.

As I did then, I still now think it highly unlikely. His parents were Irish, yes, and his father Catholic, but he was too effective in his work against the IRA for it to seem plausible. He would certainly have been in a position to give them A1 inside information, but we hadn't experienced any security breaches big enough to balance out the damage he had already inflicted on them. And the meeting with McCrory wasn't really enough to draw the conclusion of him being a double-agent. For my own part, I decided to act on a conversation I'd previously had with Nairac.

We had discussed Bernadette McAliskey (née Devlin). She was now a councillor for the IRSP (Irish Republican Socialist Party) who were the political wing of the Republican paramilitary organization the Irish National Liberation Army (INLA). The IRSP's relationship with INLA was much the same as Sinn Fein's with the IRA.

At the end of the previous year, after feuding within the Official IRA (who had themselves split from the Provisional IRA), Devlin and others had broken away and formed INLA and the IRSP. This happened every so often. Bickerings and disagreements on how to wage the war would lead to some members taking their bat and ball home and forming their own little murderous gang. It was just the same terror being traded under another name. There are only so many ways you can kill someone and most of those had been exhausted already. The victims, whether they had been killed by the IRA, INLA, UVF or UDA, were all equally dead. That's one thing that death is pretty good at: reducing everyone to the same level (approximately six feet under). And we'd be left with more bloody initials to memorize and add to the list that included all the others. I half expected the day when the local cub scouts would form their own provisional wing and start planting cow-shit bombs.

In the end the INLA turned out to be as efficient a killing machine as the IRA, if not more so. As so often happened after a new organization formed, they set about trying to establish their credentials in as swift and as vicious a form as possible. They baptized their birth in the blood of others. They were saying, 'Look how important we are. We can bomb holes in the country as well as the next group.' Northern Ireland was rapidly turning into Swiss cheese. I fully expected it to sink by the end of the decade.

McAliskey was the IRSP's 'acceptable' negotiating face for the INLA. I came up with the idea of approaching her for a meeting with me in the guise of a special security officer from Dungannon. I rang her and explained how we had information that she was being targeted to be hit by Loyalist paramilitaries and as she was in my area her safety was my responsibility. There was enough truth in this for it to be believable. Her emergence to political prominence meant she had become a viable target. Still, I was surprised when she agreed to it and arranged for me to visit her at home.

She lived in an isolated house in the Washing Bay area of

Coalisland. The area being as Republican as it was I couldn't just drive in unannounced. I didn't want to go down in British army history as their first and only kamikaze pilot. McAliskey assured me that she would make sure of my safe passage in and out. I described the car I would be using and she would inform her body-guards and the local bad boys of my arrival.

This assurance wasn't enough, though. I had to cover my arse. I arranged for a unit of soldiers to patrol near by: not too close to the house itself to give anyone the jitters but close enough to be on hand for back-up. The brigade helicopter would also hover high above as a further measure. There was only one way in and out of her house so any unusual arrivals would be easily spotted.

I also roped in another intelligence officer to accompany me. He was a tall, ex-guardsman called John who had earned the nickname 'Long Pod' because of his height. He hadn't really that much history of operating 'in the field' so when the day came I could see he was pretty skittish about the whole thing. He obviously didn't relish the idea of driving into the unfriendly heart of Republican country protected by nothing more than McAliskey's assurance and the thin steel of a Ford Escort estate.

Someone else's nervousness can affect you in two ways: it either makes you equally jumpy (making you just want to slap them and tell them to calm down) or it has the opposite effect of adding a little extra steel to your own resolve. Fortunately, I'd never been one to be much affected by other people's jitters. It just made me take command more fully than normal. Although I was aware of the old line that, 'If you can keep your head whilst others around you are losing theirs – maybe they know something you don't!'

But that didn't apply here. Having instigated it myself, I knew enough about this op not to be concerned with Long Pod's nerves. Even if you couldn't be 100 per cent sure of anything here, he should have known I wouldn't get myself into a situation I could-n't reasonably expect to get out of.

As we approached McAliskey's house his bladder finally gave up the ghost. He turned to me and said, 'Can we just pull over here for a second?' He unfolded his full lankiness from the car and took a piss in a nearby hedge. I don't know how long it had been since he'd last gone but he gave a damn good impression of Niagara Falls.

'Shame I didn't put a stopwatch on you,' I said when he clambered back in. 'We might have got you in the *Guinness Book of*

Records for the longest piss!' He just smiled weakly in embarrassment.

Before we reached the door it was opened by a heavy-duty guy in black who completely filled the door frame. Fuck me, I thought, it's Lurch out of the *Addams Family*. He was obviously one of McAliskey's bodyguards. We were ushered through to the living room. Through the open door to the kitchen, I saw two more guys in attendance, both in black leather jackets. The first went off to join them but the door remained ajar.

Bernadette McAliskey rose to greet us. I was struck by how small she was, but she had a large and open face that immediately put you at ease. Her manner was friendly. I introduced myself by the name I had decided to adopt, 'Captain White'. John arranged his long limbs in a small armchair beside me. He was probably even more thankful for his recent piss when I accepted her offer of tea. This was an Irish tradition familiar to me. You couldn't visit someone without being offered a constant supply of tea and buns. She called through to the kitchen.

There was something absurd about seeing this big, hard-faced bastard come out carrying a tray of dainty, clinking teacups. He'd probably left his gun on the kitchen table with the others. You can't make up stuff like this, I thought, you really can't.

I went through my pre-arranged patter of telling her to remain vigilant and offering advice on security lighting, deadlocks on the doors to prevent them being kicked in and break-in alarms. 'Although,' I said, 'I notice you've got your own personal, human alarms in the kitchen.' She just smiled quietly.

Eventually we moved on to more informal conversation about ourselves and the situation in Northern Ireland. At one point she broke off to tend to her daughter Roisin, who was playing in another room. I took the moment to reflect on my being here.

I really didn't have any solid, predetermined ideas about what would come of this meeting. I knew there would be no useful or startling revelations in terms of usable 'hard int'; she was far too smart, of course, to let anything slip. But that wasn't the plan. Getting an insight into the political motivations which drove ground-force actions is actually the most important thing. These were the ideological roots from which stemmed the violence we had to deal with day in, day out: every atrocious killing and filling-in, even the most callous sectarian murders. It seemed to me the only way forward was to face a truth that many found impossible to stomach: if there was any chance left to stop the killing, it meant talking to those who may have had blood on their hands.

And this wasn't a realization easily come by. My past history of being at the shittiest end of the stick had left me with many reasons not to want to believe this. Cradling a dying friend in your arms isn't something you easily forget or forgive and yet this very personal experience of death was one of the major fuels to the fire. Every victim left behind friends and family aching for justice. Often this justice took the form of revenge. The people I had grown to admire the most were those parents who, even though they were utterly crushed by their son's or daughter's death, called for no retribution in their name. You'd see them on the news, their faces slack with grief and disbelief. I thought they showed unbelievable courage and dignity. Even now, I still don't know if I would have the strength not to seek revenge for the murder of a child of mine.

We continued to talk; about Catholicism and history. I'd found that if you agreed with someone on certain issues they tended to open up, and I discovered that I genuinely did agree with her on some things. And not just that the hard nuns of both our childhoods had sometimes seemed to be in league with the devil rather than the big man upstairs.

I agreed we shouldn't really be over here but the decision taken about that had been out of both our hands. We both had to cope with what already existed. We both had a job to do.

At one point I mentioned the twenty-six counties of the Republic and she felt impelled to correct me. 'It isn't a province of twenty-six counties,' she said. 'Ireland has thirty-two.' I pointed out how thousands of Protestants would disagree. She mentioned the idea of repatriation of them to Scotland. I felt this ignored the generations of Prods who had grown up here believing it to be their home, too. That was a reality.

Even when we disagreed it remained good-natured and I found myself warming to her. I had expected a different person. She was always a very up-front, high-profile operator. On TV she came across as pretty fierce. To be honest, I'd expected something of a fire-breathing bitch ramming the party line down my throat until I choked, rather than tea, buns and civilized discussion. She didn't even agree completely with Dublin. Coming very much from the socialist perspective she also found fault in the Irish government's treatment of the working class.

Long Pod John remained conspicuously silent throughout.

Despite his university education he was well out of his depth. Whenever I glanced at him over the rim of my cup he seemed to have sunk even further into the depths of the armchair with his own cup and saucer balanced uneasily on his big knees.

Initially, I had been glad of having this imposing, wardrobe of a man with me as support but I realized now that I hadn't really needed him. She must have caught my train of thought because she made some comment about our safety here only being guaranteed by her orders. If it was a veiled threat, then it wasn't needed. I knew that already. We could have been done at any time. But I also knew that she knew I wouldn't come here without back-up. At one point during the conversation I'd caught the sound of the chopper hovering high above: very faint but detectable none the less. She hadn't mentioned it (I'd already guessed from the little I knew of her that she wouldn't) but we both knew what it meant.

I said that surely the best way forward was for people to talk as we were doing today, rather than resort to the bomb.

'Of course it is.' She leaned forward now for emphasis. 'But remember, this is our country. You are an invading, occupying force. That's how you are viewed even if you don't believe it yourselves. That is how you appear to us.'

I said these opportunities to talk were too rare. In fact, the last time I'd seen her had been back in 1971 when I was in uniform.

'And that time you nearly got me killed,' I said. She looked at me quizzically. 'You were stood on the back of an open-bed truck in . . . I think it was Butler Street, actually, or somewhere near. You were addressing this crowd. I was there with my unit keeping watch, you know, like we did. Probably expecting to get another milk bottle on my head.' She smiled slightly and nodded in understanding.

'Anyway, at one point you said something like "And these Brits over here!" and you pointed directly at me. You may not have meant me personally but you pointed directly at me. It felt like the whole crowd was looking at me in particular. I remember thinking, Oh shit, what's gonna happen now?'

During my telling of it, when she saw that I was thinking back to it with some amusement, she had been smiling. As I'd finished she'd laughed.

'Well, I'm sorry about that. You're right, I didn't mean you personally, of course. You know that. It's what you represented.'

It had been a potentially dangerous moment back there in 1971. A well-phrased speech directed at a crowd could be as inflammatory as a petrol bomb or as fatal to some poor bugger as a machine-gun with a full clip. Words could also be loaded.

I was surprised she hadn't indulged in table-banging propaganda but you still had to be careful of letting your guard down too much. There's an Irish phrase on gentle persuasion: 'Strong words, softly spoken.' Opening up leaves you vulnerable – that's one of the risks of sitting down at a conference table. Everyone is wary of appearing weak.

I had been there nearly an hour and decided the time was right to leave. As we said our goodbyes the boys in the back came out and stood around her. They hadn't softened at all over the last hour. She looked even smaller standing beside them. It was a scene that seemed to sum up all we were facing: the politically committed and determined leader surrounded by the hard action boys who implemented the darker side of the 'freedom' cause.

In spite of British and Unionist politicians' unwillingness to view this conflict as 'political', the hard truth was that it was. That had to be faced. The murders were criminal, in both senses of the word, but we couldn't continue to ignore why they were being committed. Let's face it, I thought, so-called 'ordinary' criminals don't starve themselves to death in prison on hunger strikes as some of the Provos had done. The Special Category status given to imprisoned terrorists at least showed some acceptance of this.

Still being bandied about was the phrase, 'One man's terrorist is another man's freedom fighter.' Though, to me, that conveniently ignored people's freedom not to be blown up or shot down.

Behind me Long Pod dipped his head under the door frame and we walked back to the car at the front of the house. I asked him what he'd made of it and he said he'd felt like a spare part sat there.

'You should have joined those fuckers in the kitchen. I'm sure they would have amused you. They looked like fun-loving lads up for a laugh, didn't they? And, by the way, you look like you could do with another piss, but you can wait till we've driven back.'

I left with a little more hope than I'd had before but I knew there was no magical cure and there would be no immediate end to the violence. Bernadette McAliskey might have been amiable enough to conduct a discussion without resorting to bar-room bawling, but she seemed as steeled as the rest to an armed struggle.

Some months later, however, I wasn't entirely surprised when I heard that she had left the IRSP because of the terrible acts of violence committed by their military wing, the INLA. Perhaps it was a positive sign of the increasing number of people sickened by the killing machines and their never-ending search for fodder.

Time would tell.

13

LOVE AND BULLETS

Serving in Northern Ireland never really curbed your social life as much as you might think. In the early days especially, before things got heavy, we fraternized with girls at the local discos (in years to come some of the guys would even marry Irish girls and settle down in the province). When things did change, however, we could only see Protestant women. The Catholic girls, or at least the ones left that hadn't turned against us, ran the risk of being tarred and feathered. More than the immediate distress and humiliation inflicted on the victim, it was meant as a symbolic warning to others in the Catholic community that, literally, sleeping with the enemy would not be tolerated. I remembered my first encounter with this.

We were on patrol in the Ardoyne one day when we rounded a corner and saw a young woman no more than twenty feet away. She was tied to a lamppost with her arms high. I realized then what the strange sound floating over the rooftops had been. It had been crying. One side of her body and most of her face were black. My heart bumped at the sight of the dark, shiny skin because my first thought was that she'd been set on fire. As we hurried towards her I noticed the clumps of long auburn hair on the ground at her feet. The rest that hadn't been hacked off was flattened to her skull by the oil which had been slapped over her head and body. The few white feathers stuck to it fluttered in the breeze. More lay on the ground with her hair.

As we surrounded her the crowd in the street had backed off to a distance where they stopped to watch. I tried to undo the rope but the knot was pulled tight and the oil on my hands made it impossible to get a grip. All the time she kept her face bowed, eyes down. Her head only rose slightly with each inward breath she snatched out of the sobbing.

I took out my sheath-knife and lopped the rope in two. It was like cutting a puppet's strings. When her arms dropped she sagged down cross-legged on the pavement. Still crying, she rubbed her wrists.

I bent down to her and said we'd get an ambulance out as soon as possible. I said, 'Tell me who did this and we'll go get the bastards right now.' She just shook her head violently and then put her hands to her face.

We tried to comfort her until the ambulance arrived and then she was wrapped in a blanket and helped into the back. The doors closed on her sobbing. As the ambulance pulled away we carried on down the street. The witnesses still stood around either turned away or stared defiantly back at us, depending, I suppose, on how much they thought she had deserved it.

Years later nothing had changed. Except maybe now the risk was of suffering something greater than oil and pillow feathers. I thought how it would have to be a great love (or lust) to make it worth the possible consequences. Little did I realize then that an encounter of my own was to change everything.

Funny how when you think back to things you realize that turning a different corner or making another decision might have changed your life. Or prevented you from meeting someone who would.

On this evening I travelled north to Cookstown with Johnny Hill, another regimental int officer. We went for a bevvy at a Protestant bar called the Royal. The place was already heaving. The weekend was kicking off early.

We shouldered our way to the bar. I got chatting to another int officer in there whom I recognized. Johnny disappeared. When I looked around I saw him sat in a booth with two women. The one facing me was dark-haired and pretty, the other had her back to me so I could only see this long blond hair. The dark-haired one was laughing at something Johnny was saying. He caught my eye and smiled. Typical Johnny, I thought, in like Flynn with a bucket of charm. I turned back to the bar and ordered another.

I felt a tap on my shoulder and turned back to see Johnny's shiny face. He shouted over the clammer of voices, 'Are you coming over to these two birds or what? What do you want, a gold-plated invitation?'

'Are we in then?' I said. He looked back at the booth and waved, and without turning to me said, 'Well, there'll be a better bloody chance if you get your finger out! I look like Billy No-Mates sat over there by myself.'

I said a hasty goodbye to the guy I'd been chatting to. His companionship suddenly meant absolutely bugger all. He could have been the funniest, most fascinating raconteur in the world for all I cared right then. Being a bloke, he'd understand. It would have taken the presence of Georgie Best or Muhammad Ali himself to keep me at the bar. And even then . . .

I followed Johnny through the throng and we sat down either side of the dark-haired girl. She was Karen. Her friend, who was now facing me, was called Sarah. Her blond hair fell either side of her face, framing amazing green eyes. Right then they seemed the greenest things in Ireland. I felt myself beaming an unnaturally large smile – a real ear-to-ear job. She smiled back. This one's mine, I thought, and I don't care if that Karen has a peg-leg and two glass eyes, old Johnny-my-lad will just have to make do.

Johnny introduced me as a fellow sales rep from England, Nicky D'Arcy. D'Arcy! Jesus, thanks a bunch, mate. He'd pulled that one out of the bag from my nickname down at the Aughnacloy checkpoint.

We spent the rest of the evening together getting acquainted. Initially, because I was sat next to her, I talked more to Karen. We got on well enough but it was her friend I was interested in. I made a point of trying to commandeer Sarah's attention. When Karen went to the toilet I took the opportunity to move in.

She had this beautiful, soft Irish accent. I had to lean forward over the table to catch what she was saying but that was fine by me, it just got me closer to those eyes of hers. I learned that she was Protestant, as I'd expected, of course, from her being here, and she worked as a court clerk. Safe as houses.

When Karen came back I continued chatting with Sarah. Fortunately for Johnny, Karen turned out to have two good eyes and no hint of a wooden leg but the unfortunate side was that she didn't take a shine to him. She got progressively more miffed at me and her friend hitting it off. Now and again I'd catch her throwing these 'meaningful' glances at Sarah. I knew what they meant – 'When are we going home?' Sarah didn't seem to notice or, probably more accurately, decided to ignore them. Luckily, women can be just as cavalier with their friends as men when lust rears its ugly head.

Half an hour later Karen got up again to go to the lav. And she didn't come back. Sarah said she could tell her friend was scundered. I said, 'She was what?'

'Scundered. Haven't you heard that word. It means "annoyed".'

Johnny was left a little dumbstruck, sat there by himself as Sarah and I carried on chatting away. Laughing inside, I thought, Johnny, you poor bastard. And he'd set this whole thing up as well! I couldn't wait until the end of the night so I could rib him about it.

Now that is one of the major man/woman differences. When women strike out in love their friends usually commiserate with them, but when men do their friends take the piss. No wonder we got the reputation as the stronger sex. We had to be just to put up with our friends, let alone our enemies.

Her friend having left, taking the car with her, Sarah had to ask me for a lift home. This was more than OK by me but the downside was that Johnny would have to come with us. I couldn't leave him stranded up here in Cookstown. It didn't really bother me, though, to be honest. Sarah didn't seem like the kind to take things too quickly.

She was a smart one, too, that much I'd gathered over the course of the evening. I didn't find it too difficult to keep up my disguise as an electrical goods rep on another visit to my clients over here. For instance, when I said I was staying in a hotel and she asked me which one, as I knew the area I could mention somewhere she would know. Actually, I couldn't resist showing off and began to display a little more knowledge than a sales rep would have.

'I see,' she said at one point. She lifted her glass and took a sip, looking at me over the rim. Then she said, 'You're a well-travelled man Mr D'Arcy. You must shift an awful lot of TV sets over here to get to know us so well.'

'Yeah, we are quite successful,' I said. I really couldn't tell either way if she'd sussed me but I didn't want to say anything in case she hadn't. Every lie I came out with started to sound weaker than the last. Then I thought, Nah, don't worry, Nicky, you've pulled it off. Nicky D'Arcy strikes again.

The next thing she said, though, gave me more room for doubt: 'Tell me, Nicky, do you not find it an awful strain on yourself, lugging around all those TVs and God-knows-what-else?' She looked at me brightly, smiling. I thought, Is she really taking the piss now? She waited until I opened my mouth to answer before she jumped in. Her timing was spot on.

'Now don't get me wrong. I'm not saying you're not a fit fella 'cos you obviously are. But still, you don't want to go and . . . oh, I don't know . . . pull something.'

That's exactly what I was trying to do. I smiled now because I knew she knew. And she saw that I knew. I realized she'd been gently needling me all night until the bubble finally burst. But right now, I was the one who felt like a prick.

'Shall I take you home?' I said and she nodded. I looked across at Johnny who was sitting with his arms folded and a face like sin. We'd been oblivious to him for the last twenty minutes. He was resigned to being a prize gooseberry for the rest of the night.

'Ready, then?' I said.

'Well, I'll try and drag myself away.'

As Sarah walked away I leaned towards him. 'Don't be such an old woman, Johnny. I can't help it if you haven't got the D'Arcy charm!' I started laughing. I was really happy.

'Oh, just fuck off,' he said, but then he laughed too.

We'd come out in a Mini so Johnny squashed himself in the back. We drove out to her village just outside Cookstown and parked at the bottom of a track below her house. Next to the car there was a small stream and she and I stood on the bridge for a while talking. Johnny, who was half pissed as well as being pissed off, wound down the car window. As I attempted to soften her up with some romantic ramblings he kept shouting out comments like, 'Give it a rest, Romeo!'

We moved to the other side of the bridge out of earshot. Then out of the blue Sarah said, 'There's some fields over here if you want to see.'

I looked at her, thinking I must have misheard her. 'Pardon?'

'I said there are some fields over there, really lovely fields.'

Bloody hell, I thought, talk about misjudging someone. And talk about eager! Here I was thinking she was all sweet and innocent as well as beautiful and it turned out I'd pulled the easiest bird in Ireland.

Behind her back I flipped a double thumbs-up at Johnny. I saw him sigh heavily and settle back in the seat for the wait.

We moved off the bridge and towards this 'lovely field'. They all looked the bloody same to me but I'd agree with anything she said. When a little open-air sex beckoned every field was lovely. Sarah hitched up her skirt and jumped on top of a wall and then into the field on the other side. I vaulted it like an Olympic hurdler.

'There, you see,' she said, sweeping her hand over the land-scape. 'That's beauty for you.'

I didn't take my eyes off her. 'It sure is,' I agreed. She was still looking round when I moved in and put my arms around her. My eyes were half closed as I bent down to kiss her when I felt a hand crack me across the cheek.

'What in God's name are you up to?' she said. She pulled away and gave me a stare, hands on hips. 'Just what is your game?'

I knew what I was 'up to'. Well, I thought I did.

'What do you take me for, some ol' two-bob tart?' she said. 'Talk about a one-track mind!' She stormed off back towards the bridge and I ran after her trying to get rid of the puzzled expression I could feel fixed to my face. I stumbled in the field and cursed.

'But I thought . . .'

'Oh, ay. I know exactly what you thought, *Romeo!*' I caught up with her and began to apologize. I said she can't have been serious about just showing me a field, as if I hadn't seen one before. She said she thought I hadn't.

'Of course I've seen a fucking field!' I said in amazement.

'Language!' she snapped, pointing at me. 'You're in the company of a lady. Little but did you know it. Obviously.'

'I suppose this means you're "scundered", then?' I said. This broke the mood and she smiled.

'Too fucking right I'm scundered.'

Now I pointed at her. 'Language!'

We clambered back over the wall, me a lot less eagerly this time. As I walked her up the track to the house, the truth came out. She explained she'd been brought up at school to pity the poor English because we all lived in an urban hell with nothing but miles of concrete around us, supposedly. We never experienced the joy of countryside as beautiful as Ireland's. This was news to me. She had genuinely thought she was doing me a favour by showing this Englishman the beauty that he'd been so cruelly deprived of. She said she realized now I was more depraved than deprived.

'There's loads of fields around where I come from! Christ, do you lot really think we're as backward as that?'

She laughed and asked who was scundered now? I kissed her goodnight on the doorstep and I felt her hand go around my back and tap the Browning 9mm I had tucked there.

'Dangerous business this electrical goods game, eh?' she said. I took the number of the court where she worked and said I'd get in touch.

When I got back to the car Johhny was asleep, head back, mouth open. I slammed the door hard and jolted him awake. He turned to me groggily, then looked out to the field and back to me again. 'Well?' he said.

'Yeah, I'm really well.' I laughed. 'Now let's get back.'

I drove back to Dungannon whistling most of the way, much to Johnny's annoyance. I really was looking forward to seeing her again. There was something about her I hadn't really found in a girl before. She was both knowing and naïve. And that's a potent combination for any man. It intrigued me. She had a great laugh, too. Like a nun with dirty habits, I described it.

As we bounced along in the Mini with Johnny slumped in a coma beside me, I was already planning ahead. Thinking of what I could say to make her laugh again when we next met. That's one sure sign that you're hooked, Nicky boy, I thought. One sure sign.

The Green Howards were back in Northern Ireland by now, based in Armagh City as Battalion HQ and with companies in Portadown, Lurgan and Dungannon. My old company were stationed in Armagh.

I had a tooth that was giving me some chronic jip so I decided to get it seen to by the Royal Army Medical Corps in Armagh and take the chance to visit the boys as well.

The medical officer rummaged around inside in that way that dentists do with little concern that their hand is twice as big as your mouth. He said I had a diseased wisdom tooth and it had to come out. With wisdom teeth being so deeply rooted, he recommended referring me to hospital. I'd be in for three days. I thought, sod that, it's only a tooth, whatever it's called. I insisted he took it out himself.

He produced an evil-looking needle, spiked my gum and shot in two hits of anaesthetic. While waiting for it to take effect I went outside. The medical office was right on the edge of the parade ground and when I looked across who should I see but Tom Wallace and Blakesy from my old unit! They were taking a break on the edge of the square: Nigger topping up his tan and Blakesy fag-in-mouth as usual.

They didn't notice me walking over and as I approached I cried, 'Ah-ten-*shun!*' They both looked up startled and started laughing. We exchanged handshakes and back-slaps and immediately slipped back into the old patter like we'd never been away.

'I see nothing changes,' I said to Blakesy. 'Still smoking for England.'

'Yeah. What have you done, given up smoking and taken to sucking gobstoppers?' He pointed at the swelling on my jaw.

'No, this bastard tooth is playing up. I'm here to get it pulled.'

We settled down by a wall and caught up on news. They'd both been in and out on tours of duty. It was great to see them and good to see they were OK. I felt a real invalid with half of my face paralysed. They tried to make me laugh even more to see the spit dribble down my chin. We talked about old times and what we were doing now. Nigger expressed surprise at me working undercover but Blakesy didn't. 'Yeah, that figures,' he said. 'You always were a sly bastard when you wanted to be!'

We only seemed to have been talking for a few minutes when I heard a voice calling me across the square. The dental nurse was waving me over. I waved OK.

'See boys,' I said and pointed at Nigger, 'I'm nearly as popular with the women as Mr Playboy himself, here.' We said our goodbyes and I told them to make sure they covered their arses on patrol. They called out marching orders after me as I crossed the parade ground back to the dentist's.

Upstairs the nurse said she'd thought I'd had second thoughts and done a runner until she looked out of the window and saw me on the square. I'd been longer than I thought and the anaesthetic was starting to wear off. Oh, well, in for a tooth out, in for a pound.

I figured the army must draw its dentists from some of the most evil bastards in its ranks. This one climbed on top of me, knee on my chest, and practically put half his arm down my throat as he tried to yank the tooth out. He worked on it like a rusty wheel-nut. There was still enough painkiller in me to do the job but I imagined him thinking, Well, I did offer you the chance of hospital you clever sod. I heard it cracking like hardwood until it finally gave up the idea of being part of my body and popped out. He stepped back, admired it on the end of the tongs and whistled. I could see what he meant. The roots of it looked like a blood-dipped wolf fang. I thought he should have let me in on the fact that wisdom teeth are rooted directly to your boots but I wasn't in the mood for an I-told-you-so lecture.

Just outside Dungannon the anaesthetic finally wore off and the full pain of it all suddenly decided to introduce itself. I immediately saw the doctor and got a fistful of painkillers. It was nearly three days before I felt well enough to call Sarah.

I'd seen her a few times since we first met. She sounded mildly miffed that I'd left it so long before calling since our last meeting but I explained the situation and we arranged to go to a Saturday-night dance.

Despite my eagerness to see her and the fact that I felt she was 'safe', I'd already done a 'P check' on her and her family. Better to be safe than sorry, as they say. As well as being an accountant, her father was a part-time RUC member, so no worries there. Thinking that this might turn out to be a longer-term thing than usual I put her down as a numbered source, so whenever I went to see her I could put it down to business: monkey business maybe, but still business. I thought at a push I could say it was my contribution to cementing Anglo-Irish relations.

At the dance we had a great time. Sarah's sister Rosalind and her boyfriend Jack came along with her. Occasionally, when I was talking to Jack I'd look up and see the girls huddled together, obviously chatting about me. Sarah confessed that she thought her sister had taken a shine to me. Later, when we had come off the dance floor after doing the jive, Sarah went to talk to Rosalind and then returned to me giggling.

'What?' I said. 'What now?'

She could hardly speak for laughing. 'Rosalind was watching you dance. She just said to me . . .' She laughed again and put her hand to her mouth. 'She said, "I knew that boy was too good to be true – he's got epilepsy!" '

'Oh, thanks a bunch: an epileptic who's never seen a field!'

The night went well apart from one incident that I knew would take years for me to live down. We were out on the dance floor again, me with my back deliberately to Rosalind because I knew from Sarah's expression she was probably mouthing something like, 'Is he having a fit?' I guess I should have toned it down a bit because I felt something shift and then drop coldly down my leg. Before I realized what was happening my Browning slid out of the bottom of my trouser leg and shot across the dance floor. It spun on the boards, catching the light. Before the gun had even come to rest the floor emptied. It was like someone shouting, 'FIRE!' Everyone ran to the wall. There were screams and cries of, 'There's a gun!'

I thought, Jesus H Christ! What a dickhead. I calmly picked it up and tucked it back in my waistband. I led Sarah back to our table, downed the rest of my pint and suggested it might be best if we made as dignified an exit as we could manage under the circumstances. The dance hall was predominantly Protestant but not exclusively. Catholics did go there as well.

I drove with Rosalind's guy beside me and the girls in the back. At one point Sarah said, 'Nicky, Rosalind's just wondering if you have any difficulty aiming straight with that gun of yours. You know, what with that terrible affliction you suffer from!'

Over their laughter I turned to Jack and asked if these two were always like this when they got together.

'Always,' he said. 'Consider this your baptism.'

Rosalind and Jack went up the path to the door and Sarah stayed in the car for a minute with me.

'You know what my father said to me? Listen to this. He said, "Is that boy a car mechanic or a multi-millionaire or somethin'? Every time he picks you up he's in a different car." '

It was true. It was a security risk to be seen in the same one too often so I chopped and changed from the motors in the pool.

'I suppose he won't let you out of the house again when your sister tells him I'm an armed epileptic. And one that can't even keep it in his pants.'

She laughed. 'I think he's afraid there's something else you won't keep in your pants, I can tell you that for nothing. No, Rosy won't say a thing. She likes you. And . . .' she said, cutting me off before I could say it, 'don't tell me that you like her too. My eyes are green enough already without you trying to make me jealous. Anyway . . . she doesn't like you as much as I do, Mister D'Arcy.'

I looked up at her and she gave me the full effect of those eyes and that smile. I said that she could stay over in my quarters whenever she wanted. She said she would be able to visit but not stay. She didn't want to give her ma and da simultaneous heart attacks.

As I drove away, before I'd even gone half a mile I ran into an RUC checkpoint. I never carried any security ID, of course; that was too dangerous, so I went through the standard procedure in these cases. As the officer approached I showed him my fake civvie ID and said quietly that I was with the security forces. The English accent was usually enough to convince them it was true. Because other cars had now pulled behind mine, waiting their turn, they proceeded to search me anyway so as not to arouse suspicion. He tapped me down with his palms, moving over the bump of the Browning as if there was nothing there. Then they took a quick look in the boot of the car and waved me on.

I must be pretty serious about this girl to go through all this, I thought. I made a mental note to remind her of that some time.

A few days later I had to call Sarah and tell her I was due to leave for a while. I'd just been told that I was to fly out to Germany to brief an incoming regiment.

Usually what happened was that two months before the regiment was due, their commanding officer and intelligence officers would come over on a forward reccie to talk to the present officers and LINCOs like me to see how the land was lying. I'd been through the same thing when I took over in Belfast and later at Aughnacloy and Dungannon. Once they arrived the actual change-over between regiments happened very quickly, over the course of one day, in fact.

This time, however, the idea was for me to visit them before they left. I took a Hercules from Aldergrove airport. Besides myself and a couple of other officers, the only things on board were the strapped-down cargo boxes being transported. The boom inside the near-empty cabin was even louder than usual. It was an uncomfortable flight. I felt like just another piece of freight.

It was to be a night landing. This was the only part of flying that gave me the jitters. Knowledge of radar and computer-assisted flight paths held little reassurance for me when I looked out of the porthole and saw blackness. We could have been coming down over the sea for all I knew. You just had to hope the pilot knew where he was.

I spent the night in a room prepared for me in the sergeants' mess. The briefing wasn't until ten the next morning so I could even have a lie in. The incoming regiment was the Royal Hussars, or the 'Cherry Pickers' as they were known because of the red trousers of their dress uniform.

The following morning I met their intelligence officer and ambled over to the lecture theatre to brief the dozen or so officers who would be gathered there. I walked in to one of the biggest shocks of my life. All six hundred of the regiment were sat there waiting for me, row upon row. They had even assembled a small stage for me to address them from.

I felt myself turn white. Public speaking wasn't really my bag. I could handle the shallows of informal briefing but this was out-at-sea stuff. It was like being back in Buckingham bloody Palace with me as Queen! I turned to the intelligence officer. 'Are you sure there are no waifs and strays still out in the street who you haven't pulled in yet?' He gave me a puzzled look. I explained that I'd thought I was only briefing the int boys.

'No. The whole regiment,' he replied. 'Sorry. Did I neglect to mention that?'

I wondered if I should neglect to mention what a complete wanker I thought he was right then. I was suddenly aware of not only being dressed casually in civvies but of looking much the worse for wear after the flight. I hadn't even shaved. I thought this might be in my favour, though, making it look as if I'd just come hot-foot straight from an op.

My dread mounted the stage with me. I remembered reading a survey somewhere of people's greatest fears: public speaking had come second after shark attacks. That seemed about right to me. Here I was, in at the deep end where only the appearance of a great white could make things worse. I hadn't prepared a damn thing; not even a list of subject headings as a reminder.

I bumbled through the first twenty minutes with all the confidence of a whorehouse virgin, painfully aware of the twelve hundred eyes on me. I imagined they were thinking the same as I had at that meeting with the Hooray Henry from Box 5 in Lisburn. Finally, I asked if anyone had any questions, though I didn't hold out much hope. I knew in a crowd of this size people would be loath to single themselves out.

When he saw my discomfort the intelligence officer redeemed himself a little by asking questions on the regiment's behalf. After that things didn't go too badly. I loosened up and so did they and I began taking questions from the floor. The trouble was that in this setting, surrounded by the regiment's top brass, I couldn't tell the ordinary squaddies about the tricks I had used when I'd been on patrol. I couldn't really stray from the party line of the official Rules of Engagement. So I tried to stress the importance of vigilance and never underestimating the knowledge and resourcefulness of the people we were up against.

I was glad to see the back of the place and return to the airport for my flight home.

I returned to a bloody reminder of what I'd been trying to impress upon them. Only weeks later in September 1975 the IRA exploded a sequence of bombs across the six northern counties and murdered five Protestants at an Orange Hall in South Armagh. The Loyalists struck back by killing twelve Catholics. The different terrorist organizations continued to fight among themselves and with each other.

At least meeting Sarah had given me something good to dream about for a change. We saw each other more often now, each meeting a heady brew of promise, risk and thrills. During one visit to her house I found more than I'd bargained for. I walked through the hallway, telling her all about the time I'd been stopped at the RUC checkpoint after our night out, and looked up to see a familiar face in the living room. It was one of the RUC officers from the roadblock. Before I could say anything, Sarah introduced him as her father. I thought, You sly, old dog. He'd obviously arranged for the checkpoint to be thrown up so he could size me up.

I thought it was fair enough. Like all good dads he was protective of his daughter. I would have probably done the same. I imagined that in his eyes the fact that I was part of the security forces still didn't balance out me being English. And the fact that I was Catholic as well wouldn't have helped. So Sarah conveniently 'forgot' to mention that part. Despite their belief in being part of Britain, Irish Protestants still liked their kids to date their own.

It wasn't exactly an everyday courtship. The circumstances gave rise to some strange incidents. A particularly weird one happened after I'd dropped Sarah at home as usual and headed back off to Dungannon. I saw a guy trying to hitch a lift and thought, for a change, it would be nice to have some company on the drive. Unlike England, hitching was quite a common practice in Northern Ireland, in spite of the Troubles. Hitchers were never stranded for hours like back at home.

He was a guy of about my age. I had him pegged immediately as a Catholic. I used my usual cover of being a sales rep staying in a hotel in Dungannon. As we talked I started to consider the possibility of recruiting him as a source and began laying the foundations by questioning him about his view on the Troubles. I did it very carefully, of course. At this stage I didn't want to reveal too much that may compromise me.

I quickly sussed that it wasn't on when he began his own gentle inquisition of me – what exactly did I do and how often did I come over here? When I asked him where he wanted dropping off and he said the Ponderosa Estate I knew I might have got myself in some shit. The Ponderosa was renowned around Dungannon as being staunchly Republican. I thought the sooner I drop this boy off the better. I'd make sure it was right on the outskirts of the area, too.

As we neared Dungannon the conversation cooled noticeably;

ominously, in fact. Situations always seem worse at night. The image of his face partially illuminated by the glow from the dashboard remained stuck in the corner of my eye. Both my hands being occupied by the wheel and gearstick didn't help either.

I was glad when the black of the surrounding countryside began to lighten as we approached the edge of town. Then things went from not too good to a lot frigging worse.

We rounded the next bend and came across a scene that caused me to floor the brake. Half blocking the road was a dead Mini on its side, the roof bashed in and its lights out. A guy stood in the road, swaying and waving his arms around like he was directing a plane down. I got out. The hitcher made to do the same but I told him to stay in. It turned out to be my best move of the night.

As I walked into the beam of the headlights the guy in the road did the same, shielding his eyes. Then, to my horror, he began calling my name. He lowered his hand and I immediately recognized the squinting face. Christ, I thought, not him. It was a FINCO who was known as 'Saigon Sam' from his overseas days. I also knew him as a dozy bastard of the highest order.

'Nicky! Nicky! Thank Christ it's you. I rolled the bloody car!'

'You don't say.' I walked straight past him so he had to turn and follow. I wanted him out of earshot of my travelling companion and just hoped he hadn't heard anything already. If he had, he'd be wondering how a sales rep from England could just happen to know this guy. I pretended to inspect the Mini. Sam moved alongside me.

'Will you keep it down,' I hissed. 'You don't know me. There's a local in the car with me.' He swayed and made exaggerated shushing noises. That's all I needed right now, a comic-book fucking drunk! I looked at him hard and he seemed suddenly to switch on to the situation. He nodded soberly.

We could have easily tipped the Mini back on its wheels but it was long gone. The radiator was wheezing out steam and there was such a shine off the escaped oil it looked like the car had had its throat cut. I told him to lay low, well away from the car in case anyone else stopped, and said I'd phone through for back-up to pick him up as soon as I could.

When I turned to walk back to my car I saw that the hitcher was already out, leaning on his open door. I motioned him back in and shouted that everything was OK.

As we drove away I acknowledged Sam's weak wave. In the

rear-view mirror his body burned red in my tail-lights and then shrank back into the dark and disappeared.

I said, 'I don't know which one was the most well oiled – him or the car,' but the guy just smiled slightly and said nothing. I snapped the radio on to fill the car with some evidence of the outside world. The mournful Irish folk music that came out didn't make me feel any better.

As we neared the Ponderosa Estate I nearly slowed down until I remembered I shouldn't really know where it was. I waited for him to say something. I thought he might keep quiet and deliberately take me deeper into the estate than I needed to go. Then I'd have a decision to make. No big dilemma, really – I'd slow down but not stop completely and then kick him out. The fucker would have to hit the ground running.

'Here will be OK,' he said. I relaxed a little. I kept my eyes on the mirror as I pulled away but he just strolled off quite normally. No tell-tale sprint to the nearest house.

As soon as I got back in I sent out another car to pick up Saigon. I just hoped they found him before anyone else did, partly because I didn't want him to miss the 24-carat bollocking I had planned for him the next day.

Even after the fact I couldn't find much to laugh about from this incident. Sarah didn't either. As we had become more serious about each other so we began to worry about each other's safety. I realized that if I wasn't in love with her already I was pretty damn close to it. It wasn't planned or intended. The good feelings it gave me were diluted by some bad. I knew that concern for someone else could only weaken me. I wasn't used to worrying about anyone but myself and the men I commanded. But then they were soldiers and that's part of the territory. When you sign up you agree to everything that goes with it.

It's always easier to be far more cavalier about your own safety than that of the people you care for. As well as the added weight of knowing about Sarah's fears for me, there were also my fears for her safety. She ran a risk too. Of course, with her being Protestant the Provos wouldn't give a toss about her seeing an ordinary soldier, but if my position in intelligence was discovered and then also my connection to Sarah, they could use her to get to me.

The more I tried to look into the future, the more I became aware of the law of diminishing returns. Any gambler will tell you the only certainty about good luck is its tendency to run out. The smart ones got out of the game while they were ahead.

The Holy Trinity of the Father, the Son and the Holy Ghost had been replaced in my life by another three stooges. Mother Nature and Father Time I could deal with. It was the third party you had to be wary of; after the initial smile she'd bide her time, then Lady Luck would hook you and fuck you.

Lovely thought to take home for Christmas.

14

MERRY FUCKING XMAS AND A HAPPY NEW YEAR

I flew out of Ireland exhausted, sad and relieved. I took a night flight right into a white Christmas. The plane touched down on the bleached tongue of a runway running straight into the mouth of a blizzard. The cabin door hissed open to a flurry of snowflakes out of black. I was first in the queue to get off.

I ran for shelter head down, collar up. The wind flared the tip of my cig and then blew it off. The biting cold cleared my head of the horror of details and made everything seem strikingly clear. I had one more year to go. Then I had the choice of signing off and shipping out or staying on for another three years. I thought I probably already knew what I'd possibly do . . . maybe. It was as clear as that.

I'd left Sarah behind with a kiss and an early Christmas present. I could still see her unwrapping it as she tried not to cry. I had a normal man's ability for gift shopping, that is, absolutely bugger all. So I'd got an army pal of mine to stamp out a blank dog-tag for her with both our names. It was a token more than anything. Our separation felt bitter and sweet at the same time.

I changed from an inter-city to a local train that rattled me towards my home town. A midnight taxi out to the village left me on my mum and dad's doorstep. There was no one up.

I let myself into the dark of the house and flicked the hallway light switch. The bulb flared briefly and popped. I thought, Yeah, that just about says it all. As I entered the living room I jumped when I saw a pair of feet sticking out. I looked around the door and realized it was my dad. 'Bloody hell! You nearly gave me a heart attack,' I said. 'I thought you were both in bed.'

'Yer mother is, lad. I'm just reading.'

The room was in near darkness, lit only by a small lamp next to his chair. He folded the page corner and laid his book down. I sank into the armchair opposite him and let my eyes adjust to the gloom. A decorated tree stood in the corner staring back at me, looking as tired and as switched off as I felt. The seasonal cards and hung tinsel just depressed me.

Dad started that rattling coughing I'd become used to over the last few years. He suffered from chest problems now. When it subsided he did the same thing that all seasoned smokers seem to do after a good coughing session – he reached for his pack. He tapped one out and offered me one. I said that I'd stick with my own. He smoked Park Drives. As well as having no filter they were strong enough to fell a bull elephant.

I fished out one of the bottles of whiskey from my bag. He wasn't really a whiskey drinker but he decided to join me; what with it being Christmas, he said. I thought it was as good an excuse as any.

The first mouthful made me shudder slightly and then began to warm its way through to my tired brain. We sat in silence for a while at first, practically motionless apart from the odd gulp or drag. I thought we must look like a couple of carved bookends: fags in one hand, glasses in the other. Two generations of the Curtis family's contribution to the war effort. One old soldier, one new.

Before the whiskey thickened our heads it began to loosen our tongues. We sat and talked in a way that we never had before. When he asked me how I was I could detect a real concern that demanded more of me than my usual answer of, 'OK.' I didn't really know how bad his chest problems were or might get, but I'd already started to have those horrible flashes of realization into what it might feel like to lose a parent. I'd tried to ignore them. I guess like every son I thought my dad was one of those indestructible forces that would somehow be spared.

I glugged another refill into his glass and began telling him everything. I'd never actually told him that when I left my drill-training duties I'd returned to Northern Ireland to work undercover. I'd let him think I had simply gone back to Germany. He expressed a little surprise but not too much. He wasn't stupid. He knew something was going on. The increasing length of my hair was the most obvious sign. I'd never have got away with that unless I was working in civvies. He didn't know the full extent of what I was involved in, though. In fact, he didn't know the half of it.

Over the next hour I gave him a potted history of what his son had been up to for the last two years: the emergence of the intelligence war and my part in it; the ops I went on; the successes and failures; the deaths; the 'dirty tricks', as they had become known, employed by both sides. He pretty much got the guts of the truth that lay behind the news headlines (and often the headlines were bad enough in themselves).

He took it all in, nodding understandingly or occasionally shaking his head in disbelief. Towards the end his glass remained untouched on the chair arm.

'That doesn't sound like much of a way to fight a war,' he said.

'Dad, it's become the only way. I've told you what we're up against.'

'Aye, I s'pose. Things have changed a lot since my day,' he said finally. 'And not for t'better as far as I can see. At least we knew who we were fighting. Things seemed simpler then.'

He told me again of the time he'd been captured in North Africa during the Second World War. He'd been part of the rear-guard action that had dug in to fight the advancing Germans. They were finally overrun, as seemed inevitable.

'This Jerry came at me over the trench top. I can see his face now. Young bugger, too, probably younger than me. Anyway, my rifle was next to me and I reached for it, of course. Just instinctive like. Stupid really, when I think about it 'cos he had the drop on me.' He paused to stub out his cig in that way that always reminded me of him when I saw someone else do the same, squashing it flat against the ashtray bottom with his thumb pad.

'Any road, he just shouted "Nien!" and levelled his rifle at me. You know, warning me off. Lucky for me, thinking back. I used to wonder if I'd 'ave done t'same in his position. Anyway . . . that were that. I were captured then of course.'

I hadn't heard this part of the story before. I guess it was his way of describing some kind of honour, even in the middle of war where all was supposed to be fair, that he thought was so brutally absent from the conflict I was involved in. I couldn't disagree with him on that.

'What's all this about Germans,' I said. 'We all know you were caught by Italians. Some Luigi caught you out in the field having a crap, didn't he?' This was an old joke of ours. I always teased him about it. Knowing the routine, he slipped into his part like he always did, half amused and half genuinely annoyed at me making fun of him. He leaned forward and stabbed the air.

'I'll have you know I was captured by Hitler's best, lad! This were a bloody panzer division bearing down on us. Not some bottle washers and shoeshine boys!'

'I've seen more action in the Naafi queue, Dad, than you ever did.'

'That's 'cos you never left the chuffing mess hall!' He was really starting to hit his stride now. The whiskey was geeing him on. I lay back laughing when, mock-serious, he came out with some really priceless, over-the-top exaggerations.

'When I did go out for a crap I'd come back with fifty captured Germans, an' I only had a bloody shovel! In a trench fight if I stuck two of 'em on me bayonet I'd say, "Move up! There's room for one more." '

I'd been taking a sip during this last one and I had to splurt it back in the glass. 'What? Only two? Last time you told this it was four. How long was this bayonet of yours, anyway? Six foot?'

He lay back himself now, smiling. 'Long enough, lad.'

'And then you went to jail for a while.'

'It weren't chuffing *jail*! It was a prisoner-of-war camp! Two years of it.'

After his capture he'd been transported to the prison camp in Italy that he escaped from during the football match.

'You mean to tell me you left your team-mates one man down?'

'Well, I did have more important things on me mind, son. Like getting back to my own forces for instance. Besides . . .' he paused before the punchline, 'our team were crap. We'd have got thrashed, anyway.'

His travels back and forth across Italy after his escape provided more humour within our family over the years. I explained the quite common notion of navigating by the sun and asked him what he thought it meant when the sun rose.

'It will shortly be up in the fucking sky!' he answered.

'Yeah, and it rises in the east and sets in the west. So you navigate by that.'

He admitted that geography and navigation were never his strong points. The American troops he eventually ran into must have realized this too when they asked why it had taken him ten weeks to find them when the POW camp was only eighty miles away!

'Bloody Yanks,' he said. 'I told them I'd taken the scenic route.'

All that time he lived off the land, which isn't too difficult to do in parts of Italy, drinking from streams and eating fruit. He said he'd never eat another pomegranate as long as he lived.

The Americans offered him safe passage to a ship home but only if he agreed to return on a reccie mission with one of their units to show them the gun positions he'd had to skirt around on his travels. If he didn't do this he'd have to stay with them until whenever they could get him out. Not much of a choice, really. So out they went under cover of night, retracing his route until they were sometimes only a few hundred yards from an enemy position.

Fortunately, the captain of the ship he was eventually put on was a little more skilled at navigation than my old man and he soon arrived back in England. And that, as he would say, was that.

I told him about how the things I'd seen in Northern Ireland had weakened my faith until it finally gave way. He expressed his regret at this. He was naturally God-fearing rather than a tub-thumping Catholic but it still saddened him. I explained how Chris had gone through an opposite conversion and found God when he'd had no belief to begin with. I tried to lessen the impact on him of the loss of my own faith by saying how, in time, what happened to Chris may happen to me, too. He just sighed and nodded.

The bottle was stood next to the lamp on the table beside his chair. The light glowed through the quarter of gold liquid left. He was sitting forward now towards me and, with his back to the lamp, his face was dark.

'Has it been worth it, Nicky, for a bit of metal?'

'I didn't do it for a medal, Dad. I was just in the right place at the right time. Or maybe the wrong place.'

He rose to his feet to go to bed, but before he did he had one last question for me. He said he'd never asked me why I'd joined the army.

'Because of you, Dad. Remember when you used to come back from the pub on Saturday night and tell me your war stories?'

'Aye. Didn't get any back-chat from you then, neither.'

'Well, after that I always wanted to join.' He looked strangely troubled when I said this, almost grimacing. I think it was a fight between pride and guilt.

'In that case I wish I'd never told you,' he said. 'I don't want any harm to come to you, son, you know that.'

'Yeah, Dad, I know.' He patted me on the shoulder as he passed. As I watched him leave he seemed smaller than I always thought of him; his back less broad, his shoulders narrower. This really got to me for some reason. I decided not to pour myself another.

He'd been pleased when I'd told him about Sarah, though. I wanted to call her right now but it was far too late. I didn't fancy dealing with her old man if he got to the phone before her.

I snapped the lamp off and the dark fell on me like a weight. I dropped back in the chair. Christ, I felt so weary. I always left Ireland more mentally exhausted than anything else. In the position I held as a major LINCO everybody wanted my ear. They all wanted something from me. The midnight knock on my door by some int officer or other had become a regular occurrence. My short times away were never enough to recharge me fully before I had to go back. I'd started becoming envious of ordinary blokes with their suit-and-tie jobs and wives and families. That life had never appealed to me before. It had always seemed like a living death to me when I was travelling the world.

Maybe seeing death first hand had changed my opinion; made me realize that real death is something on its own and not remotely like any part of life. People's faces in death, for example, were like nothing you'd ever seen before. No amount of faking when an actor played dead in a film could ever capture that look. A dead face had this peculiar slant like the muscles had shifted, slid and then frozen in mid-twitch. And the eyes: sometimes half lidded, sometimes fully open (very rarely peacefully closed), so emptied of light, so still you knew you could never get alive eyes to do that.

First love wasn't the only thing you never forgot. To that you could add your first death. I remembered mine. I could still see that body folded over itself as if for protection. And the face turned away as if in shame. And the smell of shit.

An angel's face on one of the Christmas cards slowly fuzzed out of focus as I blacked out into sleep and my first really bad dream for months. I saw someone kill my children. I didn't have any children. I couldn't see the killers but I knew who they were. I ran on ice, slipping like Bambi with my jelly-legs spreading out from under me. All my bones were soft with shock. And fear. I searched through the Ardoyne. Every house I burst into was full of empty rooms. Every switch I flicked blew a bulb. I ground my teeth till they powdered on my tongue, which I dipped sideways into the wet hole left by my missing tooth. I kept running into darkened rooms, through dark doors into empty lift shafts and dropping, my legs treading empty air. Every time I dropped and struck the ground, I bounced. And every time I bounced a ball of sick went from stomach to mouth. Like a tiny petrol bomb blowing open on my teeth and carpeting my tongue in flames. I could hear ratchets clicking as someone turned the handle on a siren. The far-off noise came closer until it bolted out of my mouth, jolting me awake.

I woke bent out of shape in the chair. It was morning. The windows were breeze-blocked with sky. It was grey enough not to hurt my eyes too much. Dad was sat back opposite me in his chair with his legs crossed and one slipper bobbing. He looked over his glasses at me with some amusement, some concern.

'You've got spit on your chin, lad.'

I exhaled slowly and lay my head back. 'Happy Christmas, Dad.'

'Your mother's gone out. Won't be long. She didn't want to wake you,' he said as he set down his mug. He'd drunk out of it for as long as I could remember. 'Y'all right, son?'

I forced a smile, not wanting it to look forced, and nodded. I ran my hands back through my hair and my fingers got tangled. My hair was over collar length now. My old man nodded towards it. 'Could do with a cut. You look like a bonfire Guy.'

I felt like one. It was good to be home, though, where you don't have to explain or take care or pretend. Or even think. Where you could be your most unforced self and not have to worry if that was good enough or not.

I rested my chin on my chest and back-heeled my shoes off. I wished I'd done it last night before I'd drifted off. My feet ached. And I had a mouth like Gandhi's sandals. Dad got up and went into the kitchen. I heard a cupboard bang and the tinkle of spoon and cup. I thought, Christ, I must look bad – he's making me a drink!

I called in to him. 'Don't let Mum catch you doing that. We don't want her to know you know your way around a kettle and teabag.'

He came out, smiling. 'Aye, could set a dangerous precedent, this,' he said, handing me the mug. 'So keep it to yoursen.'

I never realized how much I missed the old bugger until I came home. After first joining the army I'd come back feeling like my own man rather than just his son. I thought how men of strong character can sometimes have that effect on their kids. You need time to free yourself. Ours had been a household where you grew quickly, though. You were expected to leave school and get on with real life as soon as the last bell went. And real life meant work. I'd tried the pit but realized it wasn't for me. Bad enough living in a country as sun-free as Britain without spending false nights underground.

In common with a lot of lads, I think I'd felt protected because of my dad but loved because of my mum. It's not that he didn't care as much, it was just . . . different. I never needed a diagram to know when he was displeased but the signs of pleasure were a lot more subtle. I think my mum could have been an accomplished code-breaker for MI5 judging by her ability to decipher those particular grunts and looks.

I felt there was a whole history here, I guess, that I couldn't possibly find anywhere else. Certainly not in Ireland, despite my family roots there. I supposed that same family and history thing powered a lot of feeling behind what was going on there, too. I wondered what Sarah was doing right now but I didn't want to dwell on that too much. The bang of the front door stopped my mind wandering.

Mum busied her way into the room and seeing her face light up when she came in immediately lifted me.

'I'll put kettle on,' she said, smiling.

'It's OK,' I said, rising to greet her, aware of Dad's amused look at me, 'I've just made myself one.'

I had to get out eventually. The walls began to close in. That good, free feeling turned, as it usually did, to claustrophobia. I decided to visit Chris again to see how he was getting on. None too good, as it turned out.

I drove this time, not wanting to throw myself on the mercy of the Christmas bus and train timetables. He opened the door to me looking pale and thin. As he led me in I noticed he was limping.

We opened the bottle of whiskey I'd bought him and settled down to catch up. I decided to limit myself to one glass after last night's session with Dad.

Things had got worse for Chris since we'd last met. He was now suffering from a muscle-wasting affliction which the doctors were having some difficulty in isolating. It was obvious to me he was also psychologically affected by his duty. I was glad he still had his religion as some solace. Fortunately, he'd caught on to a strain of Christianity far healthier than Catholicism. I think he had enough guilt already without being crucified with more.

He'd been unable to work since leaving the forces and now

relied on invalidity pay and some pittance from the Social Security to support his wife and children. Pulling out early meant he wasn't eligible for an army pension. This made me absolutely fucking furious but I decided not to rage about it in his presence; I reckoned that would only make him feel worse. I thought, No wonder they say that old soldiers never die, they just fade away. And it wasn't even that he was old. He was too young for this.

As I'd aged within the army this was something that had increasingly begun to annoy me – the way young men were taken in, trained up and prepared as best they could be for what horrors might face them, but then apparently ignored afterwards when those same horrors stamped out the spark inside them.

In the First and Second World Wars, if you were lucky it would be called shell-shock; and, if you weren't, as was often the case, you'd be shot as a coward. Chris had always been strong under fire. He was as brave as any man I'd met in Northern Ireland and I'd always felt better with him at my side. But I think the after-shock was still running through him. Being smarter than me, or at least more intellectual (we'd both been pretty street-smart), hadn't done him any favours. I'd seen simpler lads walk in and out pretty unscathed, mentally.

'I'm thinking I might sell my Military Cross,' he said suddenly.

'Aw, you're not serious,' I said. I could tell from his face that he was. This really put the tin lid on things. It might only be a bit of minted metal and ribbon to a civilian but like any soldier I knew what it really meant. Decorations were rare enough to be treasured. That medal was heavier than its own weight with symbolism. There was no prouder moment in a soldier's life than receiving it, and deciding to sell it could only be a sign of desperation or disgust. 'You shouldn't have to do that, Chris.'

He shrugged and said he was only thinking of it but at the end of the day it didn't pay any bills and the money would. He was trying to be pragmatic about it but I could see it pained him.

We talked about what I was doing now and he expressed some envy about my undercover work. It's what he always wanted to do and we both knew he would have been good at it. I mentioned Robert Nairac and Chris nodded, 'Yes, I know of Nairac. Never met him but I knew of him.'

I told him some of the funnier tales of our operations. Well, they seemed funnier now in the retelling than they did at the time. But that was always the way. I said my first sighting of Robert – his bearing and swagger – had reminded me of another soldier I had got to know well during my early tours.

'Who's that then?' Chris asked as he poured himself another shot.

'You, you dozy sod.'

I told him about Sarah and realized that he was the first of my old friends whom I'd really discussed it with. That seemed a sure sign of something. I was glad he had his wife and family around him. I didn't like the thought of him going through this by himself.

By the time I left he seemed more like his old self. I felt he had a long haul ahead of him, but I thought his natural resilience should see him through.

I drove home steadily, and not just because of the drink singing through me. My talk with Chris had been sobering. Nothing like the cold, cruel hand of reality to slap you to your senses, I thought, especially at Christmas when most of the world felt forced into being happy. I pitied any carol singers who might have the misfortune to call at my mum and dad's while I was there. If I answered the door to them I could only imagine one response to 'Ding Dong Merrily on High' – and the second word of it would be 'off'.

I spent New Year's Eve night down the local with some pals of mine from the old days. I'd known most of them since childhood when we'd played war games together and got into bother with the nuns. Many of them still worked down the pit. They worked their hardest at the coal-face, but the effort they put into having a good time drinking was a close second.

After shouting myself hoarse over the music and noise I left the pub just before midnight to their bellows of 'Happy New Year!' and took the short and cold walk home. I wanted to see in the New Year with my parents.

The old couple from next door were there with them. They'd known me since I was a kid. We all clinked glasses as Big Ben chimed on the telly. Fireworks may have been going off around the world, there may have been thousands in Trafalgar Square and on the streets of Dublin but I was happier here in my own little plot. There was only one thing that could have made it better.

I called Sarah and her dad answered, sounding merry and light over the noise in the background of their own celebrations. Sarah came on and it was good to hear her voice. She was drink-happy and I struggled to get a word in edgeways. I didn't mind. I was content to listen. Until now I felt like I'd been away ages but talking to her brought home the fact that I would be returning in a couple of days. To be honest, seeing her was the only thing I was looking forward to about it. I told her. We'd long passed that initial stage you go through of trying to play it cool to keep one another interested.

'Aww, you ol' romantic. Yer sure that's not just the drink talking, now. I wouldn't want to get my hopes up,' she said in a coy, mock-girly voice.

'No. I mean it,' I said. She fell silent for a few seconds (a long time for her).

'Missed you, too, Mister D'Arcy. Come see me soon as you get back, will you?'

'You're second on my list,' I said.

'Second! What, you mean after that old dear you've been knocking off down the lane?' She laughed all the way through me explaining what she already knew, that I had to sign in at Dungannon as soon as I landed. She said she didn't mind being an army widow and before I knew it I said she didn't run the risk of being a widow until after we were married. Now she did pause. I squeezed my eyes tight shut. It wasn't my clumsy proposal I regretted but that awful implication of widowhood if I was killed. After the last few days' conversations with Chris and my dad this was the thing that struck me most about what I'd just said. Fortunately, Sarah was so shocked by the proposal itself that she didn't seem to pick up on it.

'Did I just hear what I thought I heard?' she said finally. The family noise all around me and that clammering down the phone line suddenly felt like an intrusion. I said she'd heard right.

We talked for a while longer until I heard Sarah's dad calling her and we had to say goodbye. I turned back to the room to find everyone smiling at me.

'Will you look at the grin on him, Mother?' Dad said. 'First time I've seen him smile!'

'Well, he's been talking to that lass of his, haven't you, Nicky?' She came over to me. She asked how serious I was about Sarah and when I answered she said she wondered if I was thinking of settling over there. Both of us knowing about my constant run-ins with the Catholic-school sisters when I was a kid, I replied, 'No, Ma. Not in Ireland. Too many nuns.'

After I'd returned there Sarah and I got reacquainted with indecent haste. We had some catching up to do.

She had now started coming back to my quarters at night. Never staying over, though. Even if it wasn't until the wee small hours, I always made sure she got home in time to keep up the pretence to her parents that she'd only been to a late-night dance. It always worked. Apart from one time, which immediately went down as a classic in our history.

This night I took her to a big regimental dinner dance. It was a black-tie affair with officers and top brass there, arm in arm with their womenfolk. I was done up in a strangulating tux, looking for all the world like the bastard offspring as a result of James Bond shagging a penguin. Sarah played Scarlett to my Rhett Butler. I thought she looked the belle of the ball in her long evening gown (or 'posh frock', as we both called it).

As was the usual manner at these dos the blokes got together for men-talk and the women formed their own groups to talk about whatever it was that women talked about when they got together. I thought it was just the natural order of things that this was some-thing we men would be forever kept in the dark about. We always conceitedly thought they were discussing us, of course, and, if they were, I'm sure it wasn't as flattering as we would have liked. I knew if I approached them then Sarah would turn around and throw back at me an old Yorkshire phrase I'd taught her – 'We're talking *about* you, not *to* you!'

Whenever she looked over at me in mid-conversation and threw me that smile I just wanted to invent an excuse for an early exit so I could find out if that dress came off as easily as it went on.

When we did get back to my base at Dungannon we headed for the fire door that I always left ajar on nights like this. That way I could slip her into my room without all the palava of using the main entrance. As we approached the door I saw a large, five-metre square of still-wet cement in front of it. I'd forgotten that workmen had been in all day relaying the area. I decided to live up to my outfit and do the gallant thing by carrying Sarah to the door. At worst I'd just have a good shoeshine job to do the next morning. Or so I thought. The combination of fresh cement, a headful of wine and Sarah's weight proved to be my downfall. And hers. Halfway across she shrieked when I went arse over elbow and slipped flat on my back with her astride me. She was already laughing uncontrol-lably before we hit the deck.

'Shit! Do you know how much this suit cost me?' She just remained sat on top of me, laughing. 'And,' I said, 'have you got any immediate plans to get your fat arse off me within the next hour?'

She flicked some cement at my face. 'Don't go blaming me, Romeo! I'm no more than seven stone, I'll have you know.' She hitched up her dress, tiptoed the rest of the way to the door and stood there pointing and laughing. 'Just look at the face on you! James bloody Bond, indeed. You look like a right dog's dinner!'

I heaved myself up, clomped forward and tried to throw my cement-heavy arms around her. She screamed and ran inside.

An hour or so later I got my own back. She had to go to the toilet and, as usual, she used the gents' just down the corridor from my room. After peeping out to make sure of the all-clear she sprinted out wrapped only in a towel. Then I heard the noise of boots and voices. It was the Special Patrol Group lads returning from a night patrol. I knew they shared a room which was right next to the toilets. I lay back smiling with my hands behind my head.

It was half an hour before Sarah dared to emerge. She bolted back into my room wide-eyed and started cursing me for not coming to rescue her. When she'd heard them arrive and the noise of their rowdy behaviour through the wall she had been frightened of coming out of the cubicle in case she ran into one of them. I said I'd swallowed some cement and it must have set inside me. She said she thought my stiffness was due to something else entirely. Ten out of ten for observation, I thought.

We set off back to Cookstown to get her home at a reasonable hour. I was so knackered, though, that about halfway there I had to pull in to the side of the road for a short kip. Sarah said she would wake me in a half-hour. When I did wake, cold and aching, I saw the first reds of sunrise tinging the sky. Sarah had fallen asleep beside me. We'd been there for hours. I shook her awake. She came round slowly and then sat bolt upright.

'Holy Christ! My father's gonna kill me!'

We raced back up to Cookstown like bats out of hell. Or more like a couple of vampires trying to beat dawn. Sarah bashed the dashboard and politely inquired (at the top of her voice) if 'this piece of crap' I was driving would go any faster. I started laughing, which didn't help any. As I pulled up the lane the car had barely stopped before she already had the door open and was out, belting up the path. The cement around the bottom of her gown had set hard and I could see it thumping against her ankles. She paused, hiked it up over her knees and leaped the steps. She turned at the door, saw me laughing and silently mouthed, 'Fuck off.' I thought, Charming, and took my chance to escape.

I had to wait until I next saw her for the full tale of what happened. She had crept into the house, shoes in hand, and tiptoed up the stairs, desperately trying to remember which ones creaked. Unfortunately it was now so late that her mother was already on her way down. They met in the middle. Her mother put a finger to her lips, indicated that her dad was still in his cave and hissed, 'Where have you been?' Whispering back, Sarah said she'd been home for hours and had just gone downstairs for a glass of water. Her mum then noticed the cement caked on the dress and was just about to open her mouth when a bellow came from the bedroom.

'Is that her, Lilian? Is that your daughter! Throw the tramp out! Does she know what time it is? Throw that tramp out of this house!'

Her mum had turned to Sarah and said, 'Notice how you're only *my* daughter when you're in trouble?'

Her dad's vendetta of silence went on for two weeks. He relayed messages to Sarah through her mother, even if they were all sat at the same table. He drove her to the bus stop every morning, as he always did, but 'without so much as breaking breath to me', as Sarah put it.

In fact, this silent treatment had only recently ended. So now I was allowed within a ten-mile radius of the house. It almost made me yearn for the comparatively easier option of fighting the IRA.

15

SAS CALLING

In what was to be the bloodiest year since 1972, 1976 began in the manner it was to continue, with five Catholics being murdered in South Armagh by the UVF. Republicans exacted swift revenge in the same area the following day when they took twelve Protestant workers off a bus and shot them all. One survived. It was still only 5 January. Happy New Year.

Two days later these two atrocities, along with the combined deaths of nearly fifty soldiers in the same area of South Armagh and the increasing sectarian violence, prompted the British prime minister, Harold Wilson, to send in 22nd Special Air Service Regiment: the SAS.

My reaction on hearing this was a double realization: that the escalation of violence had finally made it easier for Wilson to be conned by Box 5 into sending in the SAS; and that this was when the deaths would start to multiply.

In regards to the first point, I thought Wilson had been conned into deploying the SAS because I doubted whether he would have knowingly sanctioned them as death-squads. Box 5, on the other hand, would have had no such reticence. Troop levels on the streets were at their height but, with rioting much less prevalent now, they found themselves with little to do but be blown up and shot at. When the emphasis of the war had first started to shift, the importance of 'hard intelligence' became paramount. That's where the likes of myself and Nairac came in: keeping the forces fresh with information. The SAS couldn't do this. They were in no position to source information. They would merely be enforcers.

The second realization was based on none-too-secret knowledge of how the SAS operated. These boys went in hard, and never to wound or capture. Whatever HM government's policy was, 'Shoot to kill' was virtually embroidered on their pillows as something to live and breathe by.

They had been officially deployed in Northern Ireland only twice before, and both times in a much more secret capacity, the exact nature of which was only known to certain army personnel. This time there was good reason for their arrival to be made known to everyone. Their deployment was part political, part practical and part propaganda. With such a fanfare being made of the SAS's deployment, it would undoubtedly put the shits up the Provos. How successful the regiment would actually be on the ground, however, remained to be seen. I thought that if they stuck to acting on the information supplied to them by the likes of Robert then they would be very effective. They had to avoid going it alone too much.

Despite the mystique surrounding 22 Regiment, the reality was different. A lot of the int boys basically considered them nothing but 'jump and run' merchants: great stamina, strength and resolve (their training was second to none) but not especially blessed intellectually. Rather than implement actions they simply acted on orders. In their capacity as a brutally sharp and efficient tool, I could see why Nairac was rubbing his hands at the thought of using them.

The roots of the modern-day SAS lay in their emergence as a counter-insurgency force during the collapse of the empire, but the army had already mistakenly tried to apply these out-of-date tactics to Northern Ireland and only served to make things worse. The Troubles had evolved into a strange brew of urban guerrilla warfare fought with jungle tactics by underground terrorists: three wars in one. The SAS boys, for all their training, would flounder out of their depth without a good LINCO. It brought to mind something that Nairac had said to me on one of our recent ops: he mentioned 'getting the real boys in'. By this I presume he meant the SAS. He would be getting the reliable assassins he'd always yearned for. And they would be on the receiving end of the best info available from one of intelligence's top operatives. A marriage made in heaven, or hell, depending where your allegiances lay.

They arrived at Bessbrook in South Armagh, near the border with the Republic and right in the middle of the anarchy they were here to help quell. A small advance party came at first, to be joined later by a full squadron.

My stay away over Christmas had seemed to last ages at the time but now that I was back it faded quickly into the distance. The news of the SAS flying in and the ripples it created, and the constant requirements on me in Dungannon, day-in, day-out, demanded that all my concentration be directed to the present and to the immediate future.

As soon as I got a call from Nairac I immediately set up a meet with him. I knew he had now moved from 4 Troop commander to being the official LINCO between Box 5 Special Branch and the SAS. I suspected this move would mean I would see less of him. His time would now be exclusively demanded and jealously guarded.

With another intelligence officer riding shotgun I drove down to Bessbrook a few days later. I would also use it as an opportunity to see Colonel Inge.

Robert had changed his appearance yet again. Too many undercover operatives had taken advantage of the freedom of working in civvies by growing their hair and beards in a similar fashion. It had almost become a standing joke that you could tell a member of the security forces by the fact that he tried so hard not to look like one. I'd cut my hair a little and now just remained unshaven at most.

When I walked in I immediately clocked the SAS boys. They had a certain look I had come to recognize. I'd previously worked beside them in Africa, Germany and even back in Norfolk. They wore uniforms, of course, but generally just the bits of it they were happy with. In Africa their transport had been Land-Rovers, or 'Pinkoes', so-called because they were painted pink. Strangely enough, it was the colour found to offer most camouflage in the desert.

After Robert had introduced me as the LINCO operating out of Dungannon, we retired to an office he'd commandeered for the day. As we sat down, I motioned back through the closed door to the guys outside.

'Is this gonna quieten things down or make things hotter?'

'Bit of both,' he replied. 'One should lead to the other.' I noticed he didn't say in which order. To a certain extent it depended on the IRA's reaction. Things had calmed down noticeably in this area since news of the SAS's arrival had become public, but I put it down to initial nerves. It wouldn't be long before something happened. Then we'd see the weight of the SAS's response.

Even though the regiment was deployed only in South Armagh, I asked if there was any possibility of me using them further north, around my area of Dungannon. Robert said no. They were under strict instructions only to operate within their mandate, particularly during this high-profile stage. I thought it was understandable but

I knew it wouldn't last. You didn't bring in the SAS to play by the rules. Cross-border reccies would probably be their first ops.

Crossing the border was illegal, of course. The Republic of Ireland was – and still is – a foreign land, another country, and incursions there meant serious trouble both legally and politically. That didn't stop us from doing it, though. Half the time it was accidental, because the borderline wasn't clearly defined. The other half was deliberate, because we knew we'd get away with it.

When I'd been at the Aughnacloy checkpoint I'd sometimes taken out the brigadier's helicopter for reconnaissance missions. The chopper and pilot were made available to me every Sunday when the brigadier didn't use them. There was usually bugger-all else to do on that day anyway.

We'd swoop down over hills and fields like surfers on air, or hang high above a point, turning, as I peered through the bubble and shouted instructions over the clatter of the blades. Sometimes the pilot would nervously point out how far we had strayed over the border but we always managed to get away with it. When we landed and I jumped out, head-down under the downdraft, I always left feeling half deaf, half hoarse.

Pity I couldn't use the SAS back in Dungannon yet, I thought. They were the best for long-term, observational dig-ins. From these camouflage posts we learned of the movements of suspects and could also ID their associates. This was important because, as well as nailing down who was in which active service unit, we could identify the likely replacements if any of the ASU were killed. In my area of East Tyrone I knew most of the ASUs who were operational.

Observation posts were the rare occasions when you could get really good intelligence from your own lads without having either to rely on touts (who were never 100 per cent trustworthy) or put yourself at any personal risk. 'Personal risk' was a phrase that was to come back to haunt me a few weeks later.

We had been trying, and failing, to gather more information on this one particular guy who was suspected of being involved in a recent shooting. One of my sources had given me the initial nod but we still needed corroboration. I didn't yet want to send a snatch-squad into the house to pick him up and search the place in case they didn't find anything. Then he would be alerted and even more difficult to finger. I decided to go in myself, alone one night. This was quite common practice; illegal, of course, but so was blowing half the country to hell and back. Pretty soon they'd be able to twin-town Belfast with Beirut.

From these reccies we picked up information on all manner of things: contacts (some addresses as far away as America), arms, finances, associates, meetings and so on. All little jigsaw pieces that clicked into a wider picture. And if a hole remained you could imagine the rest.

The pressure on me hadn't let up any in this new year. The brigadier told his unit intelligence officers that he wanted new int tasks for the troops every time they went out. The intelligence officers got on my case. I was expected to deliver. Being good at this had only led them to expect even more of me.

Unlike the farmhouse reccies, where every strange footstep could arouse suspicion, this one was easier to approach as the suspect lived in a town house. The usual comings and goings on the street would provide a little cover. I decided to leave it until late Friday night, when he would be most likely to go out: out on the juice with the rest of the good Catholics.

I traced the house phone number and called to check that no one answered. When there was no response I used another form of trace that had been instigated during a procedure called 'Operation Vengeful'. This was when all the car registration numbers passing through vehicle checkpoints were logged and computer-linked so we could trace a vehicle's movements. I went to the ops room and heard the good news that my suspect's car had been logged leaving the area. I thought, Yeah, go on, you bastard, go get drunk and turn your fucking car over and save us all a lot of bother. That this boy was some nasty piece of work was one of the things we didn't need to corroborate.

Dave Stott, a colleague of mine, joined me as back-up. He was to carry the radio and take the tip-off from the nearest vehicle check-point when the car was returning. If we weren't gone already, then Dave would whistle me down. Simple. How could it fail? It's not like people were being butchered over here on a regular basis for getting things wrong, was it?

Tonight, being tooled-up meant carrying more than just the Browning 9mm that was laid out before me on the table along with all the other equipment I needed. Finding some comfort in ritual, I went through the usual routine. I picked up the 9mm, slid the clip out of the handle to make sure it was full, clapped it back, latched a round up the spout, checked the safety catch was on so I didn't blow my own arse off and then tucked it in the hollow of my back. I picked up the thin, silver micro-camera (only five-by-one inches), snapped a picture off at the floor to test the flash and pocketed it in my inside left pocket. Next, I tested the torch and weighed it in my palm like the club I knew it could double-up as. This slipped into my outside right pocket. Then I slid the sprung, metal ring towards me which contained various master keys for Union, Yale and mortise. Lock-picking was one of the easier parts of the op. Frightening, really, to think how easy it was for someone who knew. As well as several skeleton keys for turning the cams on a tooth-key lock, I had a thin but rigid metal card for slipping the wedge on a Yale; unlike in the movies this wasn't done with a credit or cheque card. Finally, I put on the thin, black cotton gloves, first pulling them down tight from the wrist and then flexing my fingers. It was hard to get men's gloves that weren't like cumbersome gauntlets but I found that large-size women's gloves fitted like a second skin.

I zipped and fastened all the pockets on my leather jacket. I was dressed dark but not overdramatically so. I didn't want to look like a cat-burglar.

By the time we got to the house it was late. Most people were already where they were going to be for the rest of the night: slumped either in their front rooms or in the booth of a pub. There were still enough stragglers on the streets to give us cover, though. We moved around the house and into the enclosed, paved area at the back. Dave settled down on his haunches by the bins. From here he could whistle me a warning when the checkpoint radioed through or, with it being an end house, if anyone entered through the front unannounced.

I slipped the Yale lock quickly and eased the door open – good, no bolts. I'd have had to go in through one of the windows otherwise. I moved into the dark of the kitchen, closing the door softly behind me. The house and its rooms were small and I felt cramped even more by the dark over my shoulders. I edged out of the kitchen to a place at the foot of the stairs. Here it was safe to use the torch without any tell-tale signs to outsiders. After checking the curtains were drawn I moved into the front room and flashed the searchlight over its surfaces. The beam hit some glass and flared up the wall – a pair of kind eyes flashed at me. Christ! And it was. A picture of him smiling benignly, his Sacred Heart on offer. No good looking at me like that, I thought, I don't play for your old man's team any more.

I ran the beam over the dusty screen of the TV and then down an old chest of drawers. This looked like the kind of place where papers would be kept. I didn't know how much time I had. I'd have to work fairly quickly to allow for an unexpected early return.

Ignoring all the usual domestic clutter that seems to clog up everybody's life, I photographed letters and notes that may have held clues to other connections. I didn't have time to sift it and examine it too closely. That would be done back at base after we'd been in the darkroom, having watched the photos emerging from the fluid.

I spread the papers on the carpet and bent low, squinting behind the camera. Every time the flash went *pupp!* it blew out a cloud of light that chased shadows round the room. My own shape jumped up and fell on the wall beside me. Every now and again the back of my neck would itch with a sound or movement that made me spin around, half expecting to see an axe or the torn edge of a shovel heading for my skull.

As thin as these gloves were, they made everything feel thicker, even time. The normal progression of time always became twisted into something stranger during these affairs. A minute could stretch out like a spring; so I might be examining a diary, for example, and suddenly come alive to the feeling I'd been there for hours – time snapped back – I'd tug the sleeve back off my watch and find it had only been minutes. The adrenalin score was immense, like being in a gunbattle; like being alone again in danger, because that's exactly where you were. My heart beat and trilled like an alarm hammer; partly out of fear and hype, partly out of thrill and promise. I didn't know what I might find. Maybe there was some bad bastard upstairs who was dead-to-the-world asleep until he heard noises below and then decided to lay in wait for me with a razor. I rose up to the dark landing. Some of the stairs squeaked but I ignored them. Or tried. If you let each noise spook you pretty soon the whole house seemed to groan and creak like a ship at sea. I thought of that dead old man I'd found upstairs back in the Ardoyne. The image of his eaten face jumping out of these shadows suddenly flashed into my mind.

I reached behind and pulled the Browning out just to be on the safe side. I pushed each door open with the barrel. I found the same dark nothingness in each room staring back at me. The dark itself seemed animated – buzzing almost – like some low-intensity static humming through the air, just on the edge of registered sound. I crouched then and, elbows on knees, rested the cold spine of the gun against my lips. Then I stood and sheathed it back in my waistband and moved to search the rooms one by one.

In the bigger bedroom I bent and pulled a handle that stuck out from under the bed. The suitcase hit the bedframe and jolted me back. I pulled again a few times until it shot out. It was ominously heavy. I could smell oil. The lid was thin and buckled. I unzipped it and whipped it back. Yeah, this guy was tooled-up all right, but only for DIY. I stared down on a power drill, cutters and chisel blades. But why keep this stuff upstairs? I flashed the torchlight over the humped contents of the case. It glinted over the hard edges. No stains or smears on the metal though; none that I could see, anyway. Maybe it was innocent. Maybe they had been wiped clean. Kidnappings and victim-torture had brought a whole new and grisly meaning to 'do-it-yourself'. Only recently I'd heard of the kidnapping of a prominent Protestant businessman. All of his fingers on one hand had been lopped off with a bolt-cutter and then dropped into a padded envelope along with a ransom note.

I reached into the case, fished out the chuck-key for the drill and pocketed it. That would inconvenience the fuckers if nothing else. Or maybe, I thought, these are just the improvized equivalents of sex toys for this guy and his old lady. She must be a tough nut to crack, I thought, just as the door downstairs flew open against the inside wall and someone yelled 'Bastard!' I froze – then heard laughing as she fell in after him shouting, 'Ye daft bastard! *You* daft bastard!'

I dropped the lid, zipped it (even the rasp sounded loud) and slid it back under the bed. I moved behind the door, flattened myself against the wall and prepared to deck him with the butt-end of the Browning as soon as he appeared and slap her senseless if she started screaming the alarm. The last thing I wanted to do was run out into the approaching arms of an army patrol.

Then it suddenly occurred to me – what the fuck happened to Dave? I heard them laughing again as their drunkenness made it a major operation for both of them to mount the stairs. I chanced a glance out. They were still halfway down. She was as big, ugly and drunk as he was. I knew I didn't even have time to dart into one of the other rooms where I could have lain in wait until the right time to make my escape. I was in their room and they were coming up into it. Simple as that. No use moaning. End of story. Fuck!

With a sinking feeling I gave in to the inevitable and climbed into the large wardrobe behind me. Even as I was doing so I was almost smiling at the absurdity, thinking, This is such a joke. I felt trapped in some bad Benny Hill comedy sketch. Things were about to get a lot funnier, I knew that much.

They entered the bedroom. I pressed myself to the back of the wardrobe and pulled the clothes inside in front of me. No chink of light came through the crack in the doors so at least they'd left the light off. I thought, Even if he opens the doors to throw his clothes in here, I might still get away with it. Providing he doesn't notice the extra pair of shoes.

My heart hammered at my chest to the point where I was sure it could be heard. At least I'd have the element of surprise on my side, especially if he opened these doors in his underpants. A sharp kick to the knackers should do it.

Even out of sight in the hidden depths of the wardrobe the next thing that happened really shocked me. The guy let rip with a fart like someone tearing cloth. She began laughing and I began to realize I was probably in for one of the longest nights of my life. He didn't stop there either but went for a full twenty-one-gun salute. I stood there thinking, You dirty bastard – if even one whiff of that comes through these doors I'm gonna jump out and kick your horrific, fat arse right back down those stairs and throw your ugly bird on top of you.

I heard the bedsprings moan under the weight of the pair of them and realized they must have just cast their clothes where they'd stood. Unfortunately, the bed wasn't the only thing that began moaning. My first thought was, 'Oh, thank you God. Is this your revenge? Making me listen to these two fuckers rutting like warthogs. The final straw, I thought, would be if I heard him drag that suitcase out and start the drill.

When the snorting and squealing finally died down I gave it another half an hour. Or so I thought. To be honest, I'd now completely lost track of time: funny the things it can do to your mind when you're stood in a wardrobe in the middle of the night listening to two strangers fuck.

The sound of the first deep snore being choked up was the sign for me to get out. I opened the wardrobe door gingerly and very slowly lowered myself to the floor. I glanced sideways only briefly at the two heaving mounds under the blankets. I felt if I stared too hard it might somehow wake them up. And by now I wasn't in the mood to fight one of them fully clothed, let alone the pair of them naked. I just hoped this had been worth it.

I could feel the grimace fixed on my face as I eased myself towards the door, tiptoeing over their underwear, around their shoes and on to the landing. And then slowly down each stair. I only relaxed a little back in the cool dark of the kitchen. I yanked the back door open and saw Dave exactly where I'd left him. I crouched down beside him. I really wanted to shout but I had to reduce it to a tight hiss.

'What the fuck happened!'

'I – I didn't get a sit rep from . . . from the checkpoint, Nicky,' he said, speaking with some difficulty because of the cold. 'They didn't call. And then when I heard them at the front door – it was too late. Sorry, mate.'

When I looked at my watch and saw we'd been here for three hours I could hardly believe it. It seemed much longer. I helped Dave to his feet. The cold night had nearly frozen the poor bugger solid. I thought I'd had it bad, but at least I'd seen the cabaret.

Big things were starting to happen. Within a few weeks of my search-and-find mission, we were into March: it turned out to be not only mad but absolutely insane. One thing seemed to lead to another.

On the first of the month, Special Category status for paramilitary prisoners was finally ended. It had first been conceded to them in 1972, partly because of the twin disasters of internment and Bloody Sunday and also as a result of a hunger-strike campaign by IRA prisoners. The concession of Special Category status was both important and a mistake. It meant that imprisoned terrorists were considered political rather than criminal internees: prisoners of war, if you like. It's what they had always wanted and demanded.

Now it was removed. It had done nothing but help legitimize the IRA's view of themselves as freedom fighters with the freedom to kill others in pursuit of it, which they had done with abandon. This year was already shaping up to be one of the worst.

The 'truce' that had been called in 1975, which had in reality been over for months, was finally announced dead and buried when the Falls Road Centre was closed by the army on 18 March.

Then an IRA commander by the name of Sean McKenna was arrested north of the border by an army patrol. This might not have been so remarkable if not for the fact that McKenna had been captured and kidnapped from his home in the Republic by an SAS unit. After the 'lift' they transported him over the border and presented him gift-wrapped to the uniform boys so he could be legally arrested. Job well done, all in all.

The IRA and McKenna cried 'foul', which was rich coming from them: a bit like one boxer pulling his shorts up to his chin and then complaining about a low blow. At first, McKenna might have felt badly done to about his abduction but the crying would stop soon enough. He was about to learn just how lucky he was to be alive at all.

I was to learn even more about Robert Nairac, the SAS and my position in the middle of it all. And also get an insight into future deaths.

16

HARD TARGETS – PRESENT DEATH, FUTURE LIFE

The month started off a hell of a lot better than it was to end. In fact, it was as good a start as any man could wish for. I was sitting in my office when a knock came on the door and the commanding officer's head appeared. 'I've got a young lady here to see you, Nicky. She asked for you.'

I got out of my chair, puzzled. This was strange. These offices were strictly out of bounds to anyone but the int boys: no visitors, no squaddies, no unauthorized personnel. I don't think a single woman had ever been near here. As I reached the door the CO opened it fully to reveal Miss World. The former Miss Puerto Rico, recently crowned Miss World, was standing there in all her gold-skinned glory, giving me a smile that made my bones soft. I had seen her photograph in the papers, of course, but to see her in the flesh was something else. I felt like I'd suddenly been hit with the realization of how drab my whole life had been. I can only remember her first name Wilemina, and she had the kind of beauty you just don't see in the streets where you live. Unless you live in Puerto Rico, I guess.

She extended her hand to me, we shook and she then walked into my office, followed by the grinning CO. I looked at him, totally gob-smacked. I'd already heard rumours of a planned visit by her as a morale boost for the troops but never thought it would happen. It was a bit like when Bob Hope flew out to Vietnam to visit the Yanks. Except they had the double disappointment of losing the war and having to put up with Bob frigging Hope.

The CO trailed behind her like a lapdog in the almost visible wake of her perfume. God, her perfume was amazing. It was the first time I'd ever smelled a really fine, expensive scent. As the CO zoomed past me, I quickly recovered from the shock, nudged him to one side and made a bee-line for her side. She was standing by the noticeboard behind my desk examining the display of photographs pinned there of IRA members, suspect members and just the downright suspect: bad photos of worse people. Her English was pretty bad: didn't even qualify for pidgin English, really.

She pointed at the pictures on the wall and said, *'Bandidos?'* *Bandidos!* I thought, bloody hell! She can even make this bunch of cold, ugly fuckers sound romantic. Rather than answer, 'Erm, no. Actually, miss, they are the East Tyrone Brigade of the Provisional IRA,' I opted for a simple 'yes' and a nod. She seemed pleased that she had made some contact with me. I was equally, if not a hundred times more, pleased.

Our unit photographer, Frankie, came into the office then and started taking pictures of us. We shook hands finally and she wafted out with the CO in tow; he was grinning like a shit-eating fox. Frankie ran out after them before I could collar him. I knew he'd set it up. I'd been working him hard lately, processing and developing the films of evidence and ID pictures; sometimes right through the night to get the info out quick. This was him and the CO setting me up for a later piss-take. Well, if this was their idea of a joke, they could pull one every day.

I followed her out, as the rest of the camp seemed to be doing, every man just nodding absently if someone was talking to him, not answering a question if asked, straining to see as she moved out of view. Eventually she stopped to pose with some squaddies and I've never in all my life seen such a bunch of attack dogs turn so quickly into big puppies. Mind you, I did understand. I'd just been through it.

I moved over to the bar to get a drink and to stand and watch. I got chatting to a woman there who turned out to be Julia Morley, the Englishwoman who, with her husband Jack, organized the Miss World contest. Both up on bar stools watching her Miss World charm the masses, she asked how I could be a soldier looking like I did: long hair, 'tash and casual clothes. I made some vague reference to my work.

'Oh, James Bond kind of stuff?' she said.

'Well, not exactly. For a start we don't get women like that,' I said, nodding to Wilemina.

She started to tell me of the difficulties of chaperoning her. She said she practically put her to bed. Poor thing.

'Actually,' I said, 'what with Dungannon here being my area, that now becomes my job.' She laughed as if to say 'you wish'.

I suddenly remembered that I was supposed to pick Sarah up. I downed my drink and rushed out. By the time I got to her house I was very late and she wasn't best pleased. Even less so when I told her why.

'You *what*? Miss World? D'you think I fell out of a tree this morning or somethin'? Miss World? You pathetic wee man. Worst excuse I've ever heard.'

'Actually, you should feel flattered that I dropped her to come back for you!' Finally I dragged her out to the car and we returned to Dungannon in time to see Julia Morley and Wilemina as they waved goodbye from their escorted limousine.

Things could only go from good to bad. One night I returned from Cookstown after dropping Sarah back at home. As usual I was tired but satisfied. The drive from Dungannon to pick her up earlier in the night always seemed a much shorter journey than the later return. All down to what is waiting for you at the other end, I suppose.

What was waiting for me at this end was my bed and a nightcap. Entering my room, I could still smell Sarah's perfume. I poured out a final shot for myself. The other glass on the tray was ringed with pink lipstick. This last year had been a strange one. Somehow I'd had to learn how to balance my happiness at meeting Sarah with the usual dour acceptance of death and dishonour throughout the winter killing season. But knowing her made things more difficult. It made me too aware of what I had to lose if things went wrong.

Before I hit the sack I decided to go down to the ops room and check out any incoming reports. I said hi to the ops officer and signaller on late duty and walked over to the telex machine. This was where all the incident/situation reports from Brigade HQ were sent. I scanned the perforated paper that stuttered out of the telex, pulling up the reels that had spewed out into the tray. The current stuff was none too dramatic so I worked back down to earlier messages. One stood out. It had only come in a few hours before and concerned the discovery of a body near Forkhill in South Armagh. The area had already been secured, it said, and an ATO bomb-disposal expert requested.

Forkhill? That was near border country – really near. It was only a few hundred yards from the Republic. I'd only been on one reccie

241

deep enough south to come close to that area and that had been with Nairac. We had driven off that day without me knowing we'd be leaving my area and straying so far down south. His rank of captain put him in charge of any magical mystery tour he decided to take us on.

'No updates on this twenty-one hundred hours?' I said to the ops officer, holding the paper up for him to see. He angled his head for a look and then shook it. I let the paper drop and decided not to dwell on it. Sometimes I felt like I was trying to solve every single sodding thing in a fifty-mile radius.

Clocking off was never my speciality, even more so since I'd been undercover. There was no regimented daily duty like there was back in uniform. The day when war became nine to five was the day I'd get regular hours. Sometimes I'd work on reports through the night and then sleep late (if possible). Often I'd find the early hours enabled me to think better, more clearly, away from the clatter of the day. Not tonight, though. I was just too tired.

I had a spectacularly nasty dream. No specific images jumped out, it was more just an overall feeling of horrible unease that seemed to nag and gnaw at me right through the night; like being weighed down with disease. The oddest thing was also the most ordinary – the sound of someone repeatedly knocking on a door and calling my name. It got louder until it became real.

I sat up groggily and shouted, 'OK', and the knocking stopped. It had sounded insistent and panicky. In the time it took me to heave myself on to the floor, wrap a dressing gown round and pad over to the door I had already put two and two together and come up with a dead four. Dead four = four kill = Forkhill? That 2100 hours incident/sit rep on the telex sprang straight to mind.

I rested my forehead on the back of the door and massaged the bridge of my nose for a second. I could hear shuffling outside and see shadows flick under the door jamb. I opened it.

I only had a second to register the face before the guy pushed past me, bumping my shoulder, saying, 'Christ, Nicky.' It was Martin, an old colleague of mine from uniform days. He looked pale and worse for wear and was flapping badly.

'Forkhill?' I asked simply as I closed the door. He nodded.

'Yeah, you heard?'

'Read it off the sit reps. Before we go on, Martin,' I said in mid-yawn as I moved to perch on the bed edge, 'do me a favour and stop pacing the fucking room. You're making me dizzy.'

He sat down next to me, trying to still his agitation, and we both torched a cig each off a single match. I told him there was one thing I didn't know yet – the identity of the stiff. He said the name: 'Cleary.'

'Peter Cleary?' I asked. He nodded as he took a drag and blew the smoke to the ceiling. 'Fuck me, Martin. You've offed a prime bastard there, son.'

Cleary was an IRA staff captain: one of the big-time boys. I decided to hold back on the congratulations until I'd heard the full story. I poured a brandy out for him. All the way through his account of the night's events he tapped his right heel on the floor.

I already knew that Martin had been taken from his parent regiment and seconded to the SAS. What I didn't know until now was that he was part of the Special Air Service's D Squadron that had moved into South Armagh.

He said he'd been part of a four-man SAS unit that had dug-in around Cleary's girlfriend's house near Forkhill. They had split into two observation posts in a nearby field. Days passed and Cleary didn't show. Martin and the other SAS boys endured the cold and discomfort until they were relieved by another op squad. They had as little success.

I watched now how he cupped his hand around the fag, as if he was still warming himself up.

'You went back out again, though?' I said.

'Yeah. We were briefed by a Special Branch guy, same one we'd seen before. He said to go over the border this time and pick up Cleary from his mother's house in case he didn't show at the girl's. We were supplied with the directions, map locations, everything. And it was all spot-on. We dug in again and snatched him the next night. Took him back over the border to Forkhill then. We were gonna be picked up and flown out.'

'And that's when you did him?' I said. 'Before the chopper got there?'

'Yeah. That's right. I fanned the other three out to light the landing zone for the chopper and then I did him.' He became suddenly agitated again. 'That's why I've come to see you, Nicky, the CID are coming after me for it, that's definite. I know that. So I asked around for how to get in touch with you. I'd already heard you'd been down at Bessbrook with the lads but that was before I got in.'

He downed the last of his brandy, poured himself another and

said, 'I always remember the guys coming to you before when they
had to get out of some shit they'd got in. The CID are gonna fuck
me over on this one, Nicky, they really are.'

All security force shootings, even those by undercover units like
the SAS, were open to judicial inquests like anything else. I thought
if they had something to go for, they probably would. The RUC
Special Branch wouldn't really give a fuck about the knocking off of
some Provo, but their remit was political. The CID boys, on the
other hand, were criminal investigators and they went after
anything and everything. They seemed to take it as a personal
affront if they couldn't solve something. Martin and the other SAS
boys would be in line for a heavy Q and A by the CID. Sometimes
these sessions had to be prepared for. The Sibs would probably be
involved as well: these were the Military Police's own Special
Investigation Branch. If there were any major inconsistencies in
their statements, then Martin had reason to be worried. I told him
to calm down and give me all the details.

He said after the other three had spread out to flare up the landing zone he'd waited until they were out of sight and then shot
Cleary.

'Just say it was self-defence,' I said.

'He was tied up.'

'OK. Well . . . never mind, say he ran at you, tried to butt you or
kick you; anything. "When trying to escape he was shot in the
struggle" – that kinda thing.'

'I shot him eight times,' Martin said, looking at me.

'Fuck. OK . . . all right . . .' I thought this showed all the signs of
him being up shit creek without a canoe, let alone a chuffing
paddle. I could only think of one explanation. I told him to tell CID
that when he'd signed out his rifle, unknown to him he had got one
with a filed-down sear. The sear was an inhibitor pin inside the
firing mechanism of a semi-automatic rifle that prevented it from
loosing off rounds in an automatic burst. Some guys filed this pin
down to convert the rifle. Being on active service, Martin would
have already had a round up the spout so, when he fired, instead of
the expected single shot, he would loose off much more. Eight was
plausible: that would happen in a second, before you'd even
blinked.

'Remember – say the sear was filed down but you didn't know
it. And the rifle's gone back in at base. Let them try to find it if they
want to.'

He calmed down a little then. I said there was one more thing I wanted to know. This wasn't for any reason other than personal curiosity, and to answer something I had suspected right from first learning of this op. I asked him to describe the Special Branch officer who briefed them. He did so, in detail, and I listened with no great surprise as he described Robert Nairac.

I didn't reveal to Martin who Nairac was. As far as he was concerned Nairac was Irish (Robert had briefed them in an accent) and a Special Branch officer.

'Did he actually tell you to kill Cleary?' I asked. 'I mean, in those words.'

'No, that's not how it works, Nicky. They make it plain, though, in every way bar drawing you a fucking picture, just exactly what they want you to do. Cleary was painted as a bad bastard with blood on his hands. They fingered him for that last shooting of that squaddie amongst other stuff. You know, he had history, and plenty of it. And we couldn't pin the bastard down. So I did.'

He then showed me the exact grid reference by a crossroads where they had dumped the body before being lifted out.

'They tell the Sass to do this,' he said finally, 'and then we end up in the fucking firing line. Crazy . . .' (In common with some of its members he pronounced SAS as one word, Sass.)

'Play it like I told you and you should be OK. Just don't start flapping 'cos then they really will clip your wings. OK?'

I led him to the door. He left looking more reassured but still uneasy at the thought of what the next forty-eight hours might bring. I thought it would go all right. If things did hot up too much, then whichever top boys were behind this whole thing would put a lid on it. They wouldn't let an SAS unit be compromised. You needed some weight, though, to silence the CID.

My thoughts turned to Nairac. He was a slippy-tit, that one, for sure; taking me out on that reccie without filling me in on the reason. But there was a hell of a lot at stake, I had to admit. He must be in seventh heaven now, I thought, seeing all that hard-won info of his being converted into results. It wasn't so much a case of the pen being mightier than the sword as turning into one.

Mind you, if I'd been roaming through Republican bars and pubs as regularly as Nairac did, I'd want to see some results for the risks I'd run. This was the pay-off.

Everyone was thoroughly revolted at seeing known gunmen and bombers continually fleeing south to the Republic, practically leaving a trail of fresh blood back to their mothers' doorsteps. Both the Irish authorities and the Garda turned a blind eye. And you had more chance of getting a blow-job from a nun than extraditing someone from south to north.

There had obviously been a pretty quick decision made to move from simply kidnapping Provos and dropping them in the north (as with McKenna) to taking them out of action more finally (as had been done with Cleary). Just another job well done in my book. For every hard-core Republican taken out, you could almost guarantee the preservation of half a dozen lives in the future.

I heard no more from Martin and nothing hit the news, so I figured everything had gone smoothly. A sudden reminder of what might have happened was just round the corner, however. A month later the whole shebang was blown out of the water when an SAS unit was caught by the Garda down in the Republic and arrested. More men in unmarked cars were sent out after the missing unit and they too were caught, this time in a joint Garda/Irish army effort. Being armed to the back teeth with practically everything bar an A-bomb, the lads could hardly deny who they were. They said their incursion had been as a result of a map-reading error. Still, they were charged and bailed, and the news exploded like Semtex.

The propaganda men of the IRA had a field day, of course. It still hadn't been established if it was a genuine map-reading error. It was possible; in parts the border was poorly designated. But even if that was the case, it didn't really matter. They could have just as easily been on a search-and-destroy. On balance, the PR damage caused by their capture was probably equalled out, if not exceeded, by the fear it shot through the ranks of the terrorist groups. Here, in plain light of day, was evidence of heavily armed elite forces prepared to chase them to ground on the very land they believed to be some kind of sanctuary. I thought it might do the IRA the world of good to live with the same fear of assassination that they had already spread among others. I didn't see why they should be spared.

At the same time as they were condemning the activities of the SAS, they would be sanctioning such acts as, for example, the murder of an off-duty RUC sergeant whilst he was at his daughter's wedding: shot dead on the church steps in front of his children. But then that's different, isn't it? He was killed by brave and proud IRA men for the brave and proud IRA cause, so fuck him, and his family, and the God they rode in on. And praise the unholy restraint of the blessed IRA for not pumping a shell right through the bride's white veil and straight out of the back of her head. Such good Catholic boys. Talk about praise God and pass the ammunition.

I thought that at least I'd had the balls to clean myself of religion before I got my hands dirty.

Come July, and the new British Ambassador to the Republic, Chris Ewart-Biggs, was warmly welcomed by the IRA when they blew him apart inside his car outside the embassy. The TV cameras hung their heads over the wreckage in the usual manner; the scene of another human body burned out with the metal was all too familiar, all too depressing.

Funny thing about being in the army is the way it causes people to drift in and out of your life. This can happen to friends, old comrades, lovers, even family. Hopefully it is just a 'drift' away, and not something more final. Moving around, never settling, means you can't take much of anything or anyone with you: just memories, really, and the hope that you'll run into people again. Mostly, whatever happened to them was lost to history. Or sometimes you'd find out further down the line. I was always amazed at the number of times, after being told of someone's death, I'd bump into the guy years later! A rumour would start somewhere without any hard evidence and before you knew it you had written someone off, just like that. I wondered if anyone from my past was walking around now thinking the same about me.

Whenever these ghosts of the undead floated back into your life in the shape of the 'deceased' themselves they always looked surprisingly chipper, for a stiff. And then, sometimes, their real death would whip them back away from you like a kite snap-diving to earth.

I'd been set on the course of thinking about this by a recent incident in South Armagh. A culvert bomb was found on a country track between Bessbrook and Crossmaglen by a local farmer. Crossmaglen was almost on the border and the bomb was nearer there than Bessbrook, so it was right down in South Armagh: right down in what I called 'shit-creek' country because if you visited it you always took a spare paddle.

The bomb, or 'suspect device', to be more accurate (it hadn't yet been confirmed), was partially hidden in one of the small culvert tunnels. In all rural areas these were the tunnels that ran beneath roads at intervals to allow for the free-flow of stream water. The Provisionals desired equation was quite simple: culvert bomb + crossing army patrol = ambush and death. It often worked. We'd lost nearly fifty men in South Armagh alone. The bomb would always be blown under the second vehicle, leaving the first one stranded ahead and unable to pass the wreckage and give chase.

After the device was reported seen, a patrol was sent out to confirm the sighting and then a platoon followed. The area was soon secured in procedural manner with troops positioned on both sides of the road and either side of the stream that led to the culvert. A few hundred feet away an open gate at the roadside provided a natural area to set up the platoon's command post. On this occasion the command consisted of an ATO (bomb-disposal expert), two of his staff (one radioman) and a guy who was a blast from my past, Major Willis.

Back in 1968, when I had first met him, Willis had still been a captain. I was stationed with the regiment in British Honduras in the Caribbean. We were based in the northern coastal city of Belize and it was absolute heaven. Jamaica was only 500 miles east, Mexico 100 miles north and to the west stretched out the Pacific Ocean. It felt like there was more sun falling to earth there in one hour than in the whole of my life back home. The climate was tropical: warm and sticky, but with some relief from cool sea breezes brought in by the trade winds. I'd felt like I would never be cold again.

One Sunday morning the army cricket team had a match arranged against a local eleven. From an early age I had been a keen cricketer so I became the team's opening bowler. Sunday morning coming pretty soon after Saturday night, however, meant that I wasn't in top condition. During the previous night another squad member, 'Punchy' Parks, and I had been out on the razzle. And bowling with a hangover is bad news, especially in heat. The sun felt like it was bursting blood across my eyes and hot-drilling my skull. It wasn't until after a few overs that I began to come around and then another two overs before I realized something was drastically wrong. When this particular batsman wasn't hitting me all over the ground he was blocking with a skilful array of stops and parries. Before I ran my legs down to the knees one of the other players informed me that the batsman was a pro who played for the West Indies. That's me fucked then, I'd thought. He's going to wipe us out. Unless I could even things up.

Walking back for my run-in I passed Punchy, who was umpiring the match (each team appointed one umpire). Punchy didn't even really play cricket, which is why we had him officiating. I knew he'd do anything I asked. I told him I was going to rap the batsman's pad and that he should give him out leg-before wicket, whatever the line of the ball.

I lolloped down the run-in with as much of the little energy I had left and pitched. It hit his pad but was a good foot off the leg-stump. I screamed, 'Howzat?' and everyone but me and Punchy was astonished when he raised his finger for 'out'. The batsman stood glaring at us for a good thirty seconds before striding off. The crowd's dismay soon boiled up into anger and it looked like we might be facing a riot and pitch invasion.

At this point Captain Willis, who was captaining our team, had left his fielding position and approached me.

'Was that really out, Corporal?' he'd said. 'It looked awfully iffy to me.'

I replied that all I'd done was appeal, the rest was down to the umpire. As the crowd continued to bellow for blood, Willis then approached Punchy. Now Punchy wasn't the most articulate of men, hence the nickname (though he'd never even boxed), and when combined with the hangover and the fact that he'd been plonked down in the middle of a game he barely understood, this priceless conversation ensued.

'Private Parks, was that man actually out?'

'It 'it 'is pad, sir!' Punchy replied.

'Pardon?' said Willis, understandably, as he didn't speak broad Yorkshire.

'Ball, sir. It 'it 'is pad, sir.' Punchy, helpfully, tapped his shin.

'Yes ... but was the pad before the wicket, Parks?' Seeing the wilderness of incomprehension on Punchy's face, Willis rephrased the question three or four times until he got an answer.

'Oh. I di'n't know t'pad 'ad t'be in front a wicket, sir,' Punchy finally admitted. At this, Captain Willis had sighed and walked wearily over to the home side's captain. The dismissed batsman was waved back on to cheers from the crowd. Unheard of in cricket, really, for a player to be called back, even if the umpire was wrong.

But then again, no umpire had ever been as wrong as Punchy Parks, and as the crowd had been getting nastier by the minute I think it was a wise decision.

As he'd passed me on his way back across the pitch, Willis had looked at me with a mixture of disapproval and amusement. It was for things like this that I liked the man. Most of the lads did. As a commanding officer he was always firm but fair with it. He wasn't a spiteful ball-breaker like some of them.

I had always got on well with him. We both shared a love of cricket. It was while out in the Caribbean that he told me my parent regiment, the York and Lancs, were disbanding and I had to choose another. As I was out here in the sun with the Green Howards I decided they were as good as any. At least it meant I could stay longer.

Now Major Willis had gone to investigate the suspect device in South Armagh and had been blown apart. Not by the culvert bomb but by another device placed beneath the ground by the open gate, right underneath the chosen command point. The Provos had been clever. The culvert device had only been a decoy. They had rightly anticipated the unit would set up their command post by the gate and buried the real bomb there. The wires from the explosives were buried out of sight and led back to a hilltop vantage point. As soon as Major Willis, the ATO and the other staff had assembled to discuss tactics for defusing the culvert bomb, the other bomb's detonator wires were touched and up they went.

I was surprised, to be honest, that they had fallen for it. The easiest place to set up command would be the last place I would do it. If somewhere looks inviting and obvious to you, then it also will to the enemy. Personally, I would have stood ankle-deep in the stream, freezing my socks off, just to make sure I was away from any secondary devices.

The cricket incident with Captain Willis, and others with him from down the years, came back to me now, I realized, not just as a memory but as an epitaph. These stories were more than mere reminders of a life, and had now become things by which to remember the dead.

I thought how this must be what it was – this present death of a past life – that turned memories from being what reminds us into what haunts us. The image of Major Willis unknowingly stepping on to that under-wired earth as the bombers looked down on him with satisfaction, seeing him first there and then suddenly gone in an upward rain of earth, filled me with both great sadness and anger.

Mentally, I licked the end of a pencil stub and Willis became a name on the list of decent blokes I'd met along the way who somewhere down the line got sent to wherever it is we go when we die.

17

BLACKBIRD SINGING IN THE DEAD OF NIGHT

The knock at my door came at five o'clock in the morning. This is about par for the course, I thought, as I got up. It was an int officer who had come to request my presence at a 'screening'. He said they had picked up a suspected member of the Provisionals and he said he wanted to talk. After getting dressed I accompanied him down to the interview room and he briefed me on the way.

This morning at the usual ungodly hour of four o'clock the RUC Special Branch and the Army had done a series of suspect-lifts in Coalisland. These swoops were done intermittently to pull in sources for debriefing or in the direct aftermath of a shooting or bombing in order to get fresh information. And if we wanted to bring a source in to pump him for info, for example, we couldn't just lift him alone. That would arouse too much suspicion and within a week he'd be dog meat. Lift twenty others, however, and your source would get lost in the middle. If I scanned the lifts of the previous three months I could see the same names cropping up. These were the sources targeted by the lifts.

Taken from out of the back of the Land-Rovers, they would be put in the Portakabins inside the compound, kept apart and then interviewed and the details compiled or checked against a 'P card'. The knock on my door had come just after one of the men lifted had aroused the suspicion of the arresting officers. After some questioning he'd said he wouldn't say another word until he could talk to someone in charge. The other officers didn't have the back-up knowledge to enable them to ask the right questions whereas I did and, also being the gaffer, this is when they sent for me.

I entered Portakabin No. 6 and he looked up at me from his chair behind the desk. He was a youngish guy: early twenties with dark, unruly hair and eyes the same. A crowded ashtray sat on the table before him. I checked his 'P card'. Name – Jackie Lynch (well, let's call him that for the purpose of this book); address – the Meaner Park Estate in Coalisland. This was a well-known Republican breeding ground. I knew he'd have been searched already but I patted him down again to double check he was clean. If we were going to be alone in here I wanted to be the only one armed.

He told me he was from the East Tyrone Brigade of the IRA. The Tyrone brigades boasted some extremely active ASUs: the east and west of Tyrone County encompassed a corner of the Murder Triangle and part of the border with the Republic. All of these operated in the area around my base of Dungannon.

I was interested to know why he wanted to talk now, of all times. We didn't even have anything on him to use as a lever.

'I want out. I just want out,' he replied. I knew from the tired energy of his taut face that he'd had enough of whatever he had been doing. But, like the Mafia, once you're in, you're in. He knew his only way out of the IRA was death or flight. He decided to fly to a sister of his in London. He also wanted paying well, not just as an aid to his escape but as a reward for his information. I decided to make sure this boy really sang for his supper.

'Will yer help me out? Will yer ship me out? See, this is the only way I can think of doing it.'

'Depends how much you give me, Jackie,' I said, and left it at that. I wanted to make him have to work at convincing me. I hoped it would produce some instant results. He gave me a taster of things to come, to 'whet my appetite' as he put it. I tape-recorded it all for later reference. Then I asked him about the shooting of a policeman in Coalisland only a few days before. He said he could name the gunman, and he would do at a later date but only over on mainland UK.

One thing that had puzzled me about the recent shooting incident was how the gun was disposed of. That day the RUC and army troops had dropped on Coalisland like a ton of bricks, and quickly, too, but searches of every likely suspect in the area had turned up nothing.

'He threw it in the fish fryer,' Lynch said in answer to me. I must have looked quizzically back because he continued without prompting. 'You know the fish and chip shop round the corner? The boy ran in there and dunked the gun in the fryer. Picked up a bag of chips and walked out calm as fucking horses.'

That would explain it. No one would think of dipping their hand into boiling oil for a rummage around. Pretty smart. Bastards.

'So the next in line got a battered pistol with their chips?' I said.

'Aye, somethin' like that. I can tell you where it is right now as well. Where there are arms caches. You've gotta come through for me too, though, you know that, don't ya?'

I gave him my own contact number and told him to stay in touch while I checked things out. He said he could only call on Tuesday when he went to Dungannon to sign on. He would feel safe doing it from there but not from a payphone in Coalisland. I think the very first needles of the enormity of what he was about to do were beginning to sink in. He had been visibly twitchy when I'd first entered the room but over the course of our conversation I seemed to win a little trust from him.

I was already planning three steps ahead and the plan wasn't going to be entirely as he wished. I just hoped that he didn't have any surprises planned for me.

After we let him go I rang the field controller, Jack Marshall, at Brigade HQ, Lurgan. For a call of this importance, concerning highly sensitive information, I informed him we had to 'go green', which meant transferring from the normal telephone to one that scrambled conversations beyond the reach of any surveillance equipment.

Hollis was excited at the prospect of this new source and within an hour he called back to say that the G2 himself, Major Prior, wanted to see me. So, armed with Lynch's information, and also his demands, I drove up to Lurgan.

In the outer office I waited for the call to come through. These were always uncomfortable moments for me. I had something like that feeling of being back in the doctor's surgery you get when you're a kid. It was crazy really, I thought, because both these men, despite their rank, rely on guys like me and the other LINCOs and int gatherers to produce the goods. It made me realize that, though it may have felt natural for me to soldier, I wasn't natural officer material. My success at my job had won me access to army functions where I had mingled with the highest ranks, and found them none too special, actually, but I knew I'd always feel more at home in the sergeants' mess than the old boys' club.

I looked up at the arrival of another figure and immediately recognized him as the former Conservative MP Enoch Powell. He was now the Unionist MP for South Down. I was struck by the force of his presence. He appeared as formidable as his reputation suggested. His ice-blue eyes flicked over me and fixed on the wall behind me. I felt like I could almost hear the cogs of his mind clicking. (Later, when I told Sarah's dad about the encounter, he'd said, 'Aye, dripping with brains, that boy.')

An officer hurried into the reception area with an armful of papers and files and beckoned me to accompany him towards the G2's office. He turned to Powell as we passed and asked him if he was being attended to. Without bothering to make eye contact with the officer or even avert his gaze from the wall, Powell replied, 'I am always attended to.'

As we walked on by, the officer turned to me and raised an eyebrow before ushering me into the office and quietly closing the large door behind me. Jack Marshall and Major Prior were already seated, waiting.

We discussed the potential of this new source. I handed over the typed MISER of all the information he had given me. To save time, I had brought the MISER with me from Dungannon, which was a little foolish, having such compromising evidence on your person. Still, I'd felt I knew the journey well enough to make it safely.

I'd rated the source F6 because, so far, he was unproven. Among the other pieces of information, the MISER also contained important evidence regarding the recent shooting: '1 Source states that the shooting of RUC officer in Ardbow area was work of —; 2 Source states that op was by 2nd Battalion, East Tyrone Brigade whose members are as follows: —; 3 Source states that — of Meaner Park, Coalisland, was also involved in shooting of constable.'

I'd headed the report 'UK EYES ONLY'. If this evidence was to get into the 'wrong' hands, then it would be due to a decision made above me. I left them to verify the information by cross-referencing it with their own source reports on the same incidents and returned to Dungannon to await the news.

It wasn't long coming. The information proved to be good and Lynch was re-rated to A1. In the hope that he would sing like one, we codenamed him 'Blackbird'. In preparation for my next meet with him I was given a list of questions that he must answer before we could proceed with the next step of getting him out of the country.

Sure enough, Blackbird rang the next Tuesday and I arranged to pick him up at the large roundabout just outside Dungannon. He was to pose as a hitch-hiker. One of the roundabout exits led to the motorway so it was quite common to find hitchers there. What I didn't tell him was that this would be a three-car swoop.

There was no way I was going out to meet him single-handed. It could still be an elaborate trap to knock me off. Apart from the obvious risk of that, I was worried because, if Lynch was doing the double and even if I managed to avoid execution this time, they now had me clocked. My gut instinct, though, was that this was kosher.

I drove out to meet him on the day, alone in my own car but boxed in by others. I knew that seeing anyone else with me would make him skittish so I arranged cover in the shape of two other cars with two armed officers in each. One drove immediately in front of me, the other several cars behind. The idea was that when I pulled over to the side of the road the first car would slow but not stop and prepare to swerve on to the hard shoulder and reverse back up to me if I needed them; and the car following would time itself to approach from behind just as I stopped for Lynch. Hopefully this would cover the possibility of ambush from the roadside or from another vehicle. With five of us all armed, we should have enough firepower.

I saw Lynch standing at the roadside a few hundred yards away, just before the roundabout. A van ahead of us touched its brakes and pulled over to him. He moved to the window. If anything is going to happen, I thought, this will be it. I'd told him to pass up any other offers with the excuse that he wasn't going their way. I held my breath for the back doors of the van to be kicked open and the smoke and lead to come crashing through my windscreen. In the few seconds it took for me to narrow the distance between us I revisited my thoughts of a few hours before.

To know how someone might try to kill you, all you have to do is imagine how, in the same situation, you would go about killing them. And then just pray that they're not smarter. I'd imagined the possible lines of attack if this was a set up. Most of them, in fact all of them, from a gun ambush to a planted bomb, relied on the enemy having prior knowledge of the car I would be driving so they could identify me before I got to Lynch. That way they could attack me without hitting him. This assumption, however, had one major flaw – they may have already decided that he was expendable and could go down in the line of fire with me. If he was a plant, then this could quite easily happen; they would have chosen him because he was someone unimportant to them and then supplied him with just enough solid information as bait to tempt me into the jaws of the ambush. Then I wouldn't even get the satisfaction of nailing him at the roadside myself because he'd probably die in the same hail as me.

For these reasons, the most important thing was that when I had arranged to meet with him I didn't reveal what car I would be driving. This isolated and sidelined some of the more uncontrollable elements that you were always at the mercy of during an open meet like this. I had to try to control the environment as much as possible; isolate the variables and then inhibit their effect.

In the few seconds it had taken for all this to crash through my mind I was almost upon the scene. Lynch looked back from the van's passenger window and clocked me. He looked straight at me through the windscreen, then stepped back from the side of the van. I slowed. The cover car in front of me passed the van. A quick dart in the rear-view mirror revealed that the guys behind were blocked off by another car that had pulled between us. I slipped the car into neutral and let the momentum take me towards the hard shoulder. Being out of gear meant I only needed to brake, and could steer with my left hand, freeing my right to rest on the butt of the small automatic I'd earlier slid into the door pocket.

Suddenly there was a puff of smoke from the back of the van as it accelerated away into the flow of traffic. Lynch nodded and stuck out his thumb. I relaxed, pulled over, threw the door open and practically dragged him in. I sprayed gravel from the back wheels and was away before the back-up car behind had passed me. I glanced in the mirror and saw them pick up speed again while keeping their distance.

Right up to the point when I'd stopped I had been in constant radio contact with the other two vehicles. The dashboard radios in all three cars had been specially adapted to transmit, as well as still functioning as normal. After the pick-up we were to maintain radio silence, so as Lynch had got in I'd snapped the radio back to a local station.

I drove around just long enough to ask the test questions I had been given, recording his answers with the body-mike I was wearing. If the next stage went as planned, I said, then what exactly did he want?

'I won't say another word until I'm over in the UK,' he said. 'And, of course, I want money. This is costing me, y'know, and I don't mean financially, either. So I want something to soften the blow.'

I slipped him fifty quid in rolled tens. With this he said he would clear some outstanding debts and the rest would cover his travel expenses. He also wanted another drop of £300 before we left. We arranged for him to call me again and then if the answers I'd taped scanned out we would begin planning his escape.

The new information was authenticated and I told HQ of the plan to get him to London. I informed them that I would have to go, as he trusted only me. This was a mixture of truth and slight exaggeration. I knew that I had won his confidence to a certain extent, if only because so far I'd delivered what I'd promised. It's true that in situations like this (and as sometimes happened between hostage and kidnapper) a strange mutual dependency builds up. He undoubtedly needed me more than I needed him; although, on the other hand, he could also get the promised escape from another int officer whereas I wouldn't be able to find his information so easily elsewhere.

I didn't want to lose this one. Already I was getting regular calls and finding dozens of messages left for me by other intelligence units after they had got wind of this A1 source called Blackbird. I thought how the dark romance of that nickname itself probably contributed to the intrigue. I'm sure the name 'Lynch' wouldn't have stirred as many imaginations.

I played upon his request for me to be the only one with him as a way of securing Blackbird under my own wing. 'Knowledge is power' after all: his knowledge, my power.

At the next call I told him we were to proceed. We arranged to meet in McKenna's Bar in Armagh City. It was a Republican hangout but we chose to meet the following afternoon when we knew the place would be dead.

When I walked in there the next day, although apparently alone I had already placed three other undercover boys inside the place and had a uniformed unit on back-up alert in the vicinity. The bar was almost deserted apart from us and a few old men. As arranged, I sat within easy sight of him and had a quick half-pint. The next stage involved one of the lads covering me to get up and go to the toilet. Really this was just to check it was empty. He came out lighting a fag on the way which meant it was clear to go in.

As I was standing at the trough pretending to zip myself up I heard the door clang behind me. Even though I was 99 per cent sure it would be Lynch I still experienced that minor heart-burst at the thought of the unexpected. I turned and saw it was him, quickly handed him the £300 (which was rolled inside a note and banded with elastic), turned without saying a word and made for the door.

I left the bar first, followed then by the other operatives, one by one. We each sat in our cars, parked near by, to confirm the safe exit of everyone. I switched the car radio over to transmit and told the others to hold on to see if Lynch came out. When he didn't emerge after five minutes I thought he was either staying to spend some of his new-found wealth or – outside chance this, but still possible – telephoning through to an ASU to come through to pick us off. In my book every silver lining had a black cloud. I always thought how I'd rather be considered paranoid than remembered as dead. Thinking badly of people had only ever kept me alive or led me to being pleasantly surprised. You couldn't lose.

The note wrapped round the money had instructed him to ring me in five days' time on his next signing-on day at two o'clock in the afternoon.

The days till then seemed to drag. I began to wonder that if this was some kind of carefully primed trap, just how far they would go, how deeply they dare play it in order to snare and kill as many of us as possible. The longer a source was played out, the more people got involved and the greater the risk of something leaking or some chink of vulnerability opening up.

I talked to Sarah only once and very briefly just to tell her I wouldn't be calling again for a while. She was upset by this and although no news is supposed to be good news, I knew the silence of the next week or so would worry her.

I had to do this, though, in order to remove the risk of any calls I made being traced to her. One of Lynch's most intriguing and tantalizing promises was of information about steps being made by the Provos to listen-in to radio and phone communications by the security forces.

By the time the weekend had passed the few people involved in this set-up were all on edge. Even more so when, come Tuesday, the deadline for Blackbird's call to me came and went without any sign of contact. This is when the movie-scripting in my head really started to go wild – had the Provisionals sussed him out and topped him? Or had they tortured him, as they would, and been given enough information about me to leave me exposed? (And how would I know until it was too late?) Or had they forced him to play out the rest of it in order to lure us in (but then he'd have phoned on time so as not to arouse suspicion)? Maybe he'd just done a runner to London and ripped us off for a few hundred quid (but he knew I knew the address of his sister's house and we could easily trace him). Perhaps he'd become a fucking nun and dyed his hair pink! I didn't know, but by three o'clock I was sure something had gone badly wrong. Every previous meet or arrangement had gone exactly as planned. The whole scene coming apart at the seams was now a real possibility. And coming down around my ears, along with the burning scenery, would be my reputation and credibility.

Then he called, and sounded no more than slightly pissed off; which was a hell of a lot less pissed off than me.

'Where the fuck have you been, Lynch? This is no fucking game, sunshine. I've told you before to do exactly as I tell you and no different! Fuck me around again and I'll have you shitting blood for a week.'

He finally broke through the barrage with his story of how the phone he had planned on using was vandalized, as were most of the others in the area. It had taken him over an hour to find another one he felt safe using. This was sometimes the case. The local phones were the only things crapped on and pissed in more than the public lavs.

'Forget that now,' I said. 'How quickly can you move? I'm sick of fucking around with you.'

'This weekend.' There was genuine urgency in his voice, as if he was afraid of me blowing him out of the water. 'Let's do it this weekend. My fuckin' nerves are shredded!'

I said we would go on that Friday's night crossing of the Belfast to Liverpool ferry. I arranged to meet him onboard once we had set sail and then we would make our own ways to London before we met again.

I had two days to clear the decks. I needed to sort out any admin problems, go to HQ and pick up some cash and brief Jack Marshall and the G2; and then ask Jack to get in touch with MI5 on mainland Britain to pass on my travelling details and arrange cover for me and Blackbird when we met in London. They wanted to know the time of the meet, my appearance, what clothes I'd be wearing and so on.

I was also supposed to sign in my handgun but neglected to do so. The little nagging pain of it in the small of my back was far too familiar now for me to go without. That night I laid the Browning out on my table then stripped it down, oiled it and reassembled it in a noise-sequence of 'clicks' and 'clacks', each slide and rotation sounding reassuringly slick. I held it in front of my face for closer examination. The metal casing and slide-bar were silvered with fine scars and scratches. They always seemed to appear, however carefully you looked after a weapon or however often it was kept holstered; almost as if the metal was naturally ageing, like skin. I turned it through degrees in the solitary lamplight and its lines, furrows and stamped numbers deepened with shadow. Beautiful things, guns, I thought, and not for the first time. Shame they can't be put to some better use than being the ugly, last resort of human behaviour. *The ugly, last resort* - that just about caught it. By the time you picked up a gun you were fucking the last available whore in the brothel.

The last day before we travelled I tried to tie up any loose ends. A lot could unravel in a week. Whenever I went away it always felt like one of those situations where no matter who you left in charge, you thought they couldn't handle it as well as yourself. In fact, there were very few guys with enough experience to take over from me.

I made a brief call to Sarah to explain I'd be away for a week or so. I only gave an outline of why but I knew she would be able to fill in the rest. Though it was only for a week, I felt it was best for both of us if I was off the scene for a while, and especially as I was now handling the defection of an important IRA activist.

Next day, Friday, I decided I wanted to observe Lynch arriving so I got to the docks early and found a spot I could watch from. I'd always had this idea that you could learn something about a person if you observed them without their knowing. It was the idea that the body language would be more revealing or exhibit more tell-tale signs than when they were on guard.

He was late again. Only twenty minutes before boarding time he turned up in a black cab. As he got out I was surprised by this sudden feeling of sympathy I had for him which began, funnily enough, when I noticed his trousers were far too short for his legs. I couldn't decide whether this clown was funny or sad. He looked a little lost and pathetic as he paid the driver and stood shivering in a thin jacket, waiting for his change. It was the first time I'd seen that mop of hair of his combed and he kept patting it down as it blew up in the coastal wind that was whipping across the docks. He looked younger than before, like an overgrown kid going on a school trip: too young really to be caught up in the intrigue and risk-taking of this whole scene. Then again, I'd never questioned him about what he had done during his time in the IRA so this sympathy could be short-lived.

I watched him walk away, head down, hands plunged in pockets, body bent around the cold. I thought how his demeanour revealed nothing about him other than the limits of his life. And the fact that he could only afford the thinnest clothes. He certainly didn't look adept enough to be trusted with the intricacies of an ambush or double-bluff.

As he had arrived late and most of the passengers were already aboard, I couldn't put many people between myself and him as we queued to go through. He never once turned around, though, so I shuffled behind him unseen. When he got to the customs desk the Special Branch guys took one look at his ID and pulled him to one side. I stepped back out of the queue, retreated a distance and watched. They went through the usual search-and-question procedure, probably radioing through for a 'stop search'. This was the way of checking someone's details against the files of wanted suspects. If it came back as a match for a 'stop one' (or two or three) then you would be detained further. I had already done this to make sure he wouldn't be detained. They seemed to be screwing him around for some reason.

The ferry was ready to sail and they were obviously going to make him miss it. I approached the information desk, slipped my open ID across and told the girl that the guy being held was with me and he had to be let through. She moved to tell the Special Branch boys and Lynch reappeared and made for the gate. I walked quickly through after him, unconcerned whether he saw me now because they were preparing to lift the boarding ramp. We both dashed on in the nick of time.

A few hours later, close to midnight as planned, we met by the guard rail in the section between first class, where I was travelling, and his own second-class accommodation. He didn't look like he'd warmed up any and out here on deck it was bitterly cold.

I tapped a fag out for him and he flared it in his cupped hands.

'What happened earlier?' I asked. 'Are you wearing a balaclava on your bloody passport photo or something?'

'Aye, I always get that shit from you boys. Soon as you see "Meaner Park, Coalisland" address youse just think, Ah, fucking Provo!'

I started laughing. 'Yeah, but they were right!'

'Yeah, OK, but they're not to know that, are they? There's nothin' on me. They were just fucking me around as per fucking usual.'

'Story of your life, eh?' I said.

'Story of my fucking country more like, mate. Now then, you think on that.' He looked over my shoulder at something then and someone walked from behind me and passed us. We waited.

'I do think on it, Jackie-boy, believe it or not. More than you'd imagine. But you're the one who came to me remember so cut the wounded and guilty act.' He flicked his cig over the side and shoved his hands under his armpits, and nodded slowly. When he spoke next, he did so softly.

'Yeah, well . . . just don't push me for justifications or you might find you've got a man overboard, *John*.' He pronounced the false name I'd given him exaggeratedly, letting me know he knew.

We made plans to meet at 8.30 a.m. in East Croydon train station in two days' time. Just before he left I gave him another bundle of £300 and suggested he buy a jumper.

I flicked my own cig-end over the rail and watched it arc down to the rolling black glass beneath me. I felt safe onboard. As soon as you boarded a ship you were as good as in England. No one else but me should be armed on here, unless, of course, there was another guy from the security forces who had 'forgotten' to sign in his pistol.

I looked far out at where the black sky shuttered down to the black sea and met at the lost black line that would have been the horizon if it all hadn't been so fucking black. I thought, So this is now my position – on a mission, having these edge-of-the-world visions. And freezing my nuts off over the Irish Sea. It would be warmer down in London, though, I knew that. Still, I thought back to the early days in British Honduras where my greatest worry had been getting the stains of grass and cricket-ball red out of my whites.

I turned up my collar and hoped that I might strike lucky and even get info out of this boy about who blew up Major Willis. Who knows? The only thing I could be sure of was that every time I went out to bat I could guarantee it would be a sticky wicket.

I didn't see him again until London. We left the ship separately and made our own ways down south from Liverpool. We weren't due to meet until Monday so I had to amuse myself over the weekend. I booked in at a hotel and then called on an intelligence officer pal of mine from the Scots Dragoon Guards. He was from London originally so we went drinking at a few of his old haunts.

By the time Monday morning came around I was pretty relaxed.

This was home turf, after all. In fact I was so relaxed I slept in late and dashed out of the hotel without having a shave. On the way to Croydon I bought some disposable razors and cold-shaved in the railway station lavs when I got there. These plastic, disposable razors were a knew thing and they made me long for my old-fashioned badger-brush and metal-blade razor. I cut my chin to ribbons and plastered so many bits of toilet paper on my face I looked like an Egyptian mummy. This is a great image to present to Box 5 UK, I thought. Fortunately, the cuts dried up quickly, in time for me to look presentable at the meet.

I passed the appointed place, which was the waiting room on platform one, and looked in to see it was completely empty. It was now 8.25 and, with only five minutes to go, still no one had showed. I didn't mind everyone cutting it fine as long as they turned up. Before I really started to worry I went to the station kiosk to buy a paper.

The station was buzzing with the last of the early morning commuters. It was an ideal place to get yourself lost or to mingle. Again I had that uncertain feeling of whether he was going to show. If he didn't, would I look like a right 24-carat berk in front of the assembled firepower of MI5.

I returned to the waiting room to find it was full. I could barely get a seat. I thought it was a little odd but figured an inter-city train must be due out. I knew one or two of the people sitting around me would be Box 5 operatives. I checked my watch – just gone 8.30. Then Lynch walked in and sat down. I continued to read my paper for a few minutes, as planned, and then rose to leave. He did the same.

Outside the room I looked to the side in order to take things in behind me with my peripheral vision. All I expected was Lynch to be to the back of me and then a couple of the cover agents behind him: nothing dramatic. I wanted this safe but low key. Instead I glimpsed what looked like the whole of the waiting room walking in a crowd behind us. I glanced back quickly to confirm what I couldn't believe was true, but it was. Every single person in the waiting room had been there as cover for me, both men and women, and they had all risen and followed us out like I was Jesus H Christ himself and Lynch was John the chuffing Baptist. This isn't exactly inconspicuous, is it? I thought.

Lynch quickly caught up to me and as I turned to him I felt a hand on my other shoulder. I heard a voice say, 'Follow me,' and then saw a guy overtake me and head for the exit. It was one of the guys from the waiting room. I stopped in my tracks, dumbfounded, Lynch stopped beside me and the crowd caught us both. They were uncertain then whether to pass us or just surround us in a protective scrum.

Lynch was twitching like a cat on needles and demanding to know what was going on. I grabbed him by the elbow and steered him outside. All the way he was saying, 'Fuck me. What's going on?' The first thing I saw was a row of eight police cars waiting for us and an interested crowd of commuters eye-balling and rubber-necking. Lynch was flapping big-style now and I didn't blame him. We both just wanted to slip into London as unobtrusively as possible and instead we were practically being given a twenty-one-gun salute. I half expected the Queen Mother to sail by in a pink hat, waving from an open-top carriage.

The character that had tapped me on the shoulder stood by the lead car, holding the door open. I had a real sense of Lynch being on the verge of making a dash for it so I virtually threw him into the back of the car. It sped off with the rest of the others tailing us. Lynch was shaking like a leaf. A head popped around between the front seats and addressed me in a south London accent.

'Don't worry, mate, we're going to Tooting nick.'

'Who ordered the fucking circus then? 'Cos I didn't!' I said. He looked startled, as if the answer should be obvious.

'He's IRA inni?' He pointed at Lynch. 'So this had to be a big operation.'

'Yeah, well you needn't have bothered,' I replied. 'It's only a big deal because you've just made it one.' The guy frowned back at me and turned away. As the procession sped through the streets I did my best to calm down Lynch. The incident seemed to spark off fears in him that he'd managed to suppress until now. I told him that everything would be OK and I'd sort it out when we got to the station.

At Tooting nick we were hussled through like underworld celebrities, people staring out of offices and down corridors at us. I could already see that most of the coppers were surprised at my protectiveness towards Lynch. To them he was just a bad bastard who, at the very least, deserved a good kicking. To me he was all that but one important thing more – the key for me to unlock the box on the others.

We escaped the attention of everyone by slipping into a side room. The guy who had accompanied us in the car followed us in and I demanded to see the officer in charge. I was led into another office, introduced to an inspector and promptly blew a gasket over the handling of the operation. I reminded him that I was the one in charge here, I was Lynch's handler, and that the high-profile pick-up had served no use other than to put everyone unnecessarily on edge.

Like the guy in the car, the officer was surprised by my attitude and began arguing that the action had been taken because Lynch was a confirmed member of the Provisional IRA. I suddenly realized that, because of the press coverage of the Troubles over the years, these mainland police, with little or no experience of dealing with terrorism (outside of cleaning up the shit and snot left behind by a bomb blast) seemed to be expecting Lynch to be some six-foot-two madman in combat boots and balaclava, rather than the much less demonic figure in odd socks that he actually was.

I tried to explain how this wasn't an arrest procedure because Lynch had agreed to be here, and also how it was in danger of completely blowing my credibility with Lynch as a reliable handler. Then I got pissed off with the whole thing and requested a private room with a phone. I telephoned Jack Marshall at Lisburn HQ and he expressed surprise at the way we had been met. I asked him to get in touch with Box 5 and make sure that all the relevant parties were rebriefed so no one else stepped on our toes. He gave me the number of Dave Collis, a Special Branch officer with the Anti-terrorist Squad on Scotland Yard's nineteenth floor. Collis was to be appointed my bodyguard during my stay in London. As I was still supposed to be unarmed, I was given a bodyguard like Collis who had a special dispensation to carry firearms on duty. So now we had two handguns at our disposal. Not that we would need them. For the first time since this episode had begun, I felt pretty safe and confident that Lynch was genuine and not some elaborate plant.

I gave Dave Collis's nineteenth-floor office number to Lynch so he could contact me through there to arrange our meets. Our Blackbird had calmed down by now and was a little less ready to take flight, more eager to sing. I reassured him again that everything would be all right. He said he would call the next day and then left to go back to his sister's, much to the consternation of the Tooting police.

I immediately called Dave Collis, who came down to the nick to meet me, and we went out for a pint to get acquainted.

Over the following week I began to debrief Lynch of all the info he had to give. Dave, Lynch and I became a gang of three. Wherever I went, Dave went. We'd get together an hour before the meet, discuss how things were progressing and then travel to the designated spot. The weather being so bright and hot, more often than not we would meet in one of London's parks. Apart from the well-known larger parks like Regent's and St James's, it never failed to surprise me how many corners of London you could still turn and find a little block of green here or a residential park there; and always edged with those railings that were fat with layers of bottle-green paint.

I think both Lynch and I were making the most of this chance to blow away some of the cobwebs and shadows of Northern Ireland. Even in the congested concrete and compressed crowds of London we always found a spot unlike the rest of it. We would sit on the grass talking whilst Dave patrolled near by, fag in hand or reading a paper on a bench. Being outside also lessened the risk of us being overheard. We could have met at my digs, but even though I was now relaxed about the meetings, I still didn't want him knowing where I was staying. That was just instinctive caution.

Quite early on I told him that I was taping our conversations. I had been doing so with a hidden mike but it seemed stupid to labour on with it. He said he understood and I then used a smaller Dictaphone recorder that I'd hide beneath a newspaper or in the palm of my hand.

Over the days I sourced all the 'hard int' from him about arms caches in Coalisland; the names of other members; who was in charge of what; who was responsible for past incidents and so on. All this was logged and reported back to Marshall at Brigade HQ in Lisburn. Some of it was acted upon, some not. This was where playing the waiting game came in, sometimes at the risk of losing. We couldn't afford to act on too much of his information immediately because it wouldn't be long before his colleagues in the IRA began to narrow down the list of possible informers, and he was already known to be off the scene and out of the country. Even though he had the legitimate excuse of visiting his sister, we couldn't afford to arouse too much suspicion.

This was because I knew something that Lynch didn't. In fact I had known it right from his very first suggestion of escaping to the UK. Despite what he had been led to believe about staying on the mainland when his work was done, this was not to be the case. We were going to take him back home and work him undercover in East Tyrone. And if he argued, as I knew he would, then I had to persuade him.

This was something I'd begun to feel less happy about the more I got to know him. He was no savage hard-case. He was actually a bright lad who had been sucked into his role first through some minor involvement and then, later, was pulled in deeper than he ever intended to go. At least this is how he described it, and he was either genuine or a bloody good liar.

I learned more about this Jackie Lynch. Our meetings gradually became part information gathering, part confession and part therapy. Back home, he said, there had been no one he could openly talk with about these things and he'd come to feel increasingly trapped. The fact that he was smarter than your average Republican volunteer meant that the big boys above him had worked especially hard to keep him in the fold. Flat-headed foot-soldiers were ten-a-penny but lads who showed enough nounce to develop into adept strategists were much rarer.

Initially he had been a look-out and bag man, then a driver and arms collector, but as he had moved up the ranks and got closer to the actions he had started to doubt his commitment to an armed conflict. The few noises he had dared to make about leaving the organization had been met with what he considered threats from the other members. Terrorist groups sometimes eat their own.

I think like many young, idealistic men, Lynch had really been seduced by the romance of 'the struggle' only to find that the killing business was more of a cold, clinical fuck. Sentiment was buried in the fields with the guns – it remained there, the guns didn't. By now I'd seen enough down the years to differentiate between the die-hards and the wayward. The die-hards found murder easy. They were violently happy. They were the ones willing to sacrifice not only their own lives but other people's. And the wayward didn't always find their way back.

He had been raised a Catholic, of course, so between taking care of 'business' we took time off and compared notes on life. Though I was nearly ten years older than him I discovered from his account that over the years the Catholic school sisters hadn't softened any. We agreed that the nuns were the provisional wing of the Roman Catholic Church.

He told me his father had died when he was a boy, leaving his mother to raise the three kids: him and his two sisters; a relatively small brood for Catholics. He said most of the money he made from his cooperation with us went to his mother. I couldn't decide whether this was a calculated ploy designed to pluck at my heart strings or if I had just become a cynical old toad.

Over the years, as I had become more knowledgeable and intimate with the workings of the paramilitary groups and their relationship to the communities they sprang from, there was something that occasionally occurred to me whenever a reminder arose, as it was doing now. I wondered about the fatherless kids who had grown up into young men looking for something they had missed, and if, in some perverse way, they found this need fulfilled in the gang mentality of the groups. I knew that once they had been taken into the fold the feeling of belonging was very strong and the younger males often looked up to the veteran leaders. I always thought, God help anyone who uses one of those guys for a father figure.

'My da was a gentle man,' he said to me at one point, 'and I started to wonder what he would think of me, you know, now . . . and I didn't like what I thought.'

I had seen brutality passed down through families in the town where I'd grown up. Passed down hand to hand, father to son, in the same way it was taught and nurtured in the ranks of the IRA. It wasn't so much a baton that was passed on as a club to beat with. The terrorist groups were like some distorted, hall-of-mirrors reflection of family values and family life, their affiliations and camaraderie based on hatred and fear rather than love.

Young Jackie Lynch wasn't going to be able to pack up his knapsack and run away from home just yet. As the end of the week neared and the information he gave us began to dry up, I knew it was time. We had exhausted him of what he already knew but he had no 'forward int', that is, knowledge of planned actions. This is why he would have to go back.

I didn't enjoy telling him. He didn't enjoy hearing it.

'You said this would be it, John!' he shouted (we'd both got used to using my false name). 'That's what you said! You know you fucking did. You've known this all along!'

We argued for a while and I was forced to play the hard man in order to get him to agree. The promise of more money didn't make up for the rest. When he refused point blank to cooperate I threatened to reveal what he'd done to his comrades back in Coalisland.

Even as I said it I knew it would work, not just because of the danger to himself but because of the potential of the violence spreading out and coming down on his family if he couldn't be found. But even as I said it I knew I wouldn't have carried out the threat to grass him up.

I couldn't decide, then, if that was worse: the fact that I had simply bluffed him. Part of me was hoping he would call the bluff and then I could end it all with a clear conscience. But he didn't. He wasn't to know, and he had too much to risk.

He jumped up and stormed off around the park where the meeting was taking place. Dave came over from where he had been watching us and asked if everything was all right.

'Do you want me to go after him?' he said. I said to leave him be. I knew he'd be back. Dave sat down next to me on the grass as Jackie paced about a few hundred yards away. I saw a cloud of cig smoke puff out as he lit one up.

'I presume this means you've just told him there's no Santa Claus,' Dave said, nodding in Jackie's direction.

'Yeah, something like that. Didn't take it too well. In his eyes I've just gone from being Fairy fucking Godmother to the Wicked Witch. Can't say I blame him, really.' I noticed that the tape-recorder was still running. As I clicked the switch, I said, 'That's the trouble with this job, Dave. It can turn you into as big a bastard as all the others.'

We saw Jackie turn and start to walk back to us. I knew what he would have to say. I got up to walk out to meet him halfway. It was the least I could do.

Two days later I saw Jackie on to a train and told him to contact me when we got back. He climbed aboard like it was the Auschwitz Express. I returned by plane. We'd both been pretty subdued during the last day and I couldn't shake the horrible feeling plaguing me that something was going to go violently wrong soon.

Before I left for the airport I was called to a meeting with the head of Scotland Yard's Anti-terrorist Squad. He wanted an end-of-week update on the situation. The fact that the head of Special Branch had also come down to interview Lynch had stirred things up as well. Word had obviously got around about Blackbird's potential.

During the meeting I made the mistake of showing Chief Inspector Whoever-the-fuck-he-was (I didn't really care) the MISER that listed Lynch's suspected IRA activities. He blew his top and started ranting and raving about locking Lynch up and throwing away the key. I had to explain to this high-ranking dickhead that locking up your chief source wasn't exactly the best way to handle him and tends to limit the amount of information you get back to absolutely fuck all. I thought then that maybe the phrase 'bent coppers' could be taken the other way and this bastard in front of me had slept his way to the top.

I knew that when I landed back in Northern Ireland advance word of the success of the London trip would have come through, the evidence passed on and filtered down: some of it acted upon, some of it stored. I'd probably have the Special Branch boys on my back trying to lift Lynch away from me to use as their own. I didn't want to lose any of the power and credibility that the success of this op had brought me. I also didn't want Jackie falling into the kind of hands that might drop him into the fire. I had already decided that because we were to continue using him and because he would be put in a dangerous position, I was determined to do my best to steer him through it all on the safest course. I genuinely wanted to see him come out the other side and hopefully move on to something better. Similarly, I wished the same for myself.

All of a sudden, thinking about it on the plane, I felt that these last few months of my service before I signed off were to be the most important I'd yet faced. It seemed vital to me that I pull off this last op successfully; and that didn't just mean getting good information out but getting Lynch out alive. I felt like I had seen enough decency in him to know that if he went down, it wasn't something I would forget or forgive easily. And by 'forgive' I meant myself as well as whoever might kill him.

The plane's porthole began to smoke over with cloud, the wing vanished and we dipped into the descent. I knew when the cloud wisped away I would be greeting Ireland from above for the last time. One way or another.

18

'I SMELL THE BLOOD OF AN ENGLISHMAN'

T he countdown had begun. For me at least. It was now August 1976. Only four months until I could sign out of the army if I chose to. I had to give three months' notice so I still had a month to decide. I didn't think I had really admitted to myself that I was pulling out but I felt that this new sense of urgency betrayed the fact that I had accepted it. The decision had been made. Only one thing left to do now – survive.

Things were speeding up. But I felt like I was accelerating and yet not moving. My days were filled with meetings, source rendezvous and telephone calls to gather, collate and telegraph messages and information. I thought my phone was going to melt through overuse and the panels on my room door were about to cave in with the constant rapping. The Murder Triangle continued to justify its name. And our Blackbird went back to his cage and continued to sing.

Jackie Lynch returned to the Republican fold and began to earn the kind of trust that brought information his way. However, the 'cell system' structure employed by the IRA – first engineered during their earlier regrouping – prevented us from gathering too much info about planned operations. Jackie gave me the nod on hidden arms caches, the likelihood of someone's involvement in an incident and the time and location of incoming shipments of guns and explosives. The East Tyrone Brigade worked out of Coalisland, around Cookstown and down to the border: the Murder Triangle in all its bloody glory.

The best I could do was try to assemble the larger picture from the bits and pieces I was given and then formulate what the IRA were planning. For example, Jackie informing me of someone being appointed to a surveillance unit on an RUC officer meant that the guy was being lined up for the drop. Sometimes we didn't figure it out until it was too late and sometimes we couldn't act at all. This was when reacting to information given to us by Lynch would tip off the IRA as to where the info had come from. The prevention of an incident had to be weighed against the possible risk of compromising the source that supplied the intelligence. Sometimes the source was deemed to be worth more than whoever the IRA were going to hit. These were cold, hard decisions and thank God they weren't mine to make: that was the province of the Box 5 boys above me who received my MISERs.

With the knowledge of each new terrorist act limited to the ASU involved and a few select guys above them, it became easier for the Provos to discover the sources of any leaks, and plug them. During our weekly phone conversations the tension seemed to have changed Jackie's voice, stretching it out thin and weak. I tried to reassure him that I would do everything I could to protect him but at the end of the day I knew he was out there by himself. But then again, at some point so were all of us.

On my trips out of base, particularly when I was alone, I was aware of being incredibly sensitized to the possibility of being followed. Lynch being discovered as an informer could have major repercussions for me, too. The long drives north to see Sarah were especially fraught journeys for me. If I was to be singled out for assassination I didn't want to take death to her doorstep. That was my greatest single fear: that so close to the safety of leaving here, so close to leaving with Sarah, I would fall at the last hurdle; fall murdered. The nearness of good things made me fear them. When I'd had nothing to look forward to I'd had nothing to lose. They say the greatest fear of the tightrope walker is falling in love: that other fatal descent.

I was increasingly aware of the law of diminishing returns: that the longer we played the lying game the greater the chance of discovery. If Lynch was sussed, he would certainly be tortured and shot. How much information he revealed during his interrogation would only come to light by the numbers killed after as a result.

We continued to meet whenever he had something of interest to tell. I would pick him up at the roadside somewhere, usually off the Dungannon roundabout, and we would go to some relatively safe bar in Armagh (that was not known to be staunchly Republican), a secluded car park or even the picnic areas around Cookstown.

He'd aged visibly, even over the last few months. I knew there was a natural lifespan to a source before something snapped, before everything wore out and broke down, either within them personally – mentally or physically – or from some outside variable that finally came around and bit you on the arse.

I looked in his face and all I saw was muscle slack with fear. And if I could see it, so would they. Those tell-tale signs were going to kill him.

Things were not easy. After any shooting or bombing incident I had to wait days for him to contact me. For security reasons, he was still paranoid about only using certain payphones but unfortunately this put a delay on the information. None of the other handlers, however, had a source in as deep as Blackbird, so the information was always worth waiting for. I counted the time by weeks rather than days.

A sudden flurry of killings in Armagh and West Tyrone sent up warning flares of imminent danger. I learned of increased SAS activity down in Armagh and believed they would soon be dispatched further north, perhaps even earlier than Robert Nairac told me they would.

The Provos usually killed their own without too much delay if they were discovered to be informers. Lynch would only be allowed to live if they thought he was more use alive than dead: that is, to get to me or to 'do the double' and plant false information with us in order enable their ASUs to mount a successful counter-attack.

The fact was that I was relying on someone who was an IRA member as well as a double-agent and cash-bought tout to give me the nod if he learned of my life being in danger. I was aware of the irony of this situation but that didn't make me sleep any easier or wake any happier. I was, to say the least, uneasy. On the positive side was the relationship I had built up with Jackie over the last few months. In him I think I saw a mirror of myself, at least in our shared sickness of it all and desire to escape.

During one meet outside Cookstown we sat in the car talking. I reminded him of a couple of times I had suppressed or altered information he had given me because I knew there was a chance it would be acted upon. If it had been used, the safety of his position would have been in doubt. It wasn't often that I did this and only then if I was certain it was for the best.

He sat next to me silently. I think that, like me, he realized that the naked truth of it was that both our fates were entwined to the extent we couldn't afford to let each other down. Like two moun-tain climbers roped together. The fall would be heavier for him, of course, but I didn't want to get dragged down.

'Look,' he said, 'if I hear of anything going down that's gonna endanger either of us, I'll let you know. I can't promise any more than that. I only know what I know.'

'I need to know everything you know, Jackie.'

'Yeah, but the better I am the longer you're gonna keep me in, aren't yer?'

'And whatever you hold back from me might be the information that I could use to save your life. This isn't gonna go on for ever.'

'How much longer *will* this go on?' he asked then, as he asked at every meeting. As usual I made some noises about it being wrapped up sooner rather than later and, as usual, I knew he knew I was lying. He didn't look like he had too much more to give. And I didn't really want to be around when the wheels came off.

Two weeks later the brakes went. A body was found in a shallow stream. It was a young lad, half stripped, bagged and stabbed and then finally shot in the head for good measure. When I read the victim's name I felt my blood chill: he was one of our touts, one of their betrayers, and someone who was known to Jackie Lynch as Lynch was known to him. The dead guy's body was striped with knife marks from some pre-death torture session. Between these lines I saw myself and Jackie moving further into view. This was the uncertainty we experienced whenever a source was offed. We never could be sure how much they had got out of him during interroga-tion. This most recent guy to be killed had always seemed more of a liability to me. He was run by the RUC Special Branch. From what I could gather, he wasn't the brightest button in the box and it was when using someone like this, with delusions of adequacy, that things could start to fall apart.

Things became worse when a sit rep came through stating that a car had been seen outside Lynch's house. When a number plate check was run, it was found that the car belonged to a guy we suspected of being the head of the local Provos.

Blackbird's next call was due in three days. I awaited it on needles. It came two days early: bad sign.

As soon as I answered I knew something was wrong. Jackie's voice sounded white with fear and he spoke hesitantly, as if reading from a prewritten script.

'You OK?' I said.

'Yeah, yeah. Everything's fine.'

An elephant syringe of adrenaline emptied into my chest. Everything was far from being OK. He'd been rumbled. I knew that much. He was almost certainly being held captive right now, probably being forced at gunpoint to make this call to arrange the next meet. And that next meet would be an ambush.

I knew the following two minutes of conversation would decide whether he lived or died. I had to think quickly and act calmly. They would also be listening in and if I gave any sign of knowing what was going on his usefulness would be over and he wouldn't make it to the end of the day.

'I've got something for you, John,' he said. 'We need to meet.'

'Usual spot,' I said, 'next Tuesday at the same time.' The 'usual spot' was the main roundabout off the Dungannon Road, and the same place I had picked him up the first time. Jackie began to resist my suggestion of this location which meant the guys at his side didn't like the sound of it and were prompting him to change.

'I might find it difficult to get out there,' he said. He sounded unconvincing. He was either a terrible actor or just crippled with fear. Both probably. All colour had drained from his voice He had definitely been discovered, I had no doubts about that now.

Usually the meeting spot was chosen for ease and safety for both of us but this time I had to insist on my choice. I knew I could talk to him as harshly as I wanted (despite the fact that we were usually quite friendly) and not alert their suspicions because they had no idea how our conversations normally went. Anyway, it probably fitted in with their notion of how some 'Brit bastard' would talk to his source.

'Just do as I fucking-well say,' I replied, 'like you always do and no one will get hurt.' Not yet anyway, I thought. He hung up before I did. The dialling tone in my ear sounded like a faraway alarm.

The way they had decided to play it told me everything about the situation. They had somehow discovered the ID of our first source, tortured and killed him and then realized that between him and Lynch, the guy they'd killed was the lesser of the two evils (the first guy had obviously bubbled Lynch). After pulling him in the temptation to kill Jackie too must have been great, but they decided to feed him back to us instead: make use of him then kill him. They obviously didn't trust him enough to use him long term. His use was going to be on a strictly temporary basis – as bait. If he'd thought they were going to feed him back in and use him over a longer period, then there would be no panic. All he'd have to do was turn up for the next meet, inform me he'd been sussed and then we'd help him disappear. The fact that he'd tipped me off meant that the next meeting was for only one reason, and that was to whack us both. Jackie knew they were going to do him one way or the other, if not before the ambush, then during or after it. The only chance he had of getting out alive from the room where they were holding him was to hope that I'd realize something was wrong and then get him lifted out to safety during the meet. He, of course, didn't know of the additional information we had of the car spotted outside his home.

It suddenly occurred to me, though, that there was one other possibility here, but one that would require greater resourcefulness from the Provos to pull off than an ambush. This was the possibility of an attempted kidnap. For that they would have to be sure they could control the area enough to disable whatever back-up I had with me. I thought there was a chance they might try this, but it was unlikely. It depended on how much they had learned of my position from interrogating Lynch, and how much nerve they had.

For them to capture an intelligence officer would undoubtedly be a real coup and allow them to interrogate for further security information. This would certainly be something they would like to pull off (I expect the torture session alone would be especially relished), but come the time when the shouting started and the adrenalin kicked in, carefully laid plans often went out of the window. In the panic of gunfire the easiest and safest thing to do was always shoot to kill, whether you were paramilitary or army. I don't think capturing came naturally to either side.

The ambush could either be by hidden gunmen or a pre-planted bomb. Explosives can be detonated from a vantage point, and by their nature decimate a big enough area to make pin-point accuracy unimportant, but the Dungannon Road wasn't quiet enough for this to be done unobserved. I thought it was most likely to be a drive-by attack from a vehicle just as I was picking up Lynch; in fact, the same kind of attack I had feared on that first meeting.

There were now only four days to go. I called Jack Marshall at Brigade HQ and filled him in on the situation. We couldn't use uniformed troops for this. They were too obvious, too easily seen. As we had a good chance here to wipe out one of their ASUs, I immediately thought of Nairac. I knew him and his boys would jump at the chance of getting their hands dirty on this one. I asked Hollis to set up a meeting between me and Nairac. Within the hour I got a call back. It was Robert. He sounded distant but said he was already near by so he'd swing around to Dungannon on his way back south. The line went dead mid-call but I'd heard enough to know that things were already rolling.

He arrived an hour later, unshaven and in his long black leather coat, looking like a down-at-heel gangster; pretty much like most of the local Provos, in fact. I ran the whole story past him in greater detail and he listened intently, occasionally interrupting to clarify a point.

'Yeah, they've already pulled the spring on this one, Nicky,' he said as I finished. 'I agree they don't have any intention of using Blackbird as anything other than bait.'

'Can you pull some of the boys out of Bessbrook for this?' I wanted a unit of the newly deployed SAS to help carry this out but I knew the recent furore over their incursions over the border had given them far more publicity than they needed. Even now they were only supposed to be operating, officially, in South Armagh.

'Well, "officially" a lot of things are supposed to happen – doesn't always mean they do, though, you know that,' he said.

'Yeah, that's why I'm asking.'

He looked at me for a second before saying, 'I think you do need them, but you know how things have been over these last few months. If I can't get it handled directly then, at the least, they'll liaise with you on the planning.'

'Look, Robert, I know as well as you do that those boys are moving around. We're talking about taking out an ASU here, maybe two; we could use 4 Troop for the reccie but not to go in at the death. I've got a suggestion. Take the Sass out of uniform and put them in civvies. Afterwards we can say it was a reccie that turned into more, or we stumbled on the ASU, or whatever. As long as we get it done.'

He decided to travel straight back down to Bessbrook to start drawing up the bones of the op. He took with him my description of the 'ambush' area and road maps of the same. Nairac knew of the Dungannon roundabout spot but not as well as I did. If needs be he would ring Jack Marshall to clear the SAS with Box 5. I knew that since their arrival here everybody in intelligence had wanted to use them.

That evening I drove up to see Sarah. I didn't want to make too big a deal of it but I really wanted to see her before this whole deal happened. She was happy, if a little tired after work, and we just sat in the house talking. There was another big army dance the following week so we made plans to go.

I fired my car back down through the dark to Dungannon and whatever lay ahead.

I was now at 4 Troop's HQ in Loughgall near Lurgan. I had travelled over from Dungannon the day before to meet Robert and the SAS. We had gone over the plans for the day and discussed the various possibilities. One reason for me coming up here was because we didn't know exactly what Jackie had told them. Did they know I operated out of Dungannon and, if so, would they try to hit me as I left there to go to the meet? So I had left a day early to be on the safe side.

4 Troop's role, supposedly, was to provide maps and aerial photographs for the army. In reality this was a cover for the 14 Intelligence operatives who worked out of 4 Troop. This was Robert's old unit. In fact it was only quite recently that he had left after being seconded to work with the SAS upon their arrival at the beginning of the year. Still, this was home ground for him. When I'd first arrived I had been shown through to the special, secluded quarters that had been set aside for him to work from.

We decided it was going to be like this, exactly like this, or as near as we could control: a four-car swoop; my car and three others on back-up. My car, a red two-litre Triumph automatic (on loan to me from Robert), would be driven by myself with another officer, Dave Stubbs, in the back on the floor. I would carry my Browning 9mm in a shoulder holster and have another weapon in the car's door pocket; Dave would be armed with a sixteen-round Uzi automatic machine-gun. The car radio was closed frequency adapted to communicate with the other three cars. These were all what I called the 'firm's' vehicles, or 'Q cars' as some called them, pulled from the car pool to be used by the SAS boys whom Robert had drafted in from Bessbrook: three of them in each vehicle. They'd bring their own firepower: 'Come As You Are', it would have said if we had sent out invites. Finally, a surveillance helicopter would hover high, out of sound and sight.

The Dungannon roundabout was like a large wheel with a grassy central hub and six entrances/exits splayed out in spokes. It was positioned on a flyover above the M1 motorway. The four corner roads were the exit and entrance ramps for the motorway, south and north. Between these were the southbound dual-carriageway leading to Dungannon and opposite that the north road to Armagh.

As usual Jackie would wait on the outer ring of the roundabout by the railings overlooking the motorway below him. There was a chevroned waiting area there where cars could stop. Often these areas would be taken by 'share and drive' cars, that is, vehicles left there for the day after workers met each morning before travelling to work together in one car.

The normal procedure was for me to enter the roundabout off the Dungannon road, pull over, and pull away as soon as he jumped in. It was a relatively safe spot to meet and pick-up and a difficult place to plan an attack on, which is why I originally chose it. This time I would be coming down from Lurgan and entering through the opposite road from the direction of Armagh. This meant me swinging all the way around the centre of the round-about to get to Jackie on the other side.

We decided the attack must take place on or near the roundabout as they wouldn't know which exit I would take. They wouldn't lay a car in wait because the space was too open. More likely they'd have a couple of cars of their own roaming the general area until they caught sight of the pick-up and noted which exit we headed for. Then the pursuit would begin.

Our own back-up cars would be placed near by. One was to follow me on to the roundabout, far enough behind to allow me to do the pick-up without passing me but close enough to catch up. A second car would be at the side of the Dungannon road entrance with its bonnet up, as if broken down, and the third would be timed to enter the roundabout just before me, leaving by the M1 south-east-bound exit just before I did the same.

The cover cars would merge into the normal flow of traffic, which would be pretty light at this time. Each one would have three occupants but in a couple of the cars two passengers would hide from view, giving the impression of a lone driver. What could possibly go wrong? Seventeen things immediately sprang to mind, but none of them was important enough to call the whole thing off.

The meet was set for 11 a.m.: in forty minutes' time, in fact. I second-checked the pistols I was to carry, pulling the slide on the Browning 9mm to put a round in the breech and then slowly thumb-lowering the hammer back before sliding it into my shoulder holster. I pocketed the second pistol (another 9mm) until I got out to the car. I met Dave downstairs in the ops room and together we walked outside to the vehicles. The Uzi slung over his shoulder hung dead-weight against his back. At the car he snapped off the strap and tossed it in the boot. Both car doors were winged open with a Royal Engineer mechanic sitting in the front flooring the accelerator, gunning the engine. As I bent down to slip my other pistol into the driver's door pocket, he turned and smiled at me through the noise, flipping a thumbs-up. He killed the engine and got out, handing me the keys.

'Yeah, it's better now,' he said. 'It was idling too low but I've sorted it. It's running sweet. Try bringing it back in one piece, though, I was hoping for a quiet weekend.'

'This car will either come back in one piece or not at all, sunshine. Simple as that,' I said as I slipped behind the wheel. I gunned it and shouted over the roar, 'Mind you, when I say "one piece" I can't guarantee it won't have a few holes in it.' He nodded as he turned and left. Looking through the windscreen and out over the compound I saw Nairac and the SAS boys climbing into their own vehicles. Just before he bent to get into the driver's seat Robert turned, saw me and nodded.

The first car – '1-Car' – had already pulled out ahead of us to position itself beside the Dungannon road as if broken down. Now 2-Car left to go south before swinging back to head for the round-about from the M1. Five minutes later I steered us out and on our way with 4-Car, driven by Robert, close behind.

I heard a tearing noise behind and looked in the rear-view mirror to see Dave pulling off strips of parcel tape and binding a second magazine of rounds for the Uzi to the one already clicked into the gun's body. When the first was empty you just pulled it out, spun it and jammed the fresh one in.

'I never had you down for a boy scout, Dave.'

'You what?'

'Well, seeing you doing that it looks like your motto's "be prepared". But I suppose you learned that from shagging Heather.'

'Fuck off. Compared to that, this is light duty. I still owe you for that and I never did get that danger money you promised me.' The radio crackled alive, 1-Car saying it was in position. They had already noticed three cars parked outside the central hub of the roundabout. These could be the usual 'share and drive' leftovers, or maybe not; maybe more. They appeared to be empty from the drive-by but they could be using the same trick of hiding occupants as us. Difficult to tell. The surveillance chopper reported that the cars had been there for some time, so if one of them was a plant, they had obviously been prepared for a long wait.

Half an hour later we all suddenly had reason to be nervous. Through the mirror I saw 4-Car pull back a little as we began to near the roundabout. I threw my fag out of the window and wound it up fully. Dave had already dropped from view behind me. I began the running commentary, 'Just approaching, Dave. Lynch is there. Just seen him,' and there he stood, to the right, bobbing with cold and fear. The radio crackled – 'Two-Car. Coming off the motorway up to you.' I dabbed the brake, slowed us, glanced around (the parked cars to the left – empty?) and then jabbed the car out into the open arena of the roundabout. 'Passing the parked car now, Dave.' We fizzed passed – a second of blind-spot between mirror and object, us and them – and I pressed back in my seat. I saw them vanish and the nose of 4-Car behind appear and disappear as we lurched into the curve. A bar of sunlight ran across the rear-view mirror – 'Two-Car on you': they had sighted us. I pitched the car through the sweep, the slant making me flatten my hand on the passenger seat for balance as Jackie looked around, dancing at the kerbside. I threw us over to him and dropped anchors, the brakes bit and cried; we slid alongside, the back door already kicked open by Dave, the tyre smell coming through. Jackie leaped in breathless with a face like a smashed watch. He hit the seat and shouted, 'Black Capri! They dropped me! Fuckin' move it!' I floored the car out as 2-Car caught us and filled my mirror. Dave was up and braced against the door. I went for the Armagh Road exit we had arrived on. Robert was still there in 4-Car, waiting for us to pass, but a lorry was pulling alongside him on to the wrong side of the road, blocking my way. I carried us round in front of their surprised eyes, saw the blob of faces blur past, and turned us off at the next exit. In the second we flashed by the back of the parked cars I held everything tight – wheel, breath, dear life; the exhaust clanked and sparked with the speed of our drop.

'Three-Car, we're still on you!' I looked behind. Robert's car and 2-Car bounced down the exit after me. The lorry was crossing the roundabout above, back up on the flyover (no involvement?). Jackie was swearing now and raving for some reassurance or sense, flapping like a rag – getting in Dave's way and already on my frigging nerves. I said, 'Shut the fuck up!' and then, when this got no response, I said to Dave, 'Shut him the fuck up!' Dave turned and cracked him unconscious with the gun butt. Then the whole rear window blew in like snow. A blizzard of cold glass and air hit the back of my head as the motorway opened out behind us with a roar. I glanced back and saw a weaving motorbike with a pillion gunman and heard the *pok! pok! pok!* of more gunfire but felt nothing hit. I swerved for the fast lane, inadvertently throwing Dave off balance as he loosed off rounds into the barrier – 'They're on you Three-Car! Get left!' The buzz of the bike grew in volume as they gained. I heard the reports of gunfire behind. The bike flashed into my wing-mirror – I saw rider and pillion passenger struggling for balance and aim. We were screaming along now, hoovering up white lines. Dave braced himself again to fire but I had to lurch us back towards the hard shoulder to avoid getting pinned down. A bark of auto-matic fire juddered and popped into the boot. Knowing what I was about to do to him, I thought, Sorry, Dave, mate, and stamped the brake pedal hard, flat to the floor. The callipers bit deep and imme-diately heaved the bonnet to earth; the massive deceleration threw Dave forwards, slamming him into my seat. I strained into the cut of the seat-belt. The bike flew past, too surprised to stop in time. The gunman turned, strained and squeezed off a last effort but they went wide.

Then 4-Car and 2-Car banged past our smashed back window in pursuit. I watched them roar off and disappear through the next bend. I felt a sudden surge of pride at seeing them vanish in chase. I knew they would pursue like pack dogs. Things hadn't exactly gone perfectly by any means but perfection wasn't expected; 'alive' was enough. I turned to the wreckage in the back. The seat was sugared with blasted glass.

'Dave?' I said.

He straightened up, brushing glass off himself, and said, 'Yeah? I'm OK.'

Out of the back I saw the silver VW of 1-Car screech up behind us. The car shuddered under braking, still rolling as the doors sprung open and they were out and around us in seconds to see if we were hurt.

'Get him in the car!' I pointed to Jackie, who was just coming round. They dragged him out to transfer him and practically kicked him headlong into the back seat of the VW, squashing him to the floor with their boots. I wanted him in their car and safely back in Loughgall and I wasn't sure yet what damage had been done to our vehicle. The radio had knocked off for one thing. Through the VW's open door I could hear the radio click on and off and Robert reporting the pursuit, his voice raiding through the snow of crackles, high on adrenalin. The door slammed on the rest, and then the engine drowned out my voice.

I circled my hand and pointed back to indicate that we should spin back up the on-ramp and get out of here as soon as possible. I followed them up as we drove the wrong way up the ramp, scaring the shit out of a motorist on his way down. We eased up and back on to the roundabout and then, suddenly back on course, we roared off without restraint down our escape route.

The SAS blasted ahead with the VW as the pace car. My fears were now narrowed down to three – further attack by Provos, attack by our own troops, and hypo-fucking-thermia from most of the back window being over the seats and dashboard. I still heard Lynch's cry of 'black Capri!' (the car they'd used to transport him) and couldn't help wonder if its long nose would reappear in my mirror as it sharked up beside me with the windows down. The other threat, of being stopped by security forces, was equally real. In fact, I thought right now that it was more likely because, if the other ASU had seen the firefight, they would probably have taken the first opportunity to fuck right off. But I knew that two cars racing through the streets, particularly one with its back window blown out, if spotted by an army patrol, would probably be put down as Provos, and shot at. And after making it all this way without so much as a scratch I didn't want all my bad-luck days to come at once and die in so-called 'friendly fire'.

We also ran the risk of hitting an RUC or UDR roadblock. I was used to running into roadblocks virtually every other day when I was out travelling, and there was a certain way we handled them before moving on. But, then again, I didn't look like we did now – like we'd just tear-arsed out of Hades, hell-for-leather on a long tether with a short fuse. My hair alone – a windblown mess sprinkled with glass – was probably enough to get me shot on sight. And the fact that I was driving wild-eyed on the very limit of the tyres wasn't going to help any.

We got back in a fraction of the time it had taken us to make the outward journey. I sledged the car to a halt in a cloud of gravel, smoke and tyre heat. As I jumped out I saw the regiment's mechanic from earlier looking out of a window with almost comical horror. I nearly burst out laughing as the sight of his face immediately snapped the tension. I couldn't resist flipping an exaggerated double thumbs-up sign to him and mouthing, 'Thanks!' before I threw the keys on to the front seat.

Now we were safely back in Loughgall I got the medic to check out Jackie. The red swelling from Dave's blow was coming up a treat, but, apart from that, and his shredded nerves, he didn't seem too bad. He actually seemed too calm, especially in light of his performance in the car. I thought he might still be in shock. Soon enough he would be debriefed of whatever knowledge he had to give but for the time being I took him to an NCO's room where he could relax, or bounce off the walls if he preferred: whatever he needed to do to get him through. I returned to the ops room. We waited for the smoke to clear so we could assess the situation. Within an hour we learned that the gunmen had taken full advantage of their chosen transport and before they could be caught had veered off-road where the cars couldn't follow. The chopper had continued to track them, relaying directions to the pursuit cars; but as the border was only ten miles away the bike had soon crossed it and disappeared. Robert and the SAS pulled back. They didn't want to risk another cross-border incursion only a few months after the publicity of the last one. And the trail was rapidly growing cold on this chase. Nairac and the SAS returned straight to Bessbrook and contacted me from there.

He said the bike had seemed to come out of nowhere, without anyone seeing from where: probably either from under the bridge or off a side verge. Motorbikes were used commonly during hits but usually only in towns and city centres, to make the escape easier. They obviously guessed correctly that if we had any suspicions about the pick-up we'd be looking out for cars. We hadn't really considered a bike hit out there. Mind you, if it had been a car, I think we'd be dead or near to it right now. The lorry blocking my exit hadn't been involved. As Robert held his car at the give-ways, waiting for me to pass, he had stalled. The lorry driver thought he had broken down, got impatient and pulled out to pass.

'Just one of those things,' he said to me.

'Yeah, just one of those things that can get you killed,' I replied. I told him that Blackbird would be debriefed by myself and Jack Marshall and he said he'd contact Jack for an update. He complimented me on the evasive driving and joked that he wouldn't demand I be breath-tested.

As I hung up, I suddenly realized that might be the last time I'd talk to him. I'd got so lost in the aftermath of pulling off the op, already reliving the danger-spots with the others for our own benefit, that I had conveniently forgotten that in a short while I wouldn't even be here. It occurred to me then that I hadn't even said goodbye to Nairac, or good luck. Although I didn't like wishing people too much luck in this game. It seemed to imply that it played too big a role in things, and we all liked to think we were in control. Having said that, however, Robert operated in an arena where luck could make or break you.

So Blackbird was finally off the scene after his months of undercover work. I knew that this day had screwed up the plans of all the Special Branch boys who had wanted to pick his bones clean after me. I already knew they were planning to lift him from me and take over the handling. But that was all shot to fuck now. Jackie Lynch was now well and truly out of the game.

I felt secretly pleased for him that he was going to get out. I was less secretive about my own pleasure at having come through the op. It felt like the last real test I would have to take; the last risk I would have to run. In fact, right now I probably had more in common with our Blackbird than ever before. I decided to go and see him and fill him in on what happened next. And share the bottle of Bushmills Dave and I had cracked open for everyone when we got back.

He was sitting on the edge of the bunk, too agitated to relax yet. Even his hair looked on edge.

'Still picking glass out of your hair?' I said as I entered.

'I think I fuckin' swallowed some. Sure of it.'

'Well, it'll come out eventually after it's worked through you.' I sat down opposite him. 'In fact, if you really want to impress someone, just shit on a plate and say they're diamonds.'

He laughed. 'If that's your idea of impressing I'm glad I'm not your girl!'

'That makes two of us, then.'

I could see the enormity of what he had done was just beginning to bed in. We were both leaving, true, but for me it was the start of family life, for him the end. I explained how he would be put through a final debriefing in Lisburn, where we would get the last of his information: IDs of the ASU involved today, details of his questioning and what he revealed and so on. Then he'd be flown over to a safe-house in the UK, armed with a new ID, documents, passport and money, and relocated in Australia or Canada. The latter was the usual choice. It wasn't exactly near to home but was a damn sight closer than Oz.

'You'll like Canada,' I said, the forced jollity in my voice sounding as false as it was. 'I've been, you know. I really liked it.' He asked why and I joked that it was because it wasn't here, because it wasn't Ireland. He smiled grimly then.

'That'll be exactly why I won't like it, then. Won't it?'

There wasn't a lot I could say to that. This was his home not mine. I was leaving to go home; he was leaving home to go away. I knew that men fled here because their lives were in danger only to return again because the homesickness felt worse. They knew they were returning to an unstable life, a life of looking under their cars for bombs every morning, but they just couldn't stay away. These people were brought up mostly in closed villages and their own communities were so tightly knit that when they moved away they felt unravelled, like a connecting thread had been snagged on their way out of the country.

They had to return. I'd seen it time and time again. But that same love of country was one of the reasons we were all here. If the Troubles didn't exist I think Ireland, north and south, would be the closest thing Europe had to a national village.

We decided to dirty our glasses by polishing off the rest of the whiskey.

'Can I see my ma before I go?' he asked suddenly out of the silence we had fallen into.

'I could arrange it with a troop escort but I wouldn't advise it. It'd be worse for them and could have repercussions. The less they know, the better, at this stage. If they're in the dark then they can't tell anyone anything, can they?'

He tried to reassemble his face into that of someone who accepted this but he failed, and he failed miserably. 'You'll be able to contact her soon enough,' I added. I felt like I'd just buried an axe in his head. 'Really, you can ring and write to her. Just don't say where you are. Things will change. They're not always gonna be like this.'

We talked about the possibility of future peace but neither of us would lay any money down. I told him he'd done the right thing over this and the one consolation was that I think he thought the same. Trouble was, though, sometimes the price for doing the right thing seems worse than that for doing wrong. All a question of what you can live with, I suppose.

I had to leave then. We wished each other luck. On the way out I asked him how many Catholics it takes to change a light bulb.

'Don't know.'

'Five. One to change the bulb and four to feel guilty for not changing it.' His smile was more genuine this time. He ran his own version by me, asking me how many Protestants it took.

'Surprise me,' I said.

'Five hundred. One to change the bulb and four hundred and ninety-nine to go on a march about how good the old bulb was.'

I closed the door on him and tried to do the same inside. Time would tell if I could. Experience suggested I couldn't. My nightmares hadn't stopped; they'd just stopped startling me. Now I woke casually horrified: taking visions of dead children in my stride (like I did last night); and people with their eyes blown out; and black explosives stuffed in their mouths; and that church-front cross I once saw blown off the wall. It looked like two twisted girders bent in the fall, or a snapped rail track, or scrapyard crap.

Christ on a pushbike.

Time to get out, I thought. Time to get out.

19

THE LEAVING

I always found there was something sad about packing up, even if you wanted to go. Unless you're walking out of an undiluted hell there's always going to be good things you leave behind as well as bad.

As much as I was looking forward to it, the thought of Civvie Street worried me a little. I knew it took time to adapt. I'd been in the army from the age of seventeen and since 1968. I'd now done twelve years, seven of them in Ireland. The army had given me some of the best times of my life and also exposed me to the worst of human behaviour. But at least I'd felt alive. Death can do that to you. As long as it's not your own, of course. That's one of the down-sides of death – it's often fatal.

I should have already been on one of the army resettlement courses to prepare me for the leaving and help with my smooth assimilation into civilian life. Somehow, though, I never got around to going on one. The demands of the immediate present were always greater than some imagined future. Anyway, I didn't see the bloody point, to be honest. I couldn't see there would be much call for my sort out in the world of nine to five. I mean, what was my CV going to say for a start? 'Qualified Small Arms Instructor, very experienced in gunbattles and handling paramilitary sources during counter-insurgency warfare. Bad language and nightmares a speciality. Met the Queen' – and bingo! the job's mine? A job doing what, though; late-night security guard at some frigging super-market?

I had already been offered promotion, and a bloody good one at that, when the Green Howards' adjutant came to see me in Dungannon near the end of my term. On the table was the offer of accelerated promotion to warrant officer class 1, and the chance to help run the Intelligence unit in Berlin. And even before that offer there was another. One of the cavalry officers at Dungannon was familiar with the work I'd done and said he'd put a word in for me at Box 5. That was the next obvious step, to move out of the firing line and into the organizational backroom. He came back with the answer I'd expected, that I would have made it but for three things: wrong school, wrong accent, wrong class. The old boys' network in full and pathetic effect. The only thing I regretted about not being offered a position was missing the chance personally to tell each and every one of them to stick it up their arse and twist it.

I wanted neither job. I'd had enough. I'd managed to get out but I didn't feel like I'd won. It didn't feel like anyone had. Bit easier to spot the obvious losers, though. They were all sunk in the ground, their possessions shared, their clothes bagged for Oxfam or, if needs be, passed on to the still living.

I thought of Stan, shot at the tyre ambush, then wired up in hospital; Johnny, wounded with him on the same op; Kev Crosier shot right beside me that time up on the rooftop; Tapper catching one in the head; and Paul, poor old Paul Austin (daft bugger), my ex-radioman, 'ex' everything right now, apart from presently being pretty fucking dead.

Good lads every one of them. Being in the wrong place at the wrong time their only crime, in my view. Hear it told by a Republican and you'll get a different story. That's their view. This is mine. But when you start killing people for holding a different view, worshipping a different God, you realize that money isn't the root of all evil, it's just one of the fruits.

And those dead men I remembered were only the ones I knew well. The roll-call of others would go on well into the night if I included every ditched and bullet-riddled body I'd seen; every anonymous burned-out corpse I'd smelled; and every poor bastard blown inside out that I'd heard about. This isle was as good as any at breeding long, long lines of life-takers and widow-makers.

My old pal Chris had got out physically intact only to have to live with his own mental scars. 'Mental': that just about summed it up at times.

But I'd got this far. Even the body of Christ had been left out there. For me. God was just another casualty of war.

So I packed up my kit and prepared to leave Dungannon and journey up to HQ at Lisburn. Zipping the lid on my suitcase, I took one last look around the near-empty room, realized it barely even justified that, and left. The case slapped against my shin as I walked; I'd made sure to squeeze in every last thing I wanted to take, including a still half-full bottle of whiskey. That was one taste I'd acquired over here that had seen me through many a long night.

The drive up to Lisburn was like any other, with one exception. As I rounded a bend I saw half a dozen dead birds in the road. I'd often seen the odd one but never so many at once. They were scattered across the tarmac like discarded gloves, their wind-blown wings tapping like fingers. Before I could avoid them I was running over the bodies. The flat red stars appeared behind me in the rearview mirror, and then I left them all behind.

At Lisburn HQ I went through the whole routine. I handed in my newly cleaned Browning to the 24 Int Arms Corps officer and went to see the regiment's doctor for my final medical. This was nothing more than him asking me how I was feeling and me answering, 'OK.' I didn't even consider mentioning my recurrent nightmares. I mean, what could he do?

I had to leave a forwarding address so the army could send me my 'red book'. This is the book that contains all details of your service: name, rank, courses attended, exact dates of service and locations, tours of duty, decorations and so on. The full history, in fact, for everyone to read, should anyone in the future but me be remotely interested. It was a bit like a combination of a potted biography and a school report. In best headmasterly fashion it also included a write-up about me by my commanding officer, Major White. I hadn't seen the bugger for two years.

I left the address of my parents' house for the book to be forwarded to. I was going to visit my mum and dad as soon as I got back to Britain but then I wanted to go straight down to London to get a place for me and Sarah. She was due to follow me over in a month's time. It would probably take her that long to talk her dad round and get her name back in the will.

Finally I picked up my resettlement allowance from the finance room. This was a cheque for one thousand pounds. I could hardly believe it. I felt like I wouldn't have to work for a year, and I knew I would feel like doing just that.

I decided to sail out rather than fly. I wanted something more leisurely, something less stressed than the flights always were. I wanted some time to myself, too, and lapping across the water would at least give me that. Train and boat journeys relaxed me while plane trips wired me out.

It was a day-crossing, unlike the last time I'd been on this ferry when Jackie Lynch and I had crossed over that night on the way to

London. The breeze was light now and the waves low and heavy; their walls and ridges sparkled in the sun. That lapping sound against the boat's side took me back to being a kid at the coast and going out on fishing trips with my dad.

I was really starting to look forward to being a civilian now, knowing that for a while at least I'd be totally unanswerable to anyone, even the big man in the sky. My earthly responsibilities would return when the time came to knuckle down and find work, support myself and Sarah and plan for the future. Any other 'answering' I had to do would only be on the rediscovery of my faith, but when I woke these days it felt like an achievement to find my feet, let alone anything else. Anyway, I thought, I could always find time later to solve the meaning and mysteries of life. Isn't that why the pubs closed so early?

I stood on the deck. The only thing on me now was my treasured guitar, which I'd carried around for years and had protected successfully. It was slung across my back like a polished rifle, the angle of the neck dug between my shoulder blades. Compared to the orderly madness of army life that I was leaving behind, I felt like a hobo drop-out about to hitch across America. Even the sky was wearing its light, faded denim.

The boat began to turn away slowly from the shore of Ireland. And that's how I left it. Not looking back: leaning on the boat's guard rail, looking down into the water, down on to the shifting glass; hypnotized by the sparkles. Me, breathing heavy – the sun, dancing light.

EPILOGUE

*'Prisoners of the past
remain hostages for ever'*

Six months after I left the army I heard of the death of Robert Nairac. At the grave sound of a newsreader's voice, I turned to the TV and saw a photo of Robert in his Guardsman's uniform. Because of the way he worked and the risks I already knew he took, the news of his murder wasn't a complete surprise and yet at the same time I was deeply shocked. Surprised, as well, by how shocked I was, even though there was the sickening feeling of an inevitability fulfilled. I was used to thinking the worst (pessimists are never disappointed) but I guess I still couldn't help hoping against hope for the better. Still, my gut feeling had been that it was a death waiting to happen.

The facts of his death came out gradually, becoming sadder and more ominous as they did. On Saturday, 14 May 1977, he left the base at Bessbrook to go to Drumintee. He was armed with his Browning and driving the Triumph I had used during the rescue of Blackbird. He said he was going out to the Three Steps Inn in South Armagh and would return to Bessbrook that evening. When he didn't return to base his commanding officer, concerned for Nairac's safety sent out an SAS-led search squad on a reccie of the Three Steps. He wasn't found and it wasn't until the next morning that his car was discovered still in the inn's car park. It had suffered some damage and the blood beside it suggested that Robert had, too. An extensive search by both police and army followed. Nothing was found and everyone knows the more time that elapses between disappearance and discovery, the less chance there is of a happy ending. When the truth finally did come out it was even sadder than expected.

It was a week after he went missing, on 21 May, that the IRA newspaper *Republican News* ran a front-page picture of Robert under the headline 'SAS CAPTAIN EXECUTED'. It read:

> The elimination of Nairac is an obvious breakthrough in the war against the Special Air Service. Sources close to the IRA refuse to say how much detailed knowledge they now have of the SAS but they are obviously highly pleased with what Nairac has either given them or confirmed. IRA sources revealed that Captain Nairac was a high-ranking officer . . . when arrested, he gave as his identity that of a Republican Clubs' Member; this identity was broken almost immediately by an IRA officer. SAS morale must now be shattered as one of their most high-ranking officers has been arrested, interrogated, executed and disappeared without a trace.

Unusual in these circumstances was the fact that no body was found. Whenever the Provos offed someone they'd always dump the body as proof and warning. I realized immediately why, in this case, they hadn't. It was another part of the psychological war that by now had become as important as the physical one. By not producing the body, the IRA knew that army intelligence would think there was a chance he was still alive and being interrogated for information. Although this was unlikely, it was a possibility that had to be considered and, in doing so, it threw up the real chance of current and future operations being compromised: had he given information on informers and other operatives? At the time there was no way of telling, so plans were put on hold and even undercover operatives pulled out for their own safety.

From what I could gather from the people I talked to during a few calls I made, the prevalent feeling was that Nairac would not have cracked under interrogation. I felt the same; I knew he was a tough bastard. But I also knew that this was my heart talking. My head told me otherwise – that every man has his limits and any man, however hard, can give under torture. An IRA torture team would be experts at finding those limits and going beyond them. It was something that all of us working undercover had feared, which is why we always tried to operate with back-up; it was our safety net. Nairac, on the other hand, tightrope-walked over Niagara Falls with nothing below him but water.

At the end of May a Provisional called Liam Townson was picked up and soon charged with the murder of Robert Nairac. On

8 November he was found guilty and jailed for life. And still no body had been found. At the time Townson said:

I shot the British captain. He never told us anything. He was a great soldier. I had been drinking in a pub in Dundalk. Danny O'Rourke came in. He told me to get a bit of hardware and there was a job to be done . . . I fired a shot from the gun (a 3.2 revolver) on the way out to test it. They were all there when I got there . . . I asked the captain who he was and he said he was a sticky. I asked him who he knew and he said Seamus Murphy from Drumintee. I told him I didn't believe him, that he was a British soldier and I had to kill him. I hit him on the head with my fist and then the butt of my gun. He said, 'You're going to kill me. Can I have a priest?' He was in a bad state. I aimed at his head I only put one in him. The gun misfired a few times. I left the body there and went home across the fields. I don't know where the body is and that's the truth.

It wasn't until a year later that more details of the full horror of Nairac's death came out. The ongoing investigation led to the arrest of five other men from South Armagh who were charged in connection with the killing. Three were charged with the murder, two with kidnapping.

According to their statements, Nairac was suspected of being SAS whilst in the bar, followed outside, beaten and driven away. During the struggle in the car park, Robert drew his Browning but was overpowered. He was driven to Ravensdale Forest. There, against a wall by the side of a bridge he was kicked and beaten about his body and face, all the time with a gun trained on him. He continued to insist on his cover story of being an Official IRA member. They continued to disbelieve and beat him. At one point he tried to escape but was too weak from his injuries. He was beaten some more. Townson knelt over him and beat him around the face and head with a gun until Robert was covered in blood. The first beating had gone on for ten minutes; this one lasted another five.

Finally, Robert was led to the middle of a field by Townson, who by this time was using the captured Browning. Robert made one last lunge for his own gun. Townson shouted to the others and then felled Nairac with another blow. One of the others, Pat Maguire, then beat him over the head with some wood as he curled on the ground. This was when he must have realized his execution was seconds away and asked for a priest to take his confession. It was denied by his good Catholic executioners.

The final indignity came when Townson put the Browning to Robert's head and pulled the trigger. The gun clicked but didn't fire. According to later statements, Townson shouted at Nairac, 'Fuck you! It's only blanks.' He then put the gun back to Robert's head, who had to endure hearing the Browning click three more times before it finally fired at the fifth attempt, killing him. It wasn't stated whether he died instantly.

As the details of his death emerged it cleared up some of the mystery and also created more questions. There was still no body. Gerard Fearon, one of the Provos involved, said that Nairac's body was left where it lay as they didn't want to run into Garda or army patrols with it in their car. Fearon said that he was later told by one of the others that the body had been 'taken care of'. Under further questioning, he finally admitted to hearing a rumour that Nairac's body had been dumped near Forkhill, at the same place the IRA staff captain Peter Cleary had been shot just over a year before. Shortly after that, the SAS boy responsible for shooting Cleary had come to me in the middle of the night for advice on how to get CID investigators off his back. And also told me that the shooting was sanctioned by Nairac.

When I got to hear this last piece of information, of Robert's body being dumped at the same spot as Cleary's, I was astounded. Very few people knew of this exact location. It convinced me that either Nairac had talked or that the IRA were sending a coded message to the security forces. Significantly, Robert's body was not found at Forkhill so it was either dumped there temporarily before being removed and put through a mincer, or, more likely, the IRA simply said it had been there to show what they knew.

The controversy raged on with many different theories being held – had Nairac really been killed? Did he survive the single bullet (unusual that he was only shot once), play dead and then escape? Or, in the most contentious scenario, was he 'doing the double' all along and was spirited away to safety in the south by the IRA? Over the following years, when I had conversations with Protestants who had been involved in paramilitary activity, the strong feeling from them was that this last theory was true.

For myself, I didn't think it likely, although that moment I had discovered him deep in conversation with McCrory in McCrory's Bar did come back to me. But in reality he had been far too successful operationally and done too much damage to the Republican cause for that theory to ring true.

His death also brought into the public domain wider knowledge of the deployment of the SAS in Northern Ireland.

In life there were many mysteries and secrets surrounding Robert Nairac, and the manner of his death created more. About the only thing that anyone agreed on (including, amazingly, the IRA) was that the courage of the man was unquestionable and evident in the way he faced his death.

In time, the truth that came out about the nature of his execution was less romantic, and even more sickening in its pathetic reality: the guys who killed him were proven Provos but only small-time members. They didn't realize the significance of the man they had taken and that is why he was killed on the night of his capture. Had they referred back to some of the Provisionals' big boys then Robert's fate would have been even worse (if that's possible to imagine): longer and more intensive interrogation and torture at the hands of the real professional pain-makers before his still certain death. If you gave those boys an inch they'd cut the smile right off your face.

But even in light of this revelation, the suffering he endured was immense. I could only wonder what he must have thought in those last minutes, blinded by his own blood, probably struck dumb with fear as his own gun misfired against his head four times before it finally went off. Half of me was furious enough to want to get back over there, while my other half, and by now the stronger part of me, was just grateful to be free of the sickness.

I talked things over with Chris. Since leaving I had made a point of keeping in touch, and over the years we have remained great friends. He is settled now with his wife and family, which I am happy about, but still suffers because of our time in Northern Ireland. He worked very little after he came out and was then wheelchair bound for many years with his illness. His condition has improved to the extent he can now walk, but he still remains on invalidity benefit. Like me, he suffers from post-traumatic stress disorder.

PTSD was first acknowledged on a wide scale by the Americans after Vietnam. Until then it was passed off with that old phrase which came straight out of the trenches, 'shell shock'. In this coun-

297

try it didn't seem to be fully acknowledged until the aftermath of the Falklands, which conveniently ignored the men who had served and suffered in the conflicts before then.

For me it began in the early 1980s when, as I became more successful in business, I began to feel guilt over simply surviving and suffered from the recurrence of my nightmares. Initially, after I'd first left, they had gradually lessened, but when they came back it was with a vengeance. It was only through chance that, years later, I got chatting to another ex-army guy who suffered from the same thing. He informed me of the war pension available to ex-soldiers who suffered as a result of their duty. Until then I hadn't known about it. It was two years before my pension finally came through from the War Pensions Authority.

I was put through a minefield of bureaucracy and tests. They torture you with brown envelopes, requesting your presence to be 'assessed'. Eventually, I saw a doctor who barely looked up from his papers as he asked me questions like, 'Can you walk up stairs?', 'Can you sit comfortably?', while he ticked boxes. After this, at first I was denied. Later, a specialist I saw wrote a damning report on the other doctor's conclusions and I was granted the pension.

It so angered me that I had a meeting with my local MP and she agreed that the current situation for ex-servicemen was appalling. She was already in the process of starting a campaign to have a minister appointed to some type of commission that could be set up to look after the interests of men who have suffered after serving their country.

This was the one thing that began to anger me after I left the army, especially when I got back in touch with Chris. The way that former soldiers appeared to be discarded and disregarded by the MoD seemed particularly unjust for someone of Chris's stature. He was a man who had served his country with dedication and bravery (and regardless of what we might now think of the rights and wrongs of us being in Northern Ireland) only to find that even after he recovered from his long physical illness he still couldn't function properly because of his mental scars. As soon as I'd learned of my eligibility for a war pension I informed Chris of his right to do the same. He is still waiting.

One of the worst things was that Chris finally had to do what he had first mentioned to me when I'd visited him that Christmas; he sold his Military Cross. It was bought by a war memorabilia dealer for next to nothing and the dealer then flogged it through auction for God-knows-what profit. It was bought by the Imperial War Museum in London. At the time I wrote to the Green Howards' regimental headquarters in Richmond and told them the auction was coming up, expecting them to buy it back for the regiment, as they often did. They didn't put in a bid. And I didn't even get the courtesy of a reply, which is laughable when you consider that the Green Howards' motto is 'Once a Green Howard – always a Green Howard'. They were even known as the Family Regiment. What's that line about being able to choose your friends but not your family?

I thought it was ridiculous, and still do; why should a war hero be forced into selling his medal just because there is so little support network available?

In the years since my service in Northern Ireland ended there have always been things to remind me: sights, sounds and smells that had the ability to conjure up ghosts or jump-start corpses back to life. It might be the back-firing of a car, the small swell of panic felt in a close crowd or something as simple as the sound of breaking glass.

In the early 1980s I returned to Northern Ireland with Sarah and one day we visited Belfast. Walking down a street on what was a brilliantly sunny afternoon, I got one of the shocks of my life. Walking towards me I recognized Jackie Lynch, our 'Blackbird'. I'd often wondered what became of him. At least this meant he was alive and any more than that, to be honest, I didn't really want to know. He looked back at me and remained impassive, even though I could tell he'd clocked me. We walked past each other. I hastened a protesting Sarah back to the car, explaining on the way, and we quickly left.

Even into the late 1980s I would accidentally meet people with connections. One of these occasions was while I was watching an amateur football competition on a local sportsfield. The teams had come from all over Britain and Ireland: one was called something like the Shankill Juniors (obviously drawn from one of the Protestant areas I had patrolled). I approached the three guys who were in charge of managing and coaching the team and we got chatting. With them being Protestant, I knew I was on safe ground. Initially, the talk was light-hearted; I introduced them to Sarah and they said, 'How come a pretty girl like you was nicked by an Englishman?' The more I talked to them on my own, however, the more it came out how actively involved some of them had been, and still were. Amazingly, the father of one of these men had been part of the Protestant community that day in 1971 who were fleeing their homes and attempting (unsuccessfully) to burn them down before they left. I confessed that I was the one who helpfully suggested that turning on the gas bottles might hurry things along. As we talked more and they learned of what I had been involved in, one of them made an offer to me. He said they needed men of experience to help wage their own campaign and asked if I would return over there to help with the work of the UVF. I had no hesitation in refusing. I didn't want to be responsible for putting fresh blood on top of that already dried.

Sometimes there were more obvious reminders that popped up in the unlikeliest places. Quite a few years later, I remember seeing a guy on the TV news and thinking, He looks bloody familiar. I was walking down a London high street at the time, right past an electrical shop. All the TVs in the window were tuned to the midday news and this guy was looking into camera, being interviewed; staring out at me twelve times in different screen sizes. I clocked the short, sandy hair and, because the volume was turned up on one set, even through the glass I could hear the clipped tones of his voice. But I recognized the eyes most, those distinctive grey eyes that I realized belonged to the marine commandos officer who had spoken to me in Belfast. It had happened following the machine-gun attack on our PIG, that time when I just managed to slam the doors before the bullets hit. The next day we met a unit of commandos, and their commanding officer – the guy now before me on TV – came over to examine the damage and talk to me; the general gist of his advice at the time was, 'Get back in and give 'em hell, and good luck.' Turns out he was called Paddy Ashdown and was now an MP.

And who would have thought that a young activist I encountered called Gerry Adams would tread the same path, eventually lunching with Tony Blair.

Other people from that time didn't fare as well. After leaving the IRSP because of the activities of its paramilitary wing, INLA, Bernadette McAliskey continued to be active within the Republican movement. In 1981 a UDA hit-squad burst into her house (the same house where I had visited her) and shot her and her husband. Both were badly wounded but survived the assassination attempt. An SAS team were dug in around her house but only apprehended the UDA gunmen as they left after the shooting. This led to further widespread controversy over Republican accusations that the SAS had not only allowed the gunmen to enter the house but that they were colluding with Loyalist death-squads by giving them training and information.

One small point that always struck me when I heard of these actions was that if a politician was shot it would be described as an 'assassination' or 'assassination attempt' but when some poor bugger on the ground got it, whether they were civilian or army, they were simply 'killed' or 'murdered'. Even in death, which is supposed to be the great leveller, we were segregated from the so-called 'VIPs'.

Another depressing sign of the continual march of violence down through the years was thrown up as recently as 1996 when a British army base in Osnabruck, Germany, suffered an IRA mortar attack. Wanted in Germany for questioning in connection with the attack was Roisin McAliskey. This is the daughter of Bernadette and, I realized, the same little girl who was at her mother's house at the time of my visit all those years ago. And so it goes on. This is how children can grow during war, and this is one of the major stumbling blocks to future peace: the unshakeable beliefs, the bitterness, the anger, the determination and the fanaticism all passed from parent to child.

Roisin McAliskey was eventually arrested in Northern Ireland and, while on bail, she gave birth to a daughter. I wonder if her view of her own daughter will mirror that of Roisin's mother when Bernadette said of her, 'I can think of much worse things than waking up one morning and finding my daughter is a terrorist.' As has always been the case in the past, time will tell.

In March 1998 the home secretary, Jack Straw, halted the extradition of Roisin McAliskey back to Germany on the grounds of mental health. Hers, not his.

Martin Meehan, who Chris and I had arrested in the Clover Club under suspicion of being involved in the murder of the three off-duty Scots soldiers, was arrested again in 1979 under the suspicion of the kidnapping and imprisonment of an intelligence informer. He was convicted and sentenced to twelve years.

But the fate of many during the twenty-nine years of the Troubles seemed to pale by comparison when I read of what happened to the lovely Miss World I had met in 1974.

She married Bruce Forsyth.

For myself, over the years immediately after leaving the forces I never fully severed my military connections and went on to further adventures in other parts of the world. Eventually, I returned to England and settled for good in the south with Sarah and our children.

My time in Northern Ireland is over and done. It is, in both senses of the word, historic: in the past and important to me. Those times will never be forgotten. Apart from myself (mine is just one story), there are too many people who have reasons to remember, even when they want to forget.

But forgetting isn't the major thing: more important, and more difficult, is forgiving. I've yet fully to return to the strength of my religious beliefs I had before I landed in Northern Ireland, but I still realize that the general Christian belief in forgiveness – rather than the specific Catholic belief in guilt and retribution – will be the only foundation on which any lasting peace in Northern Ireland will be built.

Amen to that.